Both/And

Reading Kierkegaard from Irony to Edification

BOTH/AND

Reading Kierkegaard from Irony to Edification

by

MICHAEL STRAWSER

FORDHAM UNIVERSITY PRESS
New York
1997

LC 96-39761
ISBN 8-8232-1700-0 (*hardcover*)
ISBN 0-8232-1701-9 (*paperback*)
ISSN 1089-3938
Perspectives in Continental Philosophy, No. 2
John D. Caputo, Series Editor

Library of Congress Cataloging-in-Publication Data

Strawser, Michael J.
Both/and : reading Kierkegaard from irony to edification / by Michael Strawser.
p. cm. — (Perspectives in continental philosophy : no. 2)
Includes bibliographical references.
ISBN 0-8232-1700-0. — ISBN 0-8232-1701-9 (pbk.)
1. Kierkegaard, Søren, 1813–1855. 1. Title. II. Series
B4377.S75 1997
198′.9—dc21 96-39761
CIP

Printed in the United States of America

For
Ann,
Cassandra Joy,
and Sebastian Michael

Contents

Key to Primary Source References

Throughout the body of this text, parenthetical references are given to the primary source material in abbreviated form.

A. Danish

BA *Breve og Aktstykker vedrørende Søren Kierkegaard* (Letters and Documents Concerning Søren Kierkegaard). Ed. Niels Thulstrup. Copenhagen: Munksgaard, 1953–1954.

EP *Søren Kierkegaards Efterladte Papirer* (Søren Kierkegaard's Posthumous Papers). Ed. H. P. Barfod and H. Gottscheds. Copenhagen: C. A. Reitzel, 1869–1881.

NRF *Nutidens Religieuse Forvirring: Bogen om Adler* (The Religious Confusion of the Present Age). Ed. Julia Watkin. Copenhagen: C. A. Reitzel, 1984.

P *Søren Kierkegaards Papirer* (Søren Kierkegaard's papers). Ed. P. A. Heiberg, V. Kuhr, and E. Torsting. Copenhagen: Gyldendal, 1909–1948.

SV *Søren Kierkegaards Samlede Værker* (Søren Kierkegaards's Collected Works). Ed. A. B. Drachmann, J. L. Heiberg, and H. O. Lange. Copenhagen: Glydendal, 1901–1906 (1st ed.), 1920–1936 (2d ed.), 1962–1964 (3rd ed.).

Unless indicated otherwise, SV references will be to the third edition.

B. English

1. The definitive edition of Kierkegaard's writings

KW *Kierkegaard's Writings*. Trans. and ed. (unless indicated otherwise) by Howard V. Hong and Edna H. Hong. Princeton, N.J.: Princeton University Press, 1978–.

For easy reference to the original text, each volume contains marginal references to the first edition of SV (or in some cases P) and a collation of the Danish editions of Kierkegaard's collected works. Therefore, when I refer to KW, I do not include the corresponding Danish reference. (The following list includes both the published and projected volumes.)

KW I	*Early Polemical Writings.* Trans. Julia Watkin (1990).
KW II	*The Concept of Irony; Schelling Lecture Notes* (1989).
KW III	*Either/Or* I (1987).
KW IV	*Either/Or* II (1987).
KW V	*Eighteen Upbuilding Discourses* (1990).
KW VI	*Fear and Trembling; Repetition* (1983).
KW VII	*Philosophical Fragments; Johannes Climacus* (1985).
KW VIII	*The Concept of Anxiety.* Trans. Reidar Thomte in collaboration with Albert B. Anderson (1980).
KW IX	*Prefaces.*
KW X	*Three Discourses on Imagined Occasions* (1993).
KW XI	*Stages on Life's Way* (1988).
KW XII	*Concluding Unscientific Postscript,* vols. (1992).
KW XIII	*The Corsair Affair* (1982).
KW XIV	*Two Ages* (1978).
KW XV	*Upbuilding Discourses in Various Spirits* (1993).
KW XVI	*Works of Love.*
KW XVII	*Christian Discourses.*
KW XVIII	*Without Authority.*
KW XIX	*The Sickness unto Death* (1980).
KW XX	*Practice in Christianity* (1991).
KW XXI	*For Self-Examination; Judge for Yourself!* (1990).
KW XXII	*The Point of View.*
KW XXIII	*The Moment and Late Writings.*
KW XXIV	*The Book on Adler.*
KW XXV	*Letters and Documents.* Trans. Henrik Rosenmeier (1978).
KW XXVI	*Cumulative Index.*

2. Other English translations

AC	*Attack upon Christendom.* Trans. Walter Lowrie. Boston: Beacon, 1944.
AN	*Armed Neutrality and an Open Letter.* Tran. Howard

V. Hong and Edna H. Hong. New York: Simon & Schuster, 1968.

AR *On Authority and Revelation.* Trans. Walter Lowrie. Princeton, N.J.: Princeton University Press, 1955.

CD *Christian Discourses.* Trans. Walter Lowrie. London: Oxford University Press, 1940.

CI *The Concept of Irony.* Trans. Lee M. Capel. London: Collins, 1966.

CLA *Crisis in the Life of an Actress.* Trans. Stephen Crites. London: Collins, 1967.

CUP *Concluding Unscientific Postscript.* Trans. David F. Swenson and Walter Lowrie. Princeton, N.J.: Princeton University Press, 1941.

DSK *The Diary of Søren Kierkegaard.* Ed. Peter Rohde. New York: Philosophical Library, 1960.

EO *Either/Or.* 2 vols. Volume 1, trans. David Swenson and Lillian Marvin Swenson. Volume 2, trans. Walter Lowrie. Princeton, N.J.: Princeton University Press, 1959.

J *The Journals of Søren Kierkegaard.* Trans. Alexander Dru. New York: Harper & Row, 1959.

JP *Søren Kierkegaard's Journals and Papers.* Trans. Howard V. Hong and Edna H. Hong. Bloomington: Indiana University Press, 1978.

PA *The Present Age.* Trans. Alexander Dru. New York: Harper & Row, 1962.

PF *Philosophical Fragments.* Trans. David Swenson. Princeton, N.J.: Princeton University Press, 1962.

PH *Purity of Heart.* Trans. Douglas V. Steere. New York: Harper & Row, 1948.

PR *Prefaces.* Trans. William McDonald. Tallahassee: Florida State University Press, 1989.

PV *The Point of View for My Work as an Author.* Trans. Walter Lowrie. New York: Harper & Row, 1962.

WL *Works of Love.* Trans. David F. Swenson and Lillian Marvin Swenson. Princeton, N.J.: Princeton University Press, 1946.

C. Additional Foreign-Language Translations

GW *Gesammelte Werke.* Trans. Emanuel Hirsch. Düsseldorf: Diederichs, 1952.

KG	*Kärlekens Gerningar* (Works of Love). Trans. Gustaf Thomée. Stockholm, 1862.
OC	*Oeuvres Complètes de Søren Kierkegaard.* Trans. Paul-Henri Tisseau and Else-Marie Jacquet-Tisseau. Paris: Éditions de l'Orante, 1975.

Epi-laugh

Something wonderful has happened to me. I was drawn up into the seventh heaven. There sat all the gods in assembly. By special grace I was granted the privilege of making a wish. "Will you," said Mercury, "have youth, or beauty, or power, or a long life, or the most beautiful girl, or any of the other glories we have in the chest? Choose, but only one thing." For a moment I was at a loss, then I addressed myself to the gods thus: "Most honorable contemporaries, I choose one thing, that I may always have the laugh on my side." Not one of the gods said a word; on the contrary, they all began to laugh. From that I concluded that my wish was granted and that the gods knew how to express themselves with taste; for it certainly would have been improper to answer seriously: "Your wish is granted."

A, EO I 41–2; SV II 44

Introduction: Reading Kierkegaard Philosophically

> The more the poet has abandoned this, the more necessary it is for him to have a total-view [*Total-Anskuelse*] of the world and in this way to be lord over irony in his individual existence, and the more necessary it becomes for him to be a philosopher to a certain degree.
>
> S. Kierkegaard, KW II 325

> All transformations of philosophy are grounded in philosophy itself.
>
> Grohmann and Vollbeding, contemporaries of Kant[1]

THE UNCERTAINTY INVOLVED in attempting an adequate reckoning of Kierkegaard as a philosopher in today's intellectual climate is considerable, especially for one who has tasted the weightiest texts of postmodernism and come away from them as from a Swedish smörgasbord, feeling overstuffed but strangely unsatisfied. So many questions arise. What could it mean to read Kierkegaard philosophically? How would this be possible? How does one begin?

"Kierkegaard" is now a name well established in the history of philosophy,[2] and yet taking him "philosophically" appears to be the least common way of taking him. There may be several reasons for this, but two come to mind straightaway. First, because Kierkegaard forcibly assailed and, in large part, rejected modern philosophy as he knew it, we would consider it unfair to subject his works to a reading that he himself disdained and fought against. This presupposes, of course, that there is but one common, fixed meaning of 'philosophy' and 'philosophical,' which, unquestionably, is not the case. Second, what a philosophical reading might mean or look like is no longer clear in the present age. It is possible, however, to be open to the discussion about the "end of philosophy" and still feel that philosophy and philosophical thinking can be put to some clear, constructive action. If Kierkegaard is to be read philosophically, then, a persuasive meaning must be given to the word 'philosophical.' Consequently, this introduction will describe the meaning that may be granted to such a query, as well as inform readers of the development to be found within the following study.

The depth and the range of the writings by Søren Kierkegaard (1813–1855) have secured his place in the history of philosophy. To oversimplify, as I must at this point: Kierkegaard stands for a turning point of sorts from a type of systematic philosophy that, by means of a conspicuous focus on objectivity, attempts to place itself on the secure path of science, to a "philosophy"—already viewed with a difference—that focuses its attention on subjectivity and openly acknowledges itself as fragmentary and provisional.[3] In the blink of an eye, with the aid of the writings of Kierkegaard, philosophy undergoes a transfiguration of character, if not a complete transubstantiation.[4] One sense, then, of reading Kierkegaard philosophically is to situate him sufficiently within the history of philosophy and to describe his attitude(s) toward philosophy in general, philosophies in particular, even individual philosophers and philosophizers. This calls for a rather detailed treatment of Kierkegaard's assessment of the two most prominent philosophers in his writings: Socrates, that ironist who did not write, and Georg Wilhelm Friedrich Hegel, that pregnant writer of all his discursive thinking.

That it is "Socratic discourse" that, in its generic, but indeterminate sense, seems to define 'philosophy,' appropriately though often vaguely, is a truth generally accepted. Despite this nearly universal agreement, however, irony, the method of Socrates, has been given short shrift. For Kierkegaard, who referred to himself as a "Magister of Irony" to the very end, the significance of irony can hardly be overstated.

Furthermore, though the shadows of Socrates and Hegel loom large in Kierkegaard's texts, one should not overlook Kierkegaard's appraisal, as scattered as it may be, of other writers within the "philosophical tradition," such as Plato, Descartes, Spinoza,

Kant, J. G. Fichte, and Schelling. Nor should one be oblivious to writers who fall outside this tradition, such as Hamann, Trendelenburg, and the most important Danish contemporaries of Kierkegaard: J. L. Heiberg, H. L. Martensen, Poul Møller, and F. C. Sibbern. Although a thorough description of Kierkegaard's appraisal of each of these writers cannot be given here, it is still important to indicate the points of view that Kierkegaard takes toward these thinkers. These considerations concerning Socrates in particular and other philosophers in general will yield a deeper significance to what it means to read Kierkegaard philosophically. No simple task, to be sure.[5]

Another obvious reason why Kierkegaard has frequently not been read philosophically is quite simply that there are more popular ways of reading him. Consider the following introductory paragraph:

> In Kierkegaard's authorship there are three motives which constantly resound throughout, sometimes more independently, sometimes collected as one into a deep and powerful triad: the religious conception he appropriated in inheritance from the father—Christianity, next the recollection of the broken engagement, and lastly, what one can briefly indicate by the name *Socrates*.[6]

Here we find three very specific references to Kierkegaard's motives in writing, and, curiously enough, each motive assumes the identity of an individual person: the father, Regine, and Socrates. But these are merely metaphors for ways of reading Kierkegaard that may be expressed more generally as, respectively, the religious, the aesthetic or poetic, and the philosophical.

Upon consideration of the first motif, a look at the vast secondary literature on Kierkegaard shows that it is all too customary to stress prosaically the religious or Christian meaning of Kierkegaard's writings. At times and at places, this stress is unwarranted; at others, it is questionable by virtue of its sheer familiarity; at still others, it verges on the overbearing. What these secondary authors inwardly doubt is that Kierkegaard had carefully calculated the possible effects of his writings and that, even if he had, he had difficulty expressing his total-view. They invariably cut Kierkegaard into pieces, preserving what they find most nourishing while forgetting or ignoring his warnings about the dangers of direct communication. In this light, a quote from Hegel is all the more significant: "What is 'familiarly known' is not properly known, just for the reason that it is 'familiar.' When engaged in the process of knowing, it is the commonest form of self-deception."[7]

Indeed, some scholars take great pains to give Kierkegaard's more "irreligious" works their "proper" context, and, in championing what they take to be Kierkegaard's cause, they inevitably distort his texts. On this particular point it is not difficult to feel Kierkegaard's well-known abhorrence of "the professor."[8] There are, however, certain grounds for such an emphasis and privileged view, so I do not think that one should too hastily call for the execution of all the professors. While Kierkegaard provided them an all too convenient "key" in the posthumously published "conclusion" to his literature (i.e., *Synspunktet for min Forfatter-Virksomhed*[9] [The Point of View for My Activity as an Author]), whether such readings are complete or even the result of a reasonable or judicious interpretation prompts the cautious reader to demur. Whether there is an alternative interpretation as plausible as (if not more so than) Kierkegaard's own remains to be seen.

To consider Kierkegaard's second supposed motive in writing—the broken engagement with Regine—in the light in which this is normally presented, it is, to be honest, regrettable, verging on the ridiculous. This narrative is all too frequently resorted to in interpreting a difficult passage rather than clearly focusing on the letter of the text.[10]

To approach Kierkegaard philosophically, then, one may follow the so-called third motive, which in turn presents an historical, rather than an anachronistic, approach to the study. By following Kierkegaard's conception of Socrates, one follows a thread of development of great moment in his thought, because this conception is constantly growing and expanding from the earliest academic writings to its culmination in *The Point of View*. This is not meant to suggest, however, that either the Christian content of Kierkegaard's writings or an aesthetic appreciation of them should be ignored. Certain well-intended but misguided efforts have at least a (negative) value in helping to sharpen one's reading of Kierkegaard; thus, a point of view will be developed throughout this text, rather than being imposed from the outset. It is simply a matter of beginning at the beginning of Kierkegaard's writings, beginning from the ground up, proceeding (reading) slowly without prejudgments and without a pre-(con)text. To quote Kierkegaard in his first published work: "What hope can one entertain that one will fall into the hands of readers wholly *ex improviso*" (KW I 57)? Is it possible to begin cleanly, without anticipations or expectations, to begin with the texts, unprepared, taking them up one by one for examination? Is such a reading attainable in practice? As difficult as this may be, it is the only reading worth a scholar's aim, for the texts alone are available for interpretation, evaluation, and criticism. That personal, solitary individual, if his self-chosen epitaph means anything, is inaccessible and buried in a *kirkegaard.*[11]

Hence, the writings of Kierkegaard alone will inform the organization of my study, not some narrowly conceived conceptual thesis on systematic issues claimed to be of utmost importance in understanding Kierkegaard. Only this type of organization will permit a point of departure that is philosophical—that is to say, Socratic—and, at the same time, a development that is historical. My reading of Kierkegaard will begin by focusing on three of his lesser-known texts in Part One: in chapter 1, his first work, *Af en endnu Levendes Papirer* (From the Papers of One Still Living [1838]); in chapter 2, his magisterial dissertation,[12] *Om Begrebet Ironi med stadigt Hensyn til Socrates* (On the Concept of Irony with Constant Reference to Socrates [1841]); and, in chapter 3, the unfinished work, *Johannes Climacus, eller De Omnibus Dubitanum Est* (Johannes Climacus, or That Everything Is Dubitable [written roughly during 1842–1843]).

Kierkegaard's early student writings, particularly *From the Papers of One Still Living*, serve partly as background for my investigation of a point of departure and partly as foreground to the expression of the need to strive to find (or create) a *Livsanskuelse*,[13] or "philosophy of life." Following this, it is easier to see how the works on irony and doubt present explorations for this "philosophy" which produce different outcomes. In addition, we shall see that *The Concept of Irony* and *Johannes Climacus* contain philosophical reflections that seriously prefigure—if not actually determine—Kierkegaard's method of indirect communication.

That this approach presents a simple, yet original, approach to a sustained reading of Kierkegaard is seen through the status accorded the works that are usually either completely overlooked or asserted to be misfits in the world of Kierkegaard's "primary" texts. The latter position is found in Mark C. Taylor's well-known study, *Kierkegaard's Pseudonymous Authorship: A Study of Time and the Self* (1975). Taylor contends that Kierkegaard presents the reader with four primary kinds of writings: (1) the pseudonymous authorship, (2) the religious discourses, (3) the late articles attacking the Danish Church, and (4) the journals. He then admits that four (he mistakenly counts five) works important for understanding Kierkegaard do not fit into these categories: *From the Papers of One Still Living, The Concept of Irony, Johannes Climacus*, and *The Point of View*. As I shall argue, it is precisely these works that are of special significance for a comprehensive reading of Kierkegaard.

If one had to label individual Kierkegaardian texts as more or less philosophical, one might begin by saying that *The Concept of Irony* and *Johannes Climacus* certainly look philosophical, as opposed to, say, theological. Whereas these works express what might be dubbed a negative philosophy, *Philosophiske Smuler* (Philosophical Fragments [1844]) and *Afsluttende Uvidenskabelig Efterskrift till Philosophiske Smuler* (Concluding Unscientific Postscript to the Philosophical Fragments [1846]) might be read as opening an apparently positive philosophical development directly relevant to problems in epistemology and the philosophy of religion.[14]

While it is true that any ultimate attempt to categorize the writings of Kierkegaard is doomed to failure, this does not preclude my making pointed distinctions in the structuring of my study, so long as it is borne in mind that an ultimate justification for these categories and distinctions shall not be forthcoming.

Having said this, I shall read *The Concept of Irony, Johannes Climacus, Philosophical Fragments*, and *Concluding Unscientific Postscript* as Kierkegaard's "predominantly" philosophical works, which provide the most interesting and lively picture both of Kierkegaard's conception of philosophy and his attitude toward Socrates (the father of philosophy), Descartes (the father of modern philosophy), and Hegel (the end-fulfillment of modern philosophy). For this reason, in Part Two I shall focus on the Climacian writings (chapter 6), and include a reading of Anti-Climacus's *Training in Christianity* (chapter 7).

Kierkegaard's more well-known pseudonymous works will be discussed more generally when I consider the problem of pseudonymity (chapter 4) and review a recent work that argues that all the pseudonymous views are bogus (chapter 5). We shall see that the pseudonymous writings take on a new light when they are read after Kierkegaard's earlier writings. They unquestionably enliven the search for a life-view and, in this way, provide a deeper expression for the *ever developing life-view* within the works called by metonymy "Kierkegaard."

I shall also deal accordingly with Kierkegaard's "religious writings," which are less widely read than his "other" texts. That these should be given at least equal weight in a fair, sustained reading ought not to present the slightest controversy. This study, then, does not follow those who read the pseudonymous authorship as the most important part of the Kierkegaardian corpus, or those who consider the religious writings as the crucial part of the literature. My approach, alternatively, will grant little actual priority to either of the two principal categories of Kierkegaard's writings. The trick is to avoid prioritizing when writing (in time), for, obviously, something has to precede something else, since it is not possible to discuss different works simultaneously—even if these works were simultaneously published—with even a marginal degree of clarity. Hence, the need to begin at the beginning, from the living papers of one now deceased who was interested in the non-concept of irony.

In a characteristically indirect way, Kierkegaard would describe his production as a positioning of irony and seriousness "together in such a way that the composite is a dialectical knot." Most readers—those who do not uncritically assume that the knot has been untied once for all—are still trying to untangle these threads. But my goal is quite the opposite. I am interested not so much in untying this knot as in tightening it, so that the tension pervasive throughout Kierkegaard's writings, throughout my reading of them, throughout "the original text of the individual, human existence-relationship," might be communicated to readers in the overall impression of this work.

Therefore, my aim is to show that no ultimate priority need, or can, be granted to any single category of Kierkegaard's works.

This will mean that neither "aesthetics" nor "religion" can dominate in a philosophical reading. The multitude of relations between any one text and any other will be emphasized over a single dominating relation adhering to any one categorization of his writings. In other words, the role of the development within

Kierkegaard's production will be critically evaluated, and the possibility of a holistic hermeneutical hypothesis will be advanced.

It has been noted that one of Kierkegaard's primary concerns in his writings is the existence of the reader. Despite this—or might it be because of this?—Kierkegaard is not, for all practical purposes, "reader-friendly." The magnificent variety in the collected works and papers, as well as in certain individual texts, accounts for this. Naturally, then, it is important to take each text on its own terms while realizing that it is a part of a larger fabric that is still dripping with ink. How, then, can a reader decipher the unnatural totality of Kierkegaard's corpus? Is it possible to read this unnatural totality? Yes—in an obvious sense, of course—for the words are but finite. And it is precisely this possibility that makes a holistic study possible.

Is such a whole, then, coherent, consistent, and/or orderly (systematic)? Kierkegaard scholars differ greatly in their answers. They have considerably divided views on the nature of the Kierkegaardian corpus as a whole. Is it not, then, still true today that "no one has attained a point of view which violates neither the whole nor the separate parts?"[15] Indeed, this is the case, and the reader's problem is to preserve the differences and inconsistencies that may arise in considering the whole of Kierkegaard's texts while still providing a sustained evaluation that nevertheless clears the way for a comprehensive reading from irony to edification, an interpretation that preserves both the aesthetic and the religious elements of each and every text. This, in a nutshell, is the problem of this study.

It is important to employ a distinction between (1) Kierkegaard's writings, works, or texts and (2) Kierkegaard's authorship. This distinction will be decisive when concluding my holistic interpretation. When referring to Kierkegaard's "authorship," the most constricted reference based on the author's own personal assessment of his literary production, what is specifically intended are the books that he himself cited in *The Point of View* as constituting his authorship. The note concerning his supposedly "whole" authorship reads as follows:

> In order to have it at hand, here are the titles of the books. FIRST CLASS (aesthetic productivity): *Either–Or*; *Fear and Trembling*; *Repetition*; *The Concept of Angst*; *Prefaces*; *Philosophical Crumbs*; *Stages*

> *on Life's Way*—and 18 edifying discourses, which came successively. SECOND CLASS: *Concluding Unscientific Postscript*. THIRD CLASS (solely religious productivity): *Edifying Discourses in Diverse Spirits*; *Works of Love*; *Christian Discourses*—and a little aesthetic article: *The Crisis and a Crisis in an Actress's Life* [PV 10; SV XVIII 85].

When speaking of Kierkegaard's "works" I shall include his early academic (Hegelian?) essay, *From the Papers of One Still Living*; his unfinished play, *The Battle between the Old and New Soap-Cellars*; his doctoral dissertation, *On the Concept of Irony*; the philosophical novel-in-progress, *Johannes Climacus*; the works written under the pseudonym Anti-Climacus, *The Sickness Unto Death* and *Training in Christianity*; and the posthumously published *The Point of View*. These, together with those works constituting the authorship, shall herein be considered the "Kierkegaard" readers have come to know. Then, although I shall frequently use "writings" and "works" interchangeably for ease in expression, one could make a further distinction in which the "works" would be a subcategory of the "writings," the largest category complete with everything that ever flowed from Kierkegaard's pen. The writings not strictly planned for publication would be included here—for example, the journals (sometimes called Kierkegaard's hidden authorship[16]) which are aphoristic and perhaps best used to supplement his works rather than to attempt a reconstruction of his life,[17] letters to friends and relatives, notes, and even doodles and scribblings.[18]

It is my hope that these distinctions will allow for greater precision in discussing and interpreting Kierkegaard's output. One knows, then, specifically which books are referred to by, say, "the dialectical structure of Kierkegaard's authorship." Moreover, there are additional, now customary, distinctions made within Kierkegaard's authorship. As evidenced in Kierkegaard's note above, there is an apparent difference between the aesthetic and the religious productivity, while simultaneously there are found to be three different classes (stages?) of the authorship. Given the formidable size of the corpus of Kierkegaard's writings, the distinctions explained thus far may assist readers in following the complex philosophical study that will develop in the following pages. In general, then, this will be a holistic study of Kierkegaard's writings which pays careful attention to the holes in Kierkegaard's interpretation of his authorship and thereupon seeks to establish a greater whole.

While the distinctions in the authorship, the works, and the writings may be viewed as quantitative, the deeper distinctions in the aesthetic, the ethical, and the religious works are qualitative. Both categories are the result of Kierkegaard's own plotting, and it is particularly the latter distinctions that produce a serious problematic for critical readers who, unwilling to accept the author strictly at his word, imagine the possibility of a deeper irony lurking within mysterious traces and written in the ubiquitous spaces.

These distinctions are not without their problems, especially when they are presented as the ultimate means of interpreting Kierkegaard. Precisely this may be the pinch of the problem of reading Kierkegaard in general, for whatever work from the authorship that one attempts to read, it seems to be already contained within a complicated dialectical structure that purportedly provides the key to both reading and understanding it. Questioning this "key" in its fullness is an overriding part of my concern here.

In very recent years, however, this key has been questioned; one must now question the questioners, for, as far as I can tell, the "problem of reading Kierkegaard" has not been solved; nor has it abated. Those interpreters who freely accept the religious meaning of Kierkegaard's authorship both as dominant and as the determining factor of all Kierkegaardian inquiry appear to be forever at odds with the interpreters who cannot freely accept Kierkegaard's religious *telos* and who would emphasize Kierkegaard's "de(con)structive"—to distinguish from "upbuilding"—productivity or view the entire corpus solely as an aesthetic production. On close reading, however, these opposing approaches cancel each other out and leave the problem of reading Kierkegaard a task still to be accomplished.

As an example of the latter type of criticism I would cite a postmodern critic who claims that the qualitative distinctions "rest on nothing more than an arbitrary privilege."[19] But the postmodern critic will find it somewhat discomforting to be in such close agreement with the dogmatic theologians who are not willing to accept Kierkegaard's religious views and have attacked his writings from the similar perspective that Kierkegaard never successfully escaped the aesthetic stage. Criticism, as it is said of politics, breeds strange bedfellows.

How does anyone avoid arbitrary privileging, and how might I deflect the reader's temptation to think that this work is already loaded with "philosophical privileging"? For me to attempt answering this, I must be allowed to say a few words on "philosophy," despite Plato's decree that one must be very old before one can have any insight into the matter.

First, although I am not in the business of ultimate justifications, I do at least hope to show that my philosophical organization of this study is not arbitrary but dictated by the sources themselves. Arbitrary privileging may be sidestepped by letting the writings speak for themselves, by taking them on their own terms and not treating them as enclosing the kernel of a doctrine that can be systematically constructed with supposedly key statements.

Second, *pace* Heidegger, philosophy, literally speaking, has no fixed subject matter (this is what makes it both distinct from and important for all other disciplines) and therefore cannot be generalized to mean simply "ontology" or "metaphysics."[20] To read Kierkegaard philosophically, then, is not to search for a fixed content following a set method of reading. Knowledge of the great many possible, often conflicting, readings (e.g., religious-Christian, aesthetic-rhetorical, idealist, ethical, Hegelian, Marxist, Freudian, deconstructionist) will not necessarily help readers, and may cloud the knotty task of reading Kierkegaard. The Kierkegaardian corpus is admittedly quite difficult to read. It always has been, and it is to be hoped that it always will be. If Kierkegaard wished this fate for himself, he would be satisfied in knowing that he got what he wanted. Neither speed-reading nor extensive reading is of use here. Only intensive close-reading can get the job done: reading slowly, over and over. To read Kierkegaard philosophically is thus, in my view, to read him *openly* (allowing for all possibilities, even that of being uplifted) and *closely* (and, if at all possible, in his native language).

In my own attempt to read Kierkegaard philosophically, I shall read the Kierkegaardian corpus both seriously and playfully, for one quite naturally attempts to be quiet and serious when reading, but—quite frequently, with regard to Kierkegaard—bursts out laughing in the attempt. Pascal's sentiment that the true philosopher makes light of philosophy and Nietzsche's epigraph to *The Gay Science*[21] present a mood that is all too infrequently expressed in professional philosophical writings. The *punctum saliens* is simply this: In a philosophical study, the problem of reading should inform one's writing, and familiar, uninteresting claims should, as much as possible, be avoided. From this view, a philosophical study is not necessarily a theoretical construction based on the critical search for grounds, reasons, or their intentions. It is, rather, a clear focus on the careful reading of original texts, and when critical claims are made, the "wherefores" for these claims must be made plain in light of the original text(s).

On this score, Richard Rorty's view of philosophy is surely not out of place:

> Interesting philosophy is rarely an examination of the pros and cons of a thesis. Usually it is, implicitly or explicitly, a contest between an entrenched vocabulary which has become a nuisance and a half-formed new vocabulary which vaguely promises great things. . . . This sort of philosophy does not work piece by piece, analyzing concept after concept, or testing thesis after thesis. Rather, it works holistically and pragmatically.[22]

Here, then, is another answer to the question, What could it mean to read Kierkegaard philosophically?

It is clear from the foregoing that I think Kierkegaard's collected works may be viewed as a whole and that some sense can be made of them, taken holistically. But Kierkegaard's own interpretation of his authorship presents a falsely comprehensive and holistic view of his writings; in other words, it leaves out too much. Nevertheless, this does not lead me into full agreement with those scholars who want to reject *The Point of View* and the dialectical structure of the authorship that appears in it, for to reject Kierkegaard's reading without replacing it with another hermeneutical hypothesis is of very little help to readers. Usually, the grounds for rejecting Kierkegaard's explanation have been puzzling. Some scholars take the rather strange strategy of wanting to prove that Kierkegaard was not a religious author from the outset of his authorship, and they see the denial of his religiousness as being strong enough to wipe out his dialectical structure. Why not accept the view that the authorship, beginning with *Enten–Eller* (Either/Or [1842]), had the religious in sight? This is not at all farfetched, especially when we consider the "Ultimatum" attached to *Or*, "The Edification Implied in the Thought that as Against God We Are Always in the Wrong"[23] (despite the fact that Kierkegaard does not draw our attention to this sermon, which would have helped his case in *The Point of View*).

If it is because Kierkegaard's reading is retrospective that we find it hard to swallow, I wonder if we would find it easier to accept had he unequivocally declared himself a religious author from the start? If one is inclined to think that the proposition *de omnibus dubitandum est* holds, then surely the statement "I am a religious author" is such to provoke an extraordinarily intense impulse to doubt. In other words, even if it were relatively easy to show that Kierkegaard had less ingeniously proclaimed his religiosity early on in his authorship, it would still be suspect to incredulous readers. I imagine Kierkegaard was well aware of this, and I could hardly suppose him saying, "With my direct communication to history, the whole matter will be settled once and for all."

Further, it hardly seems that any of today's postmodern readers would even accept an historically defensible reading showing Kierkegaard as a religious writer. In general, there is no obvious connection between Kierkegaard's real or feigned religiosity and his interpretation of his authorship. Whether Kierkegaard was a true Christian is certainly undecidable. On this point it seems that Kierkegaard and postmodernism can agree, for it would seem that if Kierkegaard's words mean anything, it is that there are no objective signs to decide the question with certainty, only traces of a hidden subjectivity that is never fully brought to the surface. Consequently, it is misleading to speak of Kierkegaard the person as either a Christian or a non-Christian. This should not even be a question.

It is possible to accept Kierkegaard's own interpretation of his authorship and still be in doubt concerning his body of works and his *Livsanskuelse*. *The Point of View* should be disregarded as much as it should be taken as providing the complete key to his works—that is to say, neither alternative works. One must not forget that *The Point of View* is also a piece of writing that requires interpretation. It possesses nothing intrinsically unique or different from Kierkegaard's other works. Whatever its goal, it needs to be interpreted as a part of Kierkegaard's works, not as standing outside them. That *The Point of View* has been read, by proponents and opponents alike, as somehow mysteriously lying outside the Kierkegaardian corpus is very well a universal mistake committed by Kierkegaardian scholarship. It is my view that this work must be interpreted as a part of the whole that itself adds up to a dialectical structure higher (and deeper) than the one Kierkegaard presented.

Although we cannot know for sure, it does not take a wide stretch of the imagination to feel that Kierkegaard considered *The Point of View* part of a greater whole, despite the fact that he withheld its publication during his lifetime. Kierkegaard must certainly have felt that this work was neither so simplistic nor straightforward as to be beyond interpretation. Readers must still work their way up to "the point of view," for, after all, "What in our time is an author? It is an *x*, often even when he is given in name" (PV 45; SV XVIII 108). Here, then, in a work whose title would seem to champion the authorial point of view, the writer paradoxically abjures any authorial or authoritarian position.

As stated above, the problem of this text is reading Kierkegaard from irony to edification. I shall try to make good on the points made above while presenting a new, differentiated, and holistic reading of Kierkegaard's collected works, from *The Concept of Irony* to *The Point of View*.

The problem of reading Kierkegaard is exceedingly complex for academic and general readers alike. The reasons are several. First,

> Kierkegaard's writings stand out, consistently enough, as a very motley and uneven textual mass with passages at a nearly inaccessible level of abstraction, formulated in an esoteric, forced, Germanic philosophical jargon, side by side passages of great simplicity and pictorial clarity, again alternating with diffusely garrulous digressions and sections bred of high-flown lyrical pathos.[24]

In other words, Kierkegaard had a very involved and particular manner of writing that encompassed several alternative styles. Second, Kierkegaard was very much at home in his mother tongue of Danish, which frequently does not translate nicely into English, especially when the level of abstraction is so high. The following rather lengthy quote will give the reader a discerning look at the importance of the Danish language for Kierkegaard:

> I consider myself *fortunate* to be bound to my mother tongue . . . a mother tongue that is rich in inner originality when it amplifies the soul and sounds sensually to the ear with its *sweet* ring; a mother

> tongue that does not moan vainly over a difficult thought . . . a mother tongue that does not puff and sound strained when it stands for the ineffable, but busies itself with it in jest and seriousness until it is exposed; a language that does not find that which lies *near* far away, or search *deep* down for that which is lying at hand, because it goes in and out like an elf in happy relation to the object, and like a child brings a happy remark to light without rightly knowing it; a language that is vehement and moved every time the right lover knows masculinely to excite the female passion of language, self-conceited and triumphant in the conflict of thought, every time the right ruler knows to lead it on, adroit like a wrestler, every time the right thinker does not let it go and does not let the thought go; a language that, if it even in one single place seems poor, yet it is not, for it has disdained like a modest mistress, who has the highest value, and is not at all slovenly; a language, that not without expression for the great, the decisive, the prominent, has a lovely, a decent, a blissful explanation for the intermediate thought and the secondary concept and the adjective, and the feeling of chitchat, and the hum of transition, and the fervor of inflection, and the concealed secretive fertility; a language that understands jest just as well as seriousness: a mother tongue that imprisons its children with a chain that is "easy to bear—yes! but hard to break" (SV VIII 277-8; KW XI 489–90).[25]

Third, not only does our author court both jest and earnestness in his play with language—and it is highly interesting that Kierkegaard sees language, his Danish language, as actively responsible for the jest and seriousness involved in exposing the ineffable—but he also practices the arts of self-concealment, self-denial, and self-effacement. How, then, is the reader supposed to approach a writer who went to the utmost lengths to distance himself from his work? The problem is intensified for one who quite innocently hopes to uncover a meaning, philosophy of life, point of view, or opinion that can be held on to and labeled "Kierkegaardian." This difficulty is evidently most conspicuous when reading Kierkegaard's pseudonymous works, texts from the same pen but under a different name. But, as we shall see, a serious sense of "indirectness" may be attributed to the writings signed by Kierkegaard as well (chapter 8).

A text from Kierkegaard's pen, pseudonymous or not, contains within it a formidable motion and richness such that one may well wonder if it is possible to rest in a circle of thoughts long enough to gather an opinion or glimpse a *Livsanskuelse* or *Lebensanschauung*. The complications increase when an author (and the author's author) tells the dear reader never to ask of his opinion, because he really does not have one; and even if he did, it would be worthless for the reader to know. In *Frygt og Baeven* (Fear and Trembling, 1843) we read:

> Next to the question of whether or not I have an opinion, nothing can be of less interest to someone else than what my opinion is. To have an opinion is to me both too much and too little; it presupposes a security and well-being in existence akin to having a wife and children in this mortal life, something not granted to a person who has to be up and about night and day and yet has no fixed income. In the world of spirit, this is my case, for I have trained myself and am training myself always to be able to dance lightly in the service of thought, as far as possible to the honor of the god and for my own enjoyment, renouncing domestic bliss and civic esteem, the *communio bonorum* and the concordance of joys that go with having an opinion [KW VII 7].

This, of course, is the "non-view" of the pseudonym Johannes Climacus, a view so light and lofty that it renounces all views (therefore one needs a ladder to reach it[26]). Climacus wants to dance, but he can dance only with himself,[27] that is, with his thoughts—specifically, the thought of death, that ultimate thought of the ultimate which has led to so much philosophy, so much writing.

Opinions are heavy things. They restrict and confine; they are the shackles of the mind. Human beings, then, with all their various opinions, are very heavy indeed. So heavy are they that Climacus begs the immortal gods to keep him off the (mortal) dance floor. "Every human being is too heavy for me, and therefore I plead, *per deos obsecro*: Let no one invite me, for I do not dance."

The thought of Climacus shares some deep similarities with the thought of Kierkegaard, for the latter was, after all, involved in the publication of the former. But more than this, Climacus and Kierkegaard both affirm and negate themselves throughout their problematic activity of religiously serving the god and aesthetically enjoying it. And Kierkegaard, like Climacus, does not dance. A case in point involves Fredrika Bremer, a famous Swedish author, who attempted to set up a meeting with Kierkegaard. She had met several of Denmark's leading cultural personalities in 1848, such as Bishops H. L. Martensen and N. F. S. Grundtvig, and thereafter contacted Kierkegaard with a letter that began: "To Victor Eremita: A person who lives alone like you (although she lives in the middle of the world of society) wishes heartily that before she drags herself away out of the country she might meet you, partly in order to thank you for the heavenly man in your writings, partly in order to speak with you about 'life's stages,' life's metamorphoses, a subject which holds for her a deep interest in this period more than any other."[28]

Victor Eremita never answered his contemporary from Sweden. "But when Fredrika Bremer later sent him her book *Liv i Norden* [*Life in the Nordic Countries*], Kierkegaard wrote in his diary: 'Now it nearly makes me angry that I did not answer as I first had thought: thank you so much, but I do not dance.'"[29] What, then, can be made of Climacus-(Eremita)-Kierkegaard? Have I reached an impasse in my groping to begin? What is now needed perhaps more than anything in working out the problem of reading Kierkegaard is a return to the earliest original source material and its cultural context in Denmark, especially if one takes seriously the thought, "One cannot connect Kierkegaard too closely to the intellectual life of Copenhagen from 1830 to 1850."[30]

The earliest works that I have in mind here are, as apparent from above, *From the Papers of One Still Living*, *The Concept of Irony*, and *Johannes Climacus*. Because Kierkegaard's journals and papers quite simply present too much to absorb in the present study, and because they quite honestly present a systematically uneditable incoherent mass, they cannot, considered as a whole, independent literary entity, be included in the present study. This disclaimer does not, however, prevent my turning to them when their (possible) relation to a particular text under discussion makes for greater intelligibility.

For the moment, then, let me not worry about Climacus, that humorist. By returning to the beginning of Kierkegaard's writings and reading *From the Papers of One Still Living* and *The Concept of Irony*, one finds that the early, polemical Kierkegaard certainly held that a life-view (*Livsanskuelse*), or even a "philosophy of truth," was worthy of a human being. Therefore, my reading will begin with an inquiry into the Kierkegaardian life-view that is developed in the early writings, and will then consider how this life-view relates to the rest of Kierkegaard's production.

Perhaps the relationship between a life-view and truth is not so obvious as one would assume. Consequently, it must be questioned along with Kierkegaard's interest in truth, an interest that is decisively expressed at the end of *Enten/Eller* (Either/Or [1842]): "For only the truth which edifies is truth for you" (EO II 356; SV III 324). An earlier well-known passage from Kierkegaard's papers expresses the point on a more personal note:

> The thing is to find a truth which is truth for me, to find that idea for which I want to live and die. . . . What good would it do me if truth stood before me, cold and naked, not caring whether I recognized her or not. . . . What is truth but to live for an idea? [J 44–5; P I A 75][31]

Although this passage is rarely scrutinized in its larger context, it is true enough that, in existential terms, the problem is *how* to live for an idea, with the "living for" having more importance and validity than "the idea"—unless "the idea" is itself defined by this "living for," in which case Kierkegaard's appropriation of his day's Hegelian-infected language leads to the philosophical misunderstanding that he is guilty of a blatant idealism. More specific reasons for why this is not the case will be given below. Regardless, as early as 1835 we see that Kierkegaard's ruminations have led to interesting literary bursts that would not be without significance for his future writings.

Would it be possible to build up and support the view that throughout his writings—or in any particular work—Kierkegaard tried to conjure the reader into (1) forgetting completely the pursuit of truth, (2) not holding any special life-view, or (3) accepting the ultimate absence of an absolute meaning in the face of the unknown? And what about Kierkegaard himself—how much may the reader surmise? It is useful and important to note that a negative answer to the tripartite question above does not entail that one must defend the idea of truth as "out there." This idea, or "absolute objective truth," is presented as being of no essential advantage to the existing individual—it may, in fact, be disadvantageous, and, therefore, we find Kierkegaard's (in)famous re-evaluation of the Hegelian thesis, "Truth is subjectivity." These words do not, however, necessarily lead to nihilism, despite the use that Kierkegaard was put to in French circles after the Second World War. The nihilist faces the impossible position of maintaining that it is manifest that there is no truth "out there." The atheist faces a similar difficulty, for in asserting that "God does not exist," the unbeliever says too much. In the words of Rorty, "To say that we should drop the idea of truth as out there waiting to be discovered is not to say that we have discovered that, out there, there is no truth."[32] In short, Kierkegaard was neither a nihilist nor an anti-realist, although finding the appropriate label for his complex position, a rather misguided task at best, is almost unachievable.

The way that Kierkegaard wrote about "truth" makes his writings highly relevant to the contemporary "philosophical" scene, and it is thus fitting that he be approximated to postmodern contexts. But, because Kierkegaard did not feel obliged to dispense altogether with the idea of absolute truth in the face of great doubt and uncertainty, he has in large measure been given short shrift by postmodernist writers. While they might drop his name here or there, a sustained, intensive reading by any renowned "postmodernist" has not yet appeared. This is at least mildly ironic when one acknowledges that Kierkegaard has surely foreshadowed their work in decisive ways.[33]

However, critical scholarship has recently been attracted by the problem of "Kierkegaard and postmodernism,"[34] and there can be no doubt as to the high degree of intellectual provocation that this scholarship presents. But despite this, one would be hard pressed to derive an unclouded exposition of the basic questions involved in the juxtaposition of Kierkegaard and postmodernism. A not-so-slight question that the most casual reader of intellectual history might pose is this: if postmodernism has developed during the advent of the "death of God," how can Kierkegaard possibly be read as finding a place in that historical context? Since a great many different points of view are possible here, one must go about reading Kierkegaard carefully before casting his works onto the postmodern scene.

In Merold Westphal's insightful view, we are currently in "the Kierkegaardian stage of twentieth-century philosophy." He explains:

> The paths that lead from Heidegger to Derrida and from Wittgenstein to Rorty are what I call the Kierkegaardian stage of

> twentieth-century philosophy, the increasingly emphatic denial that philosophy can be or should try to be scientific.[35]

At present, however, one finds a sharp tension between postmodernism, broadly construed,[36] and Kierkegaard. This tension will be considered after the tension of reading Kierkegaard's readings from irony to edification has been explored, in order to exhibit clearly in what sense Kierkegaard's writings may be read in a postmodernist manner.

In general, then, my essay will be informed by contemporary postmodern philosophical considerations—in ways that I think aid in a critical reading—but it will not be overwhelmed by them. It is my view that one cannot adequately deal with interesting contemporary questions without first furnishing a comprehensive reading of the Kierkegaardian literature, because their answers need to be based on and preceded by just such a reading. Any other method would be little more than intellectual guesswork, which should be avoided in one's own work and assailed in the growing field of Kierkegaardology.

Notes

1. Quoted from Ulrich Johannes Schneider's *Die Vergangenheit des Geistes: Eine Archäologie der Philosophiegeschichte* (Frankfurt: Suhrkamp, 1991) by Jonathan Rée in his review "The Philosopher in the Library," *Times Literary Supplement* (October 4, 1991).

2. Although I do not feel that this statement requires any serious defense, I can proffer the sensible words of Merold Westphal, who, in *Kierkegaard's Critique of Reason and Society* (Macon, Ga.: Mercer University Press, 1987), writes: "Since we are at what might be called the Kierkegaardian stage of the twentieth century, the time is ripe for putting aside doubts as to whether he is really a philosopher and for recognizing him not just as a historical figure who might be of interest to those who share his religious faith, but also as a full-fledged partner in the contemporary philosophical critique of reason and society" (p. 1).

3. To complicate, it is not too soon to etymologize. "Subject" comes from the Latin roots *sub* (under) plus *iacere* (to throw), and means a placing or a putting under, such as under the authority or control of, or owing allegiance to an(-)other. "Object" is from the Latin *ob* (before,

toward) plus *iacere*, and means a casting before or that which appears (before).

To be sure, the oversimplification involving the extreme poles of "objectivity" and "subjectivity" is misleading, and I shall suggest below that Kierkegaard's position could be more appropriately called "sub-objectivist."

4. As we shall see below, the idea of transfiguring or transubstantiating experience is dear to Kierkegaard.

5. "The task of examining Kierkegaard's work philosophically is not easy. It is only on the basis of an investigation of individual problems and a study of particular works that gives us warrant to pass judgements upon Kierkegaard's total work, a field now pre-empted by those who deal in generalizations and often without scrupulous reference to a text, which, often enough, is ambiguous and difficult to interpret even within the particular work in which it occurs." Although written in 1965 by Herbert M. Garelick (in *The Anti-Christianity of Kierkegaard* [The Hague: Martinus Nijhoff, 1965], p. 4), I find this quote to be quite appropriate and in tune with my perspective.

6. Jens Himmelstrup, *Søren Kierkegaards Opfattelse af Sokrates* (Soren Kierkegaard's Conception of Socrates) (Copenhagen: Arnold Busck, 1924), p. 9.

7. *The Phenomenology of Mind*, trans. J. B. Baillie (London: George Allen & Unwin Ltd, 1910), p. 92.

8. Three years before his death Kierkegaard wrote the following passage in his journal: "Melancholy: Somewhere in the Psalms it says of the rich man that he collects a treasure with great care and 'knows not who shall inherit from him': and so too I shall leave behind me, intellectually speaking, a not so little capital; alas, and I know at the same time who will inherit from me, that figure which is so enormously distasteful to me, who up till now has always, and will continue to inherit all good things: the Docent, the professor. . . .

"And even if 'the professor' were to come across this it would not stop him, it would not have the effect of making his conscience prick him, no, this too would be taught. And this remark again, if the professor were to come across it, would not stop him, no, this too would be taught. For the professor is longer than the tapeworm (which a woman lately got rid of and which measured, according to her husband, who gave thanks in the paper, 200 feet) longer even than that is the professor; and no man in whom there is 'the professor' can be freed by another man from that tapeworm, only God can do that, if the man is willing." Quoted by Louis Mackey in *Points of View: Readings in Kierkegaard* (Tallahassee: Florida State University Press, 1986), pp. 139–40. See also P X^4 A 628, 629.

9. This text was written during the summer of 1848, at roughly the same time as *The Sickness Unto Death* and *Training in Christianity*. Kierkegaard, however, had his reasons for not publishing this work, and they will be discussed in a more appropriate context (see the Conclusion). *The Point of View* remained hidden away in Søren's secretary until his brother, Bishop Peter Christian Kierkegaard, found it and published it, together with two "Notes" that S. Kierkegaard himself had considered publishing with the work, in 1859, four years after Søren's death.

10. This is surprisingly true of some recent "postmodern" readings of Kierkegaard which, if the label means anything at all, presumably intend to provide a much closer reading of the text(s).

A somewhat typical, non-postmodern account of the broken engagement is that Kierkegaard willfully renounced his beloved, Regine, who was ten years his junior, in an act not unlike Abraham's action against his son Isaac, because of a higher religious calling that had melancholically been determined as his task for life. As is no doubt apparent, I have difficulty sympathizing with this view, and see Kierkegaard as rather lacking in something which would enable him to love and commit to another. (This inability to commit takes on an additional significance in light of the ambiguity of his authorship.) Kierkegaard would seemingly concur, for as he writes in his journal: "If I had had faith, I would have stayed with Regine"(JP V 5664; P IV A 107). This should put a sharp halt to any attempted analogy between Kierkegaard/Regine and Abraham/Isaac.

11. "Kirkegaard" (the modern spelling is "kirkegård") literally means churchyard or cemetery.

12. Although at the time that Kierkegaard received his degree he was labeled "Magister" rather than "Doctor Kierkegaard," this title was abolished shortly thereafter so that all those who had previously received the Magister Artium degree were then officially considered Doctors of Philosophy. The simple point is that a magisterial dissertation is equivalent to a doctoral dissertation, and I shall use the terms interchangeably.

13. *Livsanskuelse* corresponds to the Swedish *livsåskådning* and the German *Lebensanschauung* (compare *Weltanschauung*) and expresses a complete and whole view of life. Lee Capel, the first English translator of *The Concept of Irony*, attempts to elaborate further on its meaning by translating it as "an organic view of life." This is both peculiar and intriguing. While *anskuelse* means "view" or "outlook," the adjective *anskuelig* means "clear" or "lucid." I shall look upon this word as expressing a clearly reflected philosophy of life, understanding "philosophy" in a sense that will be developed later.

14. The problem of classification is particularly acute with regard to Kierkegaard's writings. Unlike many other authors, Kierkegaard pres-

ents a difficult case for librarians, and to collect the complete works of our author, one must be prepared to traverse the distances between the philosophy, theology, and art/aesthetics sections in some university libraries.

15. Aage Henriksen, *Methods and Results of Kierkegaard Studies in Scandinavia: A Historical and a Critical Study* (Copenhagen: Munksgaard, 1951), p. 10. Although he presents his work as "an attempt to help to rectify this situation" (p. 36), Mark Taylor concedes in *Kierkegaard's Pseudonymous Authorship: A Study of Time and the Self* (Princeton, N.J.: Princeton University Press, 1975) that this judgment still obtains. Although he occasionally detours elsewhere, it is clear in this text that the totality Taylor is working with is the pseudonymous authorship.

16. See Gregor Malantschuk, "Søren Kierkegaard—Poet or Pastor?" (AN 4). Here Malantschuk briefly explains the place of the journals in the structure of Kierkegaard's work as a writer.

17. The first edition of Kierkegaard's journals and papers (EP) was edited by H. P. Barfod and H. Gottscheds from 1869 to 1881. According to the editors of this edition, all the papers up to 1843 are "an incoherent mess." Thus, one responds incredulously to the later edition by P. A. Heiberg and Victor Kuhr, who appear to know how to rearrange the incoherent papers into their aesthetic, philosophical, and religious divisions. Henning Fenger presents a carefully researched argument in *Kierkegaard-Myter og Kierkegaard-Kilder* (Kierkegaard Myths and Kierkegaard Sources) (Odense: Universitetsforlag, 1976) that exhibits a very reasonable doubt concerning the usefulness and decidability of Kierkegaard's papers.

18. Mark Taylor provides an original discussion of Kierkegaard's doodling in *Altarity* (Chicago: The University of Chicago Press, 1987), pp. 305–22. He also points out that Kierkegaard's writing, strictly speaking, was not work, and that Kierkegaard had never worked during his entire life. Taylor writes, "Had his writing become work or his writings works, he no longer would have been a writer" (p. 307). While I can agree with this statement, I shall continue to write "works" occasionally, as Taylor himself does. The reader need only remember that the works were not work in the strict sense of employment for which one is paid; they were, rather, work in the sense of play, for the author's enjoyment. But to call them "plays" would be too awkward, however suggestive it may be.

19. Christopher Norris, "De Man Unfair to Kierkegaard? An Allegory of (Non-)Reading," in *Kierkegaard: Poet of Existence*, ed. Birgit Bertung (Copenhagen: C. A. Rietzel, 1989), p. 90.

20. Philosophy in the sense that I am trying to develop here may be defined as a practice lacking any proper subject matter that gets on by

attacking problems encountered in reading and thinking, which are abated through the act of writing.

21. "Any master who lacks the grace to laugh at himself—I laugh." See Friedrich Nietzsche, *The Gay Science*, trans. Walter Kaufmann (New York: Random House, 1974), p. 31.

22. Richard Rorty, *Contingency, Solidarity, and Irony* (Cambridge: Cambridge University Press, 1989), p. 9.

23. This discourse will be considered closely in chap. 9, "The Love of Edification and the Edification of Love."

24. Bjarne Troelsen, *Søren Kierkegaard: Ideens Politispion* (Søren Kierkegaard: The Idea's Political Spy) (Herning: Systime, 1984), p. 7.

25. I have sacrificed grace for awkwardness by translating this passage as literally as possible. Throughout this work I shall incorporate many of my own translations, so a word on my philosophy of translation is in order. In contrast to the famous Swedish writer, aesthetician, and theologian Esais Tegnér (1782–1846)—who wrote: "Translations are like women, the most beautiful ones are not always the most faithful"—I sacrifice beauty for grammatical fidelity, which will no doubt explain the occasional nagging feature in my translations.

26. The name Johannes Climacus comes from a monk (ca. 570–649) who wrote "the celebrated" *Ladder of Paradise*. "Climacus" has the meanings of "climax" and "ladder," and the Hongs maintain that it symbolizes the "structure of logical sequence" in the writings under this name (KW VII ix).

27. Another pseudonymous author who danced alone is Simon Stylita. The following is from a draft of the title page of what became *Fear and Trembling*.

Between Each Other (*)
by
Simon Stylita
Solo Dancer and Private Individual

———

edited
by
Søren Kierkegaard

(*) In margin: *Movements and Positions* (KW VI 243; JP V 5659; P IV B 78).

28. Nils Åke Sjöstedt, *Sören Kierkegaard och svensk litteratur* (Søren Kierkegaard and Swedish Literature) (Göteborg: Elander, 1950), p. 87.

29. Gunnar Aspelin, *Tankens vägar* (The Ways of Thought) (Stockholm: Almqvist & Wiksell, 1958), p. 224.

30. Paul V. Rubow, *Kierkegaard og hans Samtidige* (Kierkegaard and

His Contemporaries) (Copenhagen: Gyldendal, 1950), p. 10. For the English-speaking world, the historian Bruce Kirmmse has recently published *Kierkegaard in Golden Age Denmark* (Bloomington: Indiana University Press, 1990), an important work that goes a long way in placing Kierkegaard firmly in the context of his social, political, and intellectual environment. With regard to Kierkegaard's writings, however, Kirmmse's main concern is the authorship after 1846.

31. Henning Fenger raises serious doubts concerning this and related passages in his *Kierkegaard-Myter og Kierkegaard-Kilder*, specifically chap. 4, "Kierkegaards brevnovelle 'Breve,'" pp. 71–108. The traditional view is that Kierkegaard wrote this in his journal while vacationing in Gilleleje, the northernmost coastal town on North Zealand, during the summer of 1835 (August 1, to be exact). On the contrary, Fenger presents a good deal of evidence to suggest that Kierkegaard wrote this and related passages in 1836 while back in Copenhagen, and that they were poetic, fictitious writings intended to be gathered into a novel entitled simply "Letters" in the spirit of Goethe's *The Sorrows of Young Werther* and Sibbern's *Gabrielis Breve.*

32. Rorty, *Contingency, Solidarity, and Irony*, p. 8.

33. Christopher Norris makes this point in "De Man Unfair to Kierkegaard?" This stimulating essay provides a reading of a short story by David Barthelme and an unpublished essay by Paul de Man entitled "The Concept of Irony." De Man's title is slightly misleading, however, as Norris points out, for Kierkegaardian irony is treated only peripherally. Norris attempts to sketch briefly what a postmodern reading of Kierkegaard might look like. Norris's views are further discussed below, in the Conclusion, "Rereading Kierkegaard as a Postmodern Philosopher."

34. There is an interdisciplinary series, Kierkegaard and Postmodernism, published by Florida State University Press, Tallahassee, under the editorship of Mark C. Taylor (general editor), E. F. Kaelin, and Louis Mackey. The works in this series include: Louis Mackey, *Points of View: Readings of Kierkegaard* (1986); John Vignaux Smyth, *A Question of Eros: Irony in Sterne, Kierkegaard, and Barthes* (1986); Pat Bigelow, *Kierkegaard and the Problem of Writing* (1987); Sylviane Agacinski, *Aparté: Conceptions and Deaths of Søren Kierkegaard*, trans. Kevin Newmark (1988), and the first English translation of Kierkegaard's *Prefaces* (1989) by William McDonald. Other works worthy of mention here are Pat Bigelow's *The Conning, The Cunning of Being: Being a Kierkegaardian Demonstration of the Postmodern Implosion of Metaphysical Sense in Aristotle and Early Heidegger* (Tallahassee: Florida State University Press, 1991), John D. Caputo's *Radical Hermeneutics: Repetition, Deconstruction, and the Hermeneutic Project* (Bloomington: Indiana University Press, 1987), Henry Sussman's *The*

Hegelian Aftermath (Baltimore: The John Hopkins University Press, 1982), and Mark Taylor's *Altarity*.

35. The following sentence reads, "Kierkegaard should now be included as a full partner in contemporary philosophical discussion." Westphal, *Kierkegaard's Critique*, p. 2.

36. The most concise definition I know is given in three words by Jean-François Lyotard: "incredulity towards metanarratives." See *The Postmodern Condition*, trans. Geoff Bennington and Brian Massumi (Minneapolis: University of Minnesota Press, 1984), p. iv.

PART ONE

The Development of an Ironic Methodology in Kierkegaard's Early Writings

1

The Genesis of Genius

> Even if one does not share my view that an epigraph by its musical power, which to a certain extent it can well have without being verse, either ought to play a prelude, as it were, and thereby put the readers into a definite mood, into the rhythm in which the section is written (insofar as the epigraph is a verse, this is the thing about it that reminds one of vaudeville), or it ought to relate piquantly to the whole section and not form a pun on one particular expression occurring once in the chapter or be an insipid general statement about the contents of the chapter. Even if one does not share my view, one will, however, surely grant me that it requires a good deal of taste, a high degree of inwardness in one's subject and in the temperature of the mood, to choose an epigraph that becomes a little more than an exclamation mark saying nothing or a figure like those the physicians usually write above their prescriptions.
>
> S. Kjerkegaard, KW 92–93

KIERKEGAARD'S BIRTH AS A WRITER may formally be said to begin with *Af en endnu Levendes Papirer* (From the Papers of One Still Living), published against his will (*utgivet mod hans villie*) by S. Kjerkegaard on September 7, 1838.[1] The first book to be written by Kierkegaard was none other than the first book to be written on Hans Christian Andersen, Kierkegaard's contemporary, whom Kierkegaard had most likely met, although they could hardly be considered friends.

The biographical data that usually surround—and are said to explain—the book's oblique title includes the deaths of Michael Pedersen Kierkegaard, Søren's father, four weeks before the publication date, and of Poul Møller, Kierkegaard's mentor and close friend. It is also often mentioned in this connection that only two of the seven Kierkegaard children were still living and that Søren supposedly had an (irrational) assurance that he would die before turning thirty-four years old. In addition, there is gossip that Kierkegaard was contemplating suicide. Such "explanations" are presented by the editors of Kierkegaard's *Samlede Værker* (Collected Works) as well as by the Danish scholars Georg Brandes, Vilhelm Andersen, Niels Thulstrup, and Frithiof Brandt. In my view, these explanations are at best irrelevant, at worst utter nonsense, for it seems very unlikely that Kierkegaard, who strikes one from start to finish as strictly holding the reader *in mente*, would entitle his first work something that the general reader, unaware of the peculiar biographical facts, would not possibly be able to grasp. Moreover, and this is quite important, since Kierkegaard vigorously reproaches Andersen for his superficial and incidental relation to the main line of thought in *Kun en Spillemand* (Only a Fiddler)—Andersen's lack of taste and knowledge in choosing epigraphs, to cite but one example—it would be thoughtless and unreflecting of Kierkegaard to entitle his work so very accidentally. (How the Kierkegaardologists have missed this point is beyond me.) Thus, to be fair in reading Kierkegaard, an understanding of the title should be sought in relation to the central content matter, that is, the critical discussion of Andersen's work and the importance he places on the environment's influence upon the supposed genius of Christian, the main character in *Only a Fiddler*.[2]

Prior to his first "book," if I may be permitted to use this word in the ordinary sense which will soon be lost, during his early years as a student at the University of Copenhagen from 1834 to 1836 (see KW I 1-52), Kierkegaard had published several newspaper articles, some terribly witty. *From the Papers of One Still Living* was, however, his first writing to be published independently, and Kierkegaard himself paid to see it come into print. A comprehensive reading of the Kierkegaardian literature should, then, begin with this text. Somewhere between the lines, however, I can almost hear Kierkegaard rewriting:

> *Postscript* for the readers who possibly could be harmed by reading "this book": they could just as well skip over it, and if they skipped so long that they skipped over the "other books" as well (aesthetic

> productivity? entire authorship?), it is of no consequence [KW I 60, slightly altered].

Be that as it may, this writing is not really a "book," and readers may be surprised to discover that Kierkegaard's first writing is neither a poetical (lyrical) work nor a theological discourse, although elements of both can still be found within the text. It is, rather, an extensive literary review of H. C. Andersen's third novel, *Only a Fiddler*, a work that had been published nearly a year earlier, in November 1837.[3] For whatever reason, it took Kierkegaard almost a year to get his review together. (This certainly was not the fault of the publishing company, for in those days getting something published took only a few weeks to a month.)

Philosophically, *From the Papers of One Still Living* presents, on the one hand, a polemical attack on Andersen as a romantic novelist and on his view of genius and, on the other, an initial probing into the question of a *Livsanskuelse*. It is important to realize that this writing was originally intended for Johan Ludvig Heiberg's speculative journal, *Perseus*. In many respects Heiberg (1791–1860) set the tone for the 1830s in the world of Danish letters, and he is remembered primarily as the introducer of Hegel's philosophy in Denmark. Thus, it is not surprising that *Perseus*, subtitled *Journal for the Speculative Idea*, clearly represented a foothold for Hegelianism in Denmark, and had as its "*conditio sine qua non* that all contributions should be speculative, i.e., Hegelian."[4] Any doubts as to the accuracy of this[5] are clearly alleviated after reading Heiberg's nine-page introduction to the reader, which includes this passage:

> We are lacking a journal that is exclusively devoted to the ideal endeavors, and one not merely in one single direction of these, but rather in their entire scope; for the more the rising culture splinters and particularizes the various spiritual interests, the more important it becomes to collect them as new in the highest unity, in which they all, after having been stripped of their empirical differences, can meet in the service of the Idea, stand side by side, and thereby win their shared union. In order to help out our literature's ever more perceptible need of such an asylum for the ideal endeavors, the undersigned dares to make a beginning, as he hereby opens a *Journal for the Speculative Idea*.
>
> This more specific determination of the Idea as *speculative* states the present journal's plan.[6]

To be sure, Kierkegaard's essay portrays a carefully crafted exercise in something that might be labeled Heibergian-Hegelian criticism. Unfortunately for Kierkegaard *Perseus* ceased publication in the summer of 1838, which explains why Kierkegaard sought to have his essay printed independently as a book. To provide a sweeping statement for this beginning, it can be maintained that Kierkegaard started his authorial activity as a literary critic with "a mouth full of Hegel."[7] To note that Kierkegaard was driven by a strong desire to publish—to become a writer—and that his first published work was a quasi-speculative literary review provides for the lifting of certain pretenses and allows for a fresh reading of Kierkegaard, particularly in the English-reading world where these facts are only now beginning to surface.

Would Kierkegaard at this point have considered himself an Hegelian? Certainly, he could not deny the influence that Hegel's philosophy exercised upon his writing, but "was" he an "Hegelian?" How would he define an Hegelian? Answers to these questions may be sought in the reply Kierkegaard wrote to Andersen, after Andersen had produced *En Comedie i det Grønne* (A Comedy in the Open Air), "Vaudeville in One Act Based on the Old Comedy: *An Actor Against His Will*," which was first performed at the Royal Theater of Copenhagen on May 13, 1840. Andersen's play presents a parody of Kierkegaard as a babbling Hegelian, whose language was pretty well undecipherable to Andersen and the few others who might have read it. (Andersen relates in a letter to a friend that only he and Kierkegaard had read the review.[8]) Kierkegaard's reply—entitled "Just a Moment, Mr. Andersen!"—went unpublished because Andersen had recently left Denmark to tour Europe. What follows is Kierkegaard's reaction to his character portrayed as a prating Hegelian:

> Now, if I were to say to Andersen that *I* have *never* passed myself off as a Hegelian and thus far it was *foolish* of Andersen to take sentences from my little piece and put them in the mouth of a Hegelian, then I would almost think myself crazy. For *either* I would have to associate with the word "Hegelian" the idea of a man who with seriousness and energy had grasped the world-view of his thought, had dedicated himself to it, found rest in it, and now with a certain genuine pride said of himself: I, too, have had the honor of serving under Hegel—and in this case it would be crazy of me to say it in a conversation with Andersen, because *he* probably would

> not be able to attach a sensible thought to it, just as I would at least hesitate to use such a significant predicate about myself, even if I were conscious that I had tried to make myself familiar with Hegel's philosophy. *Or* by a Hegelian I would understand a person who, superficially influenced by his thought, now deceived himself with a result he did not possess—and then it would be no less foolish to say this to Andersen, provided one agrees with me that the person who does not know what a Hegelian is in truth does not know what a Hegelian is in untruth, either, that is, can have no concrete idea on the subject [KW I 220–21].[9]

What is Kierkegaard saying here? First, it is clear that he is ridiculing Andersen for not understanding what an Hegelian is. Second, an "Hegelian" may be understood in either a positive (true) or a negative (untrue) sense, and these senses are clear enough above. Third, Kierkegaard does not directly state that he is or is not an Hegelian. He hypothesizes that were he to respond negatively to someone who had no concrete conception of an Hegelian, then he would certainly appear the fool. Whether or not the "significant predicate" of "Hegelian" should be applied to Kierkegaard remains an open and complicated question.

To quote the famous literary historian and "discoverer" of Nietzsche, Georg (Morris Cohen) Brandes (1842–1927), on Kierkegaard's first work: "This critical endeavor is, despite the exceptional powers it reveals, a beginner's attempt written nearly illegibly in parenthetical language with learned, particularly theological traces expressed throughout, richly ornamented with neck-breaking Hegelian phrases and formulas."[10] Brandes had learned a great deal from Kierkegaard—as a younger scholar he was very sympathetic to his countryman—but he grew harshly critical of him and strongly opposed (what he took to be) his *Livsanskuelse*. But Brandes's work, like many others', stands or falls provided Kierkegaard has a *Livsanskuelse* that may be clearly deciphered and determined. A clever and popular writer who is sometimes credited with introducing Kierkegaard to Germany (and Nietzsche to Scandinavia),[11] Brandes presents what I would call the "typical" everyday (unreflecting) Danish view accorded to Kierkegaard during his life and even to the present day. This view grants Kierkegaard a place of literary genius based largely on three bulky works, *Either/Or*, *Stages on Life's Way*, and *Concluding Unscientific Postscript*, but considers the production to be carried out by a rather narrow-minded, contemptuous little man whose writings have little left to offer the modern person.

In keeping with this assessment, Brandes often appears to be criticizing Kierkegaard's character rather than strictly weighing the contents of the text(s). This is unquestionably the case with his presentation of Kierkegaard's "Attack on Andersen." Scarcely referring to the text itself—with the exception of its title—Brandes enlarges from a point of view on the "essence and fate" of Kierkegaard, lamenting that Kierkegaard had not been influenced by the empirical and utilitarian philosophies evolving in Great Britain. Witness the personal attack in the chapter supposedly devoted to Kierkegaard's assault on Andersen:

> Here at the beginning of Kierkegaard's career is seen at once a side of his essence which is significant for the story of his development. He had, despite all his striving to bring himself closer to the Christian ideal of love, no humane nature; he did not possess the extensive humanity of the great critical spirits, not only not Stuart Mill's, but not even Sibbern's.[12] With all his superior virtuosity in philosophizing over whoever's thesis, he was not a philosophical trying nature, not at his guard against prejudice, unfairness, and overly hasty condemnation. With the artistic expression of Hegelianism he had acquired a good deal of its tone. Here again one may proclaim: what a misfortune that our entire cultural development was so fashioned that with these talents he was excluded from every influence from England and referred to all German expressions. Nothing would have been more salutary [*helbringende*] for him than a basic immersion into English empirical philosophy, for as the theory of knowledge [*Erkendelselære*] that evolves from the ideas of reason results in prejudice, the theory of knowledge that builds on experience leads impartially to examination.[13]

Brandes's biographical work is thus more—and less—than a critical investigation; it is, at the same time, a personal writing and a kind of polemic written to check Kierkegaard's influence, as Brandes admitted in a letter to Nietzsche several years later.

Just as Brandes in his youth had been influenced by Kierkegaard and infatuated with the prospect of faith, so he later underwent a decisive change in his life which turned him into a sharp critic who felt that he best understood his melancholy countryman's viewpoint since he himself had partaken of it. Brandes reads Kierkegaard as an idealist and a fundamentalist. He became offended by the "leap of faith" and the idea that the *New Testament* offers a worthy guide to life. He was also irritated, as no doubt many others are, by Kierkegaard's "obscure aversion to the natural sciences" (*obskurantisk Modvilje mod Naturvidenskaben*).

The essay itself, as Brandes puts it, has as "its object the punishment of the sinner Andersen who has committed *Only a Fiddler*!"[14] Despite all his *ad hominem* comments and stretching of the truth with rich metaphorical formulations, Brandes rightly notes that what had agitated Kierkegaard so much in Andersen's novel was the lax view of genius, which was presented as a fragile egg needing shelter and warmth to grow and develop properly. But first, to begin at the beginning, a word before, that is, the preface.

One hardly has to turn the first page of *From the Papers of One Still Living* to be filled with a sense of puzzlement that renders one's reading problematic. There is an intrinsic complexity involved in reading this work that is produced by the author's conscious displacement through double reflection. There is not simply a single writer and a single writing; there are at least two, which, squared, equals four: the reflective consciousness, the reflected consciousness, and the alter ego's reflective and reflected consciousnesses. With each thought or textual move, a complicated set of relationships and an intertangled multiplicity of paths are created which, by and large, keep the reader in the dark as to the writer's secret. I am reading in the preface of Kierkegaard's first published work, and yet reading it leads to a general delineation of the Kierkegaardian gambit and the Kierkegaardian text—perhaps not entirely unlike the game of backgammon where two players move in opposite directions around the same board, and the roll of doubles permits four distinct moves ahead. (And one knows, of course, that despite all the criss-crossing and steps forward and backward, one player must always arrive first.) Always imponderable and difficult to grasp, the preface leads readers into the depths without overpowering or imposing upon them. Yes, Kierkegaard's short preface could even lead readers astray, as he acknowledges in the postscript to the preface.

Within the beginning of this beginning, then, the seed that will bloom into the diverse beautiful pseudonyms is planted, the seed of "indirect communication." Although this text was written under Kierkegaard's own name, in light of the preface and the phrase "against his will," the famed "indirectness" of Kierkegaard's writings may be said to be born in this text. It is no wonder, then, that certain scholars have, in their confusion, labeled this a half-pseudonymous work! In discussing Kierkegaard's production at the end of his 1862 Swedish translation of *Kjerlighedens Gjerninger* (Works of Love) (see KG), Gustaf Thomée divides Kierkegaard's works into three groups: the absolutely pseudonymous, the half-pseudonymous, and the non-pseudonymous. *From the Papers of One Still Living* finds its place in the half-pseudonymous works, which are defined as works that Kierkegaard relates to as publisher but not as author. What is even more remarkable, however, is that in Bruce Kirmmse's recent, bulky study, *Kierkegaard in Golden Age Denmark* (1990), *From the Papers of One Still Living* is explicitily cited, without any explanation, as a pseudonymous work. What, one inevitably wants to ask, is the pseudonym? Unless this simple question can be answered, it is difficult to see how this work can be viewed as pseudonymous. I would, of course, be willing to grant pseudonymity of this writing if one were to cite "S. Kierkegaard" as the pseudonym and then present the reasons why. I doubt, however, that many scholars—or Kirmmse at least—would be willing to accept this, for the point of all of the supposedly "direct" writings of Kierkegaard would then be lost. In other words, it would no longer be clear when Kierkegaard is writing ironically or when he is writing in order to edify; the simple distinctions based solely on the names of the authors would be lost. Although I believe this is the conclusion one must reach through a holistic study of Kierkegaard's writings, it is too early to disclose this truth in all its beauty.

What makes matters worse for Kirmmse (and I should note that this is really a minor point in relation to a large and valuable study essentially concerned with Kierkegaard's post-1846 authorship) is that, first, he does not argue for the pseudonymity of *From the Papers of One Still Living* and, second, he then uses the mistaken fact of pseudonymity to interpret Kierkegaard's production from *From the Papers of One Still Living* to *A Literary Review*, the latter of which contains Kierkegaard's first mention of his early book.

> Furthermore, near the beginning and the conclusion of the *Review* there are direct references to SK's first book, *From the Papers of One*

> *Still Living*, a pseudonymous work, the one work which SK had not acknowledged in his afterword to the just-completed *Postscript* and which he finally acknowledges here in the *Review*.[15]

One of the ostensible reasons for the mention of this writing in *A Literary Review* is that:

> SK wishes to call attention to the fact that the early pseudonymous review, like the present *Review*, concerns itself with the problem of the whole, ethically integrated personality. However, the most important reason that the first book review is brought up in this present *Review* is that SK is mentioning it "in conclusion"; that is, SK sees *A Literary Review* as the concluding work of his literary production. Thus, his literary work began with a lengthy and pseudonymous book review that concerned itself with the ethical questions, and it concludes—with the symbolic symmetry that SK loved so well—with another lengthy ethical-political book review which this time is, significantly, not pseudonymous but in SK's own name. By pointedly alluding to *From the Papers of One Still Living* in *A Literary Review*, SK calls attention to the symmetry of the authorship he hoped he was concluding, an authorship that had allowed for the repetition and deepening of the same themes over and over again but that had also seen the essential movement from pseudonymity to direct communication.[16]

Unfortunately, this interpretation prompts suspicion, because it is not at all clear that *From the Papers of One Still Living* is pseudonymous. On the contrary, Kierkegaard signed his own name, the spelling of which was not fixed at the time, so that it read "S. Kjerkegaard" on the title page (see KW I 206 for a facsimile of the original title page). The most that can be claimed is that this writing presents a palpable duplicity that would later become more clearly reflected through the distance of pseudonymity. The lesson to be learned—and kept in mind—is that, from the very beginning, a writing *signed by* Søren Kierkegaard contained the force of indirect communication. From this moment on, reading Kierkegaard would not be easy.

In an 1835 paper entitled "Our Journalistic Literature" and presented to the Student Association, Kierkegaard says that he is nothing more than a *réflecteur* (KW I 38). While this is a very apt designation of Kierkegaard as a writer, it may also serve to define the Kierkegaard reader as a *réflecteur de réflecteur*. It is obvious that the reader plays an integral role in establishing the problem of reading Kierkegaard, for only through the existence of the reader does this "problem" make itself known. One would therefore need to flush out the important and problematic notions of reflection, double reflection, reduplication, and so forth, in order to make the Kierkegaardian word plain. To take just the notion of "reflection," without looking too far ahead, one can be sure that Kierkegaard, from his earliest student days, is well aware of the nature and power of reflection and the general significance it has for Hegel's philosophy. (Alternatively, one cannot know with assurance the extent of Kierkegaard's direct contact with Hegel's texts at this time. It seems likely that much of his early knowledge was acquired indirectly, through others.)

Etymologically, the word "reflection" means a bending or a throwing back, such as when one talks about light rays or sound waves. For Hegel, the concept has an extraordinarily wide range of use and plays an extremely important role in his philosophical system. In his *Lectures on the Philosophy of Religion*, Hegel defines reflection as "the action that establishes oppositions and goes from one to the other, but without effecting their combination and realizing their thoroughgoing unity."[17] In this way Hegel was able to criticize the philosophies of Kant, Fichte, and Jacobi for not being able to integrate the oppositions and differences constituted through reflection.[18] Nonetheless, Hegel still uses reflection in largely the same way as his predecessors, the difference being that he is then able to mediate all of the oppositions. In Jens Himmelstrup's *Terminologisk Ordbog* (Terminological Dictionary) to Kierkegaard's *Samlede Værker*, the concept of reflection in Hegel's philosophy is explained as follows:

> As Hegel goes from his treatment of the concept of Being [*Væren*] to the concept of Essence [*Væsen*], he fixes Essence as the truth of Being, as its actual ground. In the terminology of Hegel's logic this means that Being comes over from immediacy in difference, in contrast; there it opens up the "chasm" in the concept, which was not discovered before. A species of duplicity is therefore at work in the concept of Being. "Being is abrogated," and the Essence comes forward, comes into view. To fix this duplicity one needs a special *cogitation* [*Eftertanke*], and this cogitation is precisely reflection. The concept of Being requires only an immediate thought. That every object is something, has size and a way of being does not require any further cogitation. Such cogitation is first needed when there is

> a question concerning the ground of the being [*Værende*], concerning its characteristics, powers, causes, etc. When we use our cogitation, that is, think *over* something, not merely *on* something, according to Hegel something like a doubling of the thought occurs; it first directs itself immediately toward its object, but then "is broken" and thrown back, as with our thought over the essence of the object. As Hegel says, "nämlich den Gegenstand nicht gilt in seiner Unmittelbarkeit (zu wissen), sondern wir denselben als vermittelt wissen wollen" [namely, the object is not valid (to know) in its immediacy, rather we want to know it as mediated]. Hegel emphasizes that the truth of reflection's determinations depends upon their reciprocity, "und damit darin besteht, dass jede in ihrem Begriffe selbst die andere enthält" [and thereby is such that each one in its concepts even contains the others], and he even says: "ohne diese Erkenntnis lässt sich eigentlich kein Schritt in der Philosophie thun" [without this knowledge no step in philosophy may actually be taken]. The expression and concept of reflection is thus of rich use in Hegel's works and in the System's second half where relations and concepts often "reflect themselves" in each other and become objects for corresponding conceptual reflection as described above [SV XX 176-77].

The task, then, is to discover how the Hegelian notion was brought over into Kierkegaard's writings.

Kierkegaard, in keeping with the times, has an opaque understanding of reflection and uses the word widely, which may lead to a certain obscurity not unlike that felt after reading Hegel. It is difficult to state just what the concept of reflection meant to Kierkegaard,[19] but I like to view it as the ability to fine-tune thought dialectically. Though Kierkegaard does not define reflection at this stage, there is a concrete application of his ruminations on the power of reflection directed toward the self in the opening pages of *From the Papers of One Still Living*. The duplicity of the writer/publisher is expressed in several ways. The text was "published against his will" and the "preface" is devoted to explaining the distinction between the writer and his alter ego, that is, the writer and his will, the writer and his other, the writer and his double. (Read also the writer and the reader, or the writer as critic and the reader as friend, for at the end of this writing Kierkegaard writes of the reflected distinction between "a reading and a criticizing world's judgement.") Furthermore, one finds the (necessary?) duplicity of the human soul who wrote this book reflected in the form of (contingent?) letters: Kierkegaard was Kjerkegaard, the unstable "i" was varied in "Kierkegaard." If the reader is to grasp the writer set down on page after page, is it solely through being stirred in a strangely sympathetic way explicable only by an incomprehensible *communicatio idiomatum* (communication of two natures)?

A disunity is clearly reflected in this text which has Kierkegaard begin by arguing with himself. It would have been easier for him to begin by using a pseudonym, but instead we find a publisher (*utgiveren*, person responsible for publication—i.e., Kjerkegaard) at odds with the author (Kierkegaard) published against his will. The writer "closes himself up, silent and secretive in his *ádutov* (inner sanctum), so that he seems to avoid even me" (i.e., the publisher, who is also "the reader," as distinct from the writer), "in whom he otherwise usually has no secrets, and it is only in a vanishing reflection [*Afglands*], as it were, of what is moving in his soul that I, in a strangely sympathetic way [explicable only by an incomprehensible *communicatio idiomatum*] feel what is stirring in him" (KW I 56).

On the next page Kierkegaard expresses his reservations regarding his writing and questions the possibility of falling into the hands of readers who know how to read.

> You know very well I consider writing books to be the most ridiculous thing a person can do. One surrenders oneself entirely to the power of fate and circumstance, and how can one escape all the prejudices people bring with them to the reading of a book, which work no less disturbingly than the preconceived ideas most bring with them when they make someone's acquaintance, with the result that very few people really know what others look like? What hope can one entertain that one will fall into the hands of readers wholly *ex improviso* [without expectancy]? Besides, I feel tied by the fixed form the essay has finally acquired and, in order to feel free again, will take it back into the womb once more . . . [M]aybe then it can emerge in a regenerated shape [KW I 57].

The form, however, remained unchanged, and to get over long-spun considerations, the review was sent out into the world in the misleading form of a book with Pilate's famous decree: "What I have written, I have written" (John 19:22).

Om Andersen som Romandigter med stadigt Hensyn til hans sidste Værk "Kun en Spillemand" (On Andersen as a Novelist with

Constant Reference to His Last Work "Only a Fiddler") is the title given to this work after the preface. It is in many respects a more straightforward and clearer title that comes closest to the contents of the text, and its form will be repeated in Kierkegaard's magisterial dissertation, *Om Begrebet Ironi med stadigt Hensyn til Socrates* (On the Concept of Irony with Constant Reference to Socrates).[20] The review is a writing openly at odds with Andersen's central teaching in *Only a Fiddler*.

What provoked Kierkegaard to this burst of literary criticism was the view that genius needed nurturing and loving surroundings in order to grow and produce great things. In other words, without favorable circumstances, a genius—in the case of Andersen's novel, Christian—would die without success, as a victim of cruel fate. Kierkegaard will reject this view of the environment's encroachment on life, but he will not do so straightforwardly. He is well read in the philosophy of the times and, therefore, in order to criticize Andersen he begins with Hegel, or, rather, with the definition of Hegelian logic's point of departure: Being, pure and abstract (*Seyn*), is Nothing (*Nichts*). Kierkegaard's observations on beginning from the beginning are quite general and obscure.[21] He considers two manifestations of the attempt to begin with nothing, that of Hegel and that of an unnamed "genuinely original character."

Concerning the latter, the reader, then as now, is left to puzzle over the reference. According to the German scholar Emanuel Hirsch,[22] the "Simon Stylites" in question is the German theologian Carl Daub (1765–1835), though Julia Watkin suggests instead that Kierkegaard might have had Johann Gottlieb Fichte or Johann Georg Hamann in mind.[23]

Concerning the former, Kierkegaard essentially accepts that philosophy as a system should begin without presuppositions or unweighed premises, although he remarks, without giving reasons for his view, that it is only through a misunderstanding that existence itself should be considered in this way. This is clearly the first indication of what Kierkegaard will later develop into a full-scale criticism of speculative philosophy based on a deep consideration of the nature of existence. But it is only a hint, and, for reasons that follow in the text, Kierkegaard does not chide Hegel here for failing to appreciate actuality; he criticizes the Hegelians instead. Actuality has been neglected by the misunderstanding Hegelians and thousands of the age who stand ready, waiting, and willing to get every correct and reasonable word wrong. The trouble with the recent literature, which is "so completely preoccupied with prefacing and writing introductions," is that "it has forgotten that the beginning from nothing of which Hegel speaks was mastered by himself in the system and was by no means a failure to appreciate the great richness actuality has" (KW I 62). Clearly, Kierkegaard's complaint here is not with Hegel's system but with the Hegelians who have misapprehended not only the system but actuality as well. Kierkegaard, then, is not inconsequent in wanting to follow the Hegelian strategy of beginning from the beginning and from nothing, which in this project is identified as the cycle of short novels by Mrs. Gyllembourg[24] that begins with *En Hverdags-Historie* (A Story of Everyday Life).

Kierkegaard intertwines literature and philosophy and draws this cycle of short novels under the comb of Hegelian logic. He does this neither to "raze this summit with modern philosophical bustling and transform it into a vanishing element in existence" nor "to fix them in an absolute catholicity outside which there is no salvation" (KW I 65). What he wants to bring forward through his dialectical scrutiny is the life-view (*Livs-anskuelse*) in these short novels which surely has "its corresponding element in existence (*Tilværelse*) for its presupposition as it has also an aroused element as its effect" (KW I 65).[25]

When Kierkegaard finally gets to treating Mr. Andersen, he takes up the theme of the necessity of a life-view for the writer of short novels and novels. Fortunately for readers, Kierkegaard does try to spell out what is meant by a life-view. In the first place, "a life-view is more than a quintessence or a sum of propositions maintained in its abstract neutrality" (KW I 76). Thus, a simple, impersonal expression such as "Know thyself" or "Reality is rational" does not constitute a life-view or a philosophy of life. This is a rather familiar misunderstanding committed by both intellectuals and nonintellectuals alike who often act as though a clever, well-formulated statement is equivalent to (if not greater than) a complex, toilsome, personal standpoint. "A life-view is more than experience [*Erfaring*], which as such is always fragmentary," often contradictory and unclear. A life-view is, then, "the transubstantiation of experience [*Erfaringens Transsubstantiation*]; it is an unshakable certainty in oneself won from all experience [*Empirie*]" (KW I 76).

Given this positive characterization, it becomes clear (*anskuelig*) that not every person has a life-view in Kierkegaard's sense.[26] What does it take to change the substance of one's experience into something else? Not an easy question, yet Kierkegaard believes it can be done. A person who would win a life-view "does not allow his life to fizzle out too much but seeks as far as possible to lead its single expressions back to himself again" (KW I 77). Having a life-view does not mean that one has fully understood one's life, if understanding one's life means to understand each and every particular experience in it. One can, however, open the door to a successive understanding (*successive Forstaaelse*) that sheds a strange (*be-synd-erligt*: *synd* means "sin" or "shame" in Danish) light over one's life, leaving it to be understood in the past tense. Kierkegaard cites the German theologian Carl Daub,[27] who made good use of the Hegelian dialectic, in agreement: "There must come a moment, when, as Daub observes, life is understood backwards through the idea" (KW I 78). Thus, it is Daub, that "backwards prophet," as Kierkegaard will later call him in the *Philosophiske Smuler* (Philosophical Fragments), who may be credited with the oft-cited Kierkegaardian maxim that "Life must be lived forwards, but can only be understood backwards." The "idea," in all its mystery and importance for a life-view, surfaces here and cannot be easily submerged. At the very least it indicates the reflection necessary for understanding one's life—a reflection that is very much indebted to Hegel. But how does this reflection work in time? Kierkegaard will elsewhere write:

> It is quite true what philosophy says, that life must be understood backwards. But that makes one forget the other saying, that it must be lived—forwards. The more one ponders this, the more it comes to mean that life in time is never properly intelligible, for the very reason that at no point can I find complete repose in which to take up the position—backwards [DSK 111; P IV A 164].

Although Kierkegaard thinks that a life-view proper begins at the time of one's death, since this provides the necessary repose, in the present text, he wants to avoid this annihilating consequence so that in time he can propose his philosophy of the life-view. He therefore maintains "the idea," which serves as the center for a life-view, and writes: "But there must necessarily come a moment [*et Øieblik*]" (KW I 77), "there must come a moment" (KW I 78). But one should not think that "an idea as such (least of all a fixed idea) is to be regarded as a life-view" (KW I 79). Nor should "a certain poetic mood" be considered a life-view. All this Kierkegaard will use against his contemporary Andersen. Before I turn to Kierkegaard's criticism of Andersen, however, let me go back, reflecting on this abstract consideration of a life-view, to reread the two concrete examples Kierkegaard gives of a life-view, that is, a certainty in oneself won from the transubstantiation of experience. From a purely human standpoint, Stoicism is an example of a life-view oriented toward all worldly relationships, but it misses the deeper experience of the religious, which is characterized as follows:

> [The religious] has found therein the center as much for its heavenly as its earthly existence, has won the true Christian conviction, "that neither death, nor life, nor angels, nor principalities, nor powers, nor the present, nor the future, nor height, nor depth, nor any other creation will be able to separate us from the love of God in Christ Jesus our Lord" [KW I 76–77].

Stoicism and Christianity, then, are two examples of what Kierkegaard means by a *Livsanskuelse*.

Throughout the dialectical development of Kierkegaard's review, he sketches and describes recent figures in Danish literature in preparation for his treatment of Andersen. *A Story of Everyday Life* by Mrs. Gyllembourg serves as the point of departure not only aimed at subverting the misunderstanding Hegelians but equally, if not more forcibly, directed against "the main trend of the age in the political sphere." Young, revolutionary politicians bent on attacking the present actuality are, for Kierkegaard, sorrier forms of deluded persons whom he unremittingly scorns at every turn in the text. Mrs. Gyllembourg's short novels are briefly treated as presenting a fullness and joy in life that makes them edifying studies stamped with a religious character.[28] The life-view contained in these stories befits the older generation and individuals who have "finished the race and kept the faith." A quite different viewpoint, moral rather than religious, is expressed by the short novels of Carl Bernhard. The point in briefly describing these short novels as "native to the younger generation," and as being characterized by "a certain tendency to reminisce [*snakke gammelt*]," is "merely" to evince that these stories are not the manifestation of the (political) misunderstanding of "the deeper significance of a historical evaluation" which often appears "as a lack of patience to adapt oneself to the conditions of life, as powerlessness, when filling a particular position in the state, to share the burden of history, which is light and beneficent for the reasonable" (KW I 63). Although there is in all likelihood a concealed condescension of (the Heibergian) Bernhard, as the tendency to reminisce carries with it a certain degree of self-reflection, the unreflective misunderstanding that Kierkegaard is scoping out will have to be sought after in another lyrical outburst.

Before reaching Andersen, Kierkegaard pays tribute to "that voice in the wilderness, Steen Steensen Blicher, who, however, and this is precisely what is remarkable, transformed it into a friendly place of refuge for the imagination exiled in life" (KW I 69). Blicher (1782–1848),[29] who quite generally is remembered for his strong portrayal of life's hard realities as well as his social solidarity, also marks "a certain beginning from the beginning." He unveils:

> a deep poetic mood, shrouded in the mist veil of spontaneity, the unity of an individual-popular poetic keynote, echoing in the soul's inner ear, and a popular-idyllic picture, spread out for the imagination, illuminated by mighty flashes of summer lightning. . . . [T]here is also a unity here, which in its spontaneity significantly points to the future and which inevitably must grip the present age much more than it has done and thereby perhaps come to work beneficially on the prosaic manner in which politics have hitherto been handled [KW I 69].

Having said this, Kierkegaard is now ready to criticize the favorably known H. C. Andersen.

One of the first points Kierkegaard makes in focusing his critique on Andersen is that he has missed the "proper epic development." This is to be understood as

> a deep and earnest embracing of a given actuality, no matter how one loses oneself in it, as a life-strengthening rest in it and admiration of it, without the necessity of its ever coming to expression as such, but which can never have anything but the highest importance for the individual, even though it all went so unnoticed that the mood itself seemed born in secrecy and buried in silence [KW I 71].

It is significant that Kierkegaard follows Heiberg here in viewing the epic stage as antithetic, whereas, for Hegel, the epic stage was thetic and the three stages of poetry were constituted as epic, lyric, and the higher synthesis, drama. It is thus the case that Andersen does not carry his reflection through to its proper conclusion; his life-development is stagnant, and this is because it happens to succumb to the political misunderstanding of the times, a period of fermentation (*Gjærings-Periode*) rather than a period of action (*Gjernings-Periode*).[30] Kierkegaard's criticism of Andersen is thus social and political as well as aesthetic and philosophical.

There is further significance in the fact that Kierkegaard treats of Andersen as a *Roman-Digter* and not a *Roman-forfatter*. The English translation of "novelist" for *Romandigter* misses the reflective distinction that one would suspect Kierkegaard wished to make. Rather than calling Andersen an "author of novels" (*Romanforfatter*), Kierkegaard calls him a "poet of novels" (*Romandigter*), which fits nicely with the criticism that Andersen "cannot separate the poetic from himself" (KW I 75). Kierkegaard criticizes Andersen for being a romantic poet who blends together reality and poetry in such a way that his poetry becomes prose and the reader cannot possibly obtain a unified total impression from his writings.

Following this assessment, Kierkegaard states that "Andersen totally lacks a life-view" (KW I 76). I have already gone through Kierkegaard's explanation of a life-view, an idea of great importance not only in this work but in Kierkegaard's writings taken as a whole. While a life-view comes across as something with ethical or religious significance, one finds that it also incites aesthetic determinations concerning the novel.

Kierkegaard explains that he is not overstepping his aesthetic jurisdiction by referring to Andersen personally as a personality. He justifies his references to Andersen's personality by "merely stating" that "the poetic production proper . . . is nothing but a copious second power, shaping itself in a freer world and moving about in it, reproducing from what has already . . . been poetically experienced to the first power" (KW I 83). Kierkegaard's criticism, then, is conducted in the second power—or the second power squared, if you will—and is an attack on Andersen not as a young man or personality but only insofar as he is a "novelist."

For a novelist, Kierkegaard boldly writes, a life-view is a *conditio sine qua non* (KW I 77).

The point is interesting. But if a life-view is absolutely necessary for the novel, how does such a life-view relate itself to the novel? Kierkegaard's view is clear:

> A life-view is really providence in the novel; it is its deeper unity, which makes the novel have the center of gravity in itself. A life-view frees it from being arbitrary or purposeless, since the purpose is immanently present everywhere in the work of art. But when such a life-view is lacking, the novel either seeks to insinuate some theory (dogmatic, doctrinaire short novels) at the expense of poetry or it makes a finite or incidental contact with the author's flesh and blood [KW I 81].

A life-view is thus the depth of the novel; it is immanent in the novel, and not to be sought as something transcendental to the work of art. If there were no life-view within the deeper structure of the novel, it would be either doctrinaire or subjective. The author's personality should not stand in a finite or incidental relation to his or her work.

> Instead, the poet himself must first and foremost win a competent personality, and it is only this dead and transfigured personality that ought to and is able to produce, not the many-angled, worldly, palpable one. How difficult it is to win oneself such a personality can also be seen from the fact that in many otherwise fine novels there is to be found a residue, as it were, of the author's finite character, which like an impudent third person, like a badly brought up child, often joins in the conversation at unseemly places [KW I 82].[31]

Since Kierkegaard applies this standard to the writings of others, these are grounds to suppose that one may apply it to his own works.

Kierkegaard's text *From the Papers of One Still Living* alone dictates how it should be read. If one would like to think that Kierkegaard has followed his own advice, then most, if not all, of the biographical criticism that Kierkegaard has been subjected to is irrelevant and uninteresting. If one views Kierkegaard, the poet, as the victorious champion of a life-view—yet without knowing what this life-view is (and, as Kierkegaard noted earlier in the text he is seeking not to make one life-view valid but rather to combat the complete lack of one)—or as a successful writer, then one will find references to his finite character annoying and will seek, rather, the deeper unity of his text(s). For Kierkegaard, the unity of a novel is produced by "an immortal spirit that survives the whole" (KW I 83). Thus, Kierkegaard says in a footnote that shares an affinity with "The Truth of Irony," which will be worked out in his doctoral dissertation, "a genuine poetic production should make the poet inwardly freer, richer, more certain of himself" (KW I 84). With Andersen, however, his novels stand in a misrelation to his personality; they are not freeing and are "to be regarded more as an amputation than as a production from himself."

"In Andersen," Kierkegaard writes, "there is absolutely no grip on things: when the hero dies, Andersen dies, too, and at most forces from the reader a sigh over them both as the final impression" (KW I 83). Here the reader sees how the unnecessary mystery surrounding the title of this earliest work may be cleared up without transcending the bounds of the text. Andersen has misunderstood both the art of reflectively relating oneself to one's production as a second power and the nature of genius in his "passivity theory." Concerning the latter, Kierkegaard does not mince words:

> This view implies a failure to appreciate the power of genius and its relation to unfavorable circumstances (for genius is not a rush candle that goes out in a puff of air but a conflagration that the storm only incites) and is due to Andersen's depicting not a genius in his struggle but rather a sniveler who is declared to be a genius, and the only thing he has in common with a genius is that he suffers a few trifling adversities to which, moreover, he succumbs [KW I 88].

For these reasons, Kierkegaard disdainfully proclaims his criticism of the failed genius Christian and of his author Hans *Christian* Andersen—both of whom, viewed through a critical reading of the text, have died—and affirms it as coming from one still living, one with a life-view, that *conditio sine qua non* of a writer, whose text presents the tightly worked unity of a would-be genius. Andersen's passive genius has suffered and died owing to life's cruel movements, whereas Kierkegaard's active (ironic) genius is ready and willing—do not let the subtitle fool you—to do battle with fate.

Still the question of a life-view resounds in the reader's ear. What life-view can be discerned through a careful reading which at once frees the person Kierkegaard while simultaneously unifying both his texts, taken individually, and his production, taken as a whole? To answer this question, I turn now to consider Kierkegaard's second writing, *On the Concept of Irony with Constant Reference to Socrates.*

NOTES

1. An older spelling of Søren's family name is found on the original title page (see KW I 206). The significance of this will be explored later.

2. For insight into the textual understanding of Kierkegaard's title, as opposed to the biographical understanding, I am here indebted to Søren Gorm Hansen, *H. C. Andersen og Søren Kierkegaard i dannelseskulturen* (H. C. Andersen and Søren Kierkegaard in the Culture of "Refinement") (Copenhagen: Medusa, 1976), pp. 123–24.

3. The editors of SV present the following note on *Only a Fiddler*: "It is of a strongly autobiographical character, as were his two previous novels, *Improvisatoren* and *O. T.*, but while the hero of these books becomes a hit, in *Only a Fiddler* Andersen has projected the possibility of artistic forfeiture onto the screen such that a genius, according to his view, could come to birth only if he had good luck or good fortune. The novel is, in his own words, "so much a spiritual blossom, projected by the pressure I suffered in this powerful struggle between my nature as a poet and the all too hard surroundings." The hero, who bears the author's own name, Christian, dies in misery because no one safeguards and takes care of his genius. Thus, this is the book's conclusion. Might it have been H.C. Andersen's himself if God in his goodness had not sent him protecting and influential friends on his way? Genius is like a piece of wreckage that is cast here and there without itself being in condition to form its fate" (SV I 334).

4. See Fenger, *Kierkegaard-Myter og Kierkegaard-Kilder*, p. 275, for an interpretation of the significance of this fact and an attack on those who have neglected it.

5. Such doubts are harbored by Niels Thulstrup in his doctoral dissertation, *Kierkegaards Forhold til Hegel og den Speculative Idealisme indtil 1846* (Kierkegaard's Relation to Hegel and the Speculative Idealism up to 1846) (Copenhagen: Glydendal, 1967), where he writes: "In this connection one should hardly pay too much attention to this, that Heiberg's journal represented Hegelianism" (p. 145).

6. Quoted in Fenger, *Kierkegaard-Myter og Kierkegaard-Kilder*, p. 114.

7. Georg Brandes, *Søren Kierkegaard: En Kritisk Fremstilling i Grundrids* (Søren Kierkegaard: A Critical Presentation in Outline) (Copenhagen: Gyldendal, 1877), p. 36.

8. See Andersen's *Mit Livs Eventyr* (My Life's Adventure) (Copenhagen, C. A. Reitzel, 1855), p. 198.

9. See also KW I 202–204 for an excerpt from *A Comedy in the Open Air*.

10. *Kierkegaard*, pp. 35–36.

11. In 1888 Brandes gave the first lectures on Nietzsche in Copenhagen. He also wrote to Nietzsche during the same year to call his attention to Kierkegaard. This was in vain, however, for it proved too late for Nietzsche to procure the works of Kierkegaard. See Walter Kaufmann's *Nietzsche: Philosopher, Psychologist, Antichrist* (Princeton, N.J.: Princeton University Press, 1974), pp. 4, 125.

12. Friedrich Christian Sibbern (1785–872) was the academic dean of the philosophy department at the University of Copenhagen who gave the signed approval of Kierkegaard's dissertation, *The Concept of Irony*. In a general review of Danish literature Sibbern is presented as a "quiet and lovable thinker" by Mogens Brøndsted and Sven Møller Kristensen in *Danmarks Litteratur fra Oldtiden til 1870* (Denmark's Literature from Antiquity to 1870) (Copenhagen: Gyldendal, 1963), p. 145. Sibbern is an interesting and sympathetic figure, and I shall have more to say about him later.

13. *Kierkegaard*, pp. 37–38.

14. Ibid., p. 38.

15. If Kierkegaard had actually considered *From the Papers of One Still Living* to be a pseudonymous work, it is much more likely that he would have listed it in his "First and Last Declaration" to the *Concluding Unscientific Postscript*. It seems, rather, the case that he viewed this work, much like *The Concept of Irony*, as an early, relatively unknown writing, that had clearly been presented to the reader as "by S. Kierkegaard."

16. *Kierkegaard in Golden Age Denmark*, pp. 265–66.

17. Georg Wilhelm Friedrich Hegel, *Lectures on the Philosophy of Religion*, trans. E. B. Speirs and J. B. Sanderson, 3 vols. (New York: Humanities Press, 1968), 1:191.

18. For a further elaboration of this point see Mark Taylor, *Journeys to Selfhood: Hegel and Kierkegaard* (Berkeley: The University of California Press, 1980), pp. 41–50.

19. Under the heading of "Reflection" Himmelstrup continues: "In keeping with the times' Hegelian-infected language, Kierkegaard uses this term to an extraordinarily large extent. He uses the word "reflection" in several senses: as the *general usage of reflection*, which is consider-

ation, contemplation; next, in a sense which forms a middle way between the general usage and the Hegelian meaning of the word (compare, that the development "is stopped by reflection"); and, lastly, in a sense that lies close to Hegel's yet is more psychologically-ethically oriented ("a thoroughly reflected individual" and the like); with that comes as well the use of "reflection" as a reference or indication of the Hegelian philosopher" (SV XX 177).

In order to compound meanings and witness to the complexity of Kierkegaard's reflective determinations of reflection, I cite Mark Taylor's note in *Journeys to Selfhood*: "it is essential to note Kierkegaard's distinction between 'reflexion' and 'reflection.' While reflexion differentiates previously undifferentiated opposites, reflection abstracts from concrete existence by dispassionate speculation" (p. 173*n*104).

20. It will be seen that Kierkegaard's first two writings share a deep affinity, such that they could be treated together. Thus, careful readers will gather that I am already reading Kierkegaard from irony to edification.

21. The attempt to begin at the beginning from nothing serves also as an indication of the ubiquitous reflection at work here. When starting from nothing, reflection is the fundamental requirement (or presupposition) needed to get things going.

Kierkegaard would seem to also think that beginning from nothing creates the aesthetic effect of a better writing, a writing which has its center in itself and not elsewhere. Here, then, is one way of reading Hegel—as Derrida has—as the first thinker of writing.

22. It is worth noting that Hirsch also finds an essential agreement between *From the Papers of One Still Living* and *The Concept of Irony*, particularly in relation to Kierkegaard's aesthetic theories and his ethical-religious views.

23. The evidence cited is P I A 252, 340; JP II 1188, 1541.

24. Thomasine Gyllembourg-Ehrensvärd was the mother of Johann Ludvig Heiberg and published this work pseudonymously in 1828. She also wrote *To Tidsaldre* (Two Ages) which Kierkegaard reviewed in 1846 and entitled simply *En literair Anmeldelse* (A Literary Review).

25. Here the implicit thought concerning existence is a reversal of the Cartesian *cogito ergo sum*. For Kierkegaard, even in his first published work, thought cannot prove existence. Existence is a presupposition, unquestionable and ungraspable. All thought and every life-view has as its antecedent life or existence.

26. This goes against the Swedish scholars at "the department for the science of beliefs and life-views" (*avdelningen för tros- och livsåskådningsvetenskap*) at Uppsala University who feel that all persons have a life-view which follows them throughout their life. I think particularly of

Professor Anders Jeffner who defines a life-view (*livsåskådning* in Swedish) as a mixture of three different elements: (1) a conception of what is important in life, (2) which picture of the world we have, and (3) the general feeling that follows us throughout existence. See "Vår Natur är oss en väldig borg" (Our Nature Is for Us a Mighty Stronghold), *Forskning och Framsteg* (Research and Progress), (March–April 1991).

27. On Daub see JP I 619, 1030, 1025; III 3553 (P II A 558, 624, 725; IV A 164).

28. The quote from *Ægtestand* (Matrimony) on page 19 shows the writer's attempt at intimacy with the reader through a direct address, "My dear young (female) reader . . . " Kierkegaard emulated such an attempt in both edifying and aesthetic works. See, for the first example, the beginning of *Either/Or*.

29. For a more detailed discussion on "Kierkegaard and Blicher," see the chapter of the same name in Fenger, *Kierkegaard-Myter og Kierkegaard-Kilder*, pp. 102–108.

30. In the final paragraph of his review, however, Kierkegaard assumes a conciliatory spirit and expresses his joy that Andersen has not fully fallen to "the all-embracing devil-may-care trade wind of politics" (KW I 102).

31. The "dead and transfigured personality" Kierkegaard writes of not only reminds the reader of the importance of death for a life-view, but also of the religious call to die to this world and be born again.

2

The Original Point of View for Kierkegaard's Activity as a Writer

> Irony, the ignorance Socrates began with, the world created from nothing, the pure virgin who gave birth to Christ—
>
> S. Kierkegaard, P 1 A 190 (1836)

> Ut a dubitatione philosophia sic ab ironia vita digna, quae humana vocetur, incipit.
>
> Severinus Kierkegaard, 15th thesis to *The Concept of Irony*

It is remarkable that students of Kierkegaard have, in general, had so little to do with *Om Begrebet Ironi med stadigt Hensyn til Socrates* (On the Concept of Irony with Constant Reference to Socrates).[1] The seriousness of Kierkegaardian studies appears to have precluded—and this is already mildly ironic—any serious investigation into Kierkegaard's magisterial dissertation. The lack of attention paid to *The Concept of Irony*[2] is thus inversely related to the degree of seriousness found in Kierkegaardian studies. Were *The Concept of Irony* taken more seriously, there would be less serious-mindedness in Kierkegaardian scholarship, and the appropriate mixture of irony and seriousness could find its fitting expression.

The aim of the present chapter is to show that, with regard to the Kierkegaardian corpus and Kierkegaard's developing *Livsanskuelse*, one may truly proclaim that "In the Beginning was the Word Irony." This will serve, then, as both background and point of departure for "the higher dialectical structure," which will show itself in a holistic study of Kierkegaard's writings. Given the background of the creative writer's need for a liberating life-view (chapter 1), the search for such a life-view for Kierkegaard begins with *The Concept of Irony*.

In reading this most valuable text, one finds—to anticipate a bit—that the concept of irony presents not only conceptual determinations but also existential ones. While the ramifications of the former are such that they inevitably turn on themselves to question their own conceptuality, the latter determinations solidify at the heart of existence immediately after the diaspora of the concept, and these would then seek to advance a whole "philosophy of life." The case is uncommonly clear: the initial point of view for the study of Kierkegaard's work as a writer, the study of his *Livsanskuelse*, is found in the rich text *The Concept of Irony*.

I begin near the end of *The Concept of Irony*, where Kierkegaard reminds his readers of both the necessity of a life-view and, interestingly enough, the necessity of becoming a philosopher:

> The more the poet has departed from this (the immediate standpoint of genius), the more necessary it becomes for him to have a total-view [*Total-Anskuelse*] of the world, the *more necessary* it becomes for him to be a *philosopher* in a certain degree, and thus in his individual existence to become lord over irony [CI 337; SV I 327].

To master the concept of irony and become lord over this text requires that the reader read Kierkegaard philosophically. This is fitting for a work that is itself philosophical, not theological, as Thulstrup rightly declares[3]; nor should readers forget that Kierkegaard's highest academic degree was in philosophy, not theology. For one reads on the Latin cover page that it was the Department of Philosophy, University of Copenhagen, that approved Kierkegaard's dissertation, as attested by F. C. Sibbern, Dean of the Faculty of Philosophy.

If one thus hopes to "master" Kierkegaard, one would do well to begin with what Brandes knowingly called "the true point of departure for Kierkegaard's authorship."[4] One comes, simultaneously, to the question of a beginning and the question of irony. How are these terms to be elucidated?

They must be conflated: irony is a beginning. It is not, however, a beginning for philosophy in the modern tradition, because for that to begin, one has to doubt. Although it might seem that irony and doubt are identical, they are not, as Kierkegaard makes clear. "Doubt is a conceptual determination while irony is the being-for-itself of *subjectivity* [*Subjectivitetens Forsigværen*].'' ''Irony is essentially practical'' (CI 274; SV I 272), whereas doubt is not.[5] Implicit already in Kierkegaard's engaging fifteenth and final thesis to his dissertation is a break with the philosophy of modernism, and the beginning of something different, something that takes its origin as irony. And is not that something, a writing or self-creation which takes its origin as (being) irony, the defining characteristic of the postmodern? That Paul de Man has hailed this text as ''the best book on irony that's available''[6] is not, then, of great wonder.

For irony to begin something, according to the ancient tradition, one has to speak (Greek: *eirein*). Classically, irony has always been defined by saying one thing and meaning another. But irony is not solely dependent on the speech act per se. This point hardly needs laboring when in our own day even buildings are considered ironic. All forms of irony, to put the matter into Kierkegaard's Hegelian language, are characterized by the opposition of the phenomenon to its essence (CI 264). In terms of written language, irony occurs when the phenomenon or word is opposed to the essence or meaning. Thus, it follows logically that without ''essences'' or meanings, irony could not exist. If I suffered the fate of not being able to mean anything, then I could scarcely be able to be ironic. In addition, no form of irony can be directly understood, and this grants a mark of distinction or superiority to the one ''who has ears to hear'' the ironic communication.

The mysterious Indo-European base of the word in question brings one closer to the heart of the matter. Reflect on the following etymologies:

> **irony**, n. —— L. *ironia*, fr. Gk. *eironeia*, 'irony', fr. *eiron*, 'dissembler', 'sayer' (i.e., one who speaks in order to hide his thoughts), fr. *eirein* 'to speak', which is rel. to 'public speaker, orator; rhetor', and cogn. with L. *verbum*, 'word', Goth. *waurd*, OE. *word*, 'word'. See *word*.

> **word**, n. —— ME. *word*, fr. OE. *word*, rel. to OS., OFris. *word*, Du. *woord*, OHG., MHG. G. *wort*, ON. *oro*, Dan., Swed. *ord*, Goth. *waurd*, fr. IE. **werdh-*, whence also OPruss. *wirds*, 'word', Lith. *vardas*, 'name', Mir. *fordat*, 'they say', L. *verbum*, 'word', IE. **werdh-* is an enlarged form of base **wer-*, **were-*, 'to speak', whence

> Gk. *eirein*, 'to speak', *eiron*, 'dissembler', lit. 'sayer' (i.e., one who speaks in order to hide his thoughts), *eironeia*, 'irony'. See *irony*.[7]

The lost origin of irony lies deep within the heart of "the word" itself. Here one finds a hole of missing significance through which ironies or complexities of reference issue and by which communication becomes hit and miss and indirect. To think in contemporary terms, the point is not that the phenomena—words—do not signify thoughts or meanings but that they signify so very many of them and that, of these, many will be ambiguous, imprecise, overdetermined or undetermined, and some will be concealed, obscure, and unknown. To begin, then, with "the word" is to begin with this gap, fissure, and opening of meaning. In other words, it is to begin with nothing, to start from scratch, like Socrates, and like the God, that first creator in whose image we were created.

There is, however, a major point of distinction between the ironist who begins from nothing and the God who begins from nothing. The God is able to create something out of nothing, whereas the ironist cannot. The ironist establishes nothing; he or she[8] cannot even put forward a thesis. Kierkegaard explains why:

> irony in the stricter sense of the word can never set forth a thesis, because irony is a *determination* of the *being-for-itself subject* [*forsigværende Subject*], who, with perpetual agility permits nothing to endure, and because of this agility *cannot* collect himself in the *total view* [*Total-Anskuelse*] that he permits nothing to endure. . . . In the last analysis the ironist must always posit something, but what he posits in this way is nothing. Now, it is impossible to take nothing seriously without either arriving at something (this happens when one takes it speculatively seriously), or without despairing (this happens when one takes it personally seriously). But the ironist does neither of these, and to this extent one may say he is not really serious about it. Irony is the infinitely delicate play with nothing, a play which is not terrified by it but still pokes its head into the air [CI 286–7; SV I 283].

Such is Kierkegaard's actual beginning, an "infinitely delicate play with nothing." Irony clears the stage, starts from nothing, and results in nothing. One has little doubt, then, that the dissertation designed to "let irony speak"—insofar as it is a written text and not merely an occasional, institutional discourse[9]—is itself ironic,[10] and that the author, the being-for-itself subject, is an ironist who, with his fifteen theses on irony in hand at one moment and out the window the next, is actually just playing with nothing or nothingness.[11]

How can such a complex concept as irony be said to begin that human life that each one of us wants to live, that life that is worthy of one as a human being? The fifteenth Latin thesis of Kierkegaard's dissertation is troublesome, perhaps its author is overzealous, and it is not surprising that one faculty member objected to this thesis on the grounds that it would be too difficult to discuss in Latin. One wonders if it would have been easier to discuss in Danish or German. Will it prove too tough to discuss in English?

Dialectically and existentially, Kierkegaard is saying that a human life without irony is worthless. Provided one grants that a human being wishes to live a life worthy of itself qua human being, it would seemingly be better for such a person never to have seen the light of day than to live without dignity amid a world of vanities. For, as Kierkegaard writes in the final section, "He who does not understand irony and has no ear for its whisperings lacks *eo ipso* what might be called *personal life's absolute beginning*" (CI 339; SV I 329). Irony, which for the modern philosopher was (mistakenly) viewed solely under the domain of aesthetics, appears here to acquire an ethical edge, which sets forth a possible way of life based on its implicit nature as an existential-ontological task. Irony both provides and clears the way for the authentic human life, and if this authentic life is further labeled as Christian, then irony must have some profound relevance for Christianity. Accordingly, then, it is described biblically: "Irony is, as the negative, the way; not the truth, but the way" (SV I 329). A formidable thesis indeed.

The Concept of Irony is the beginning. The "concept of irony" provides the point of departure, the point of view, and the conceptual framework, in weak outline, for the writings Kierkegaard would later produce. This text is a youthful writing, written when Kierkegaard was twenty-eight years old, but one which nevertheless portrays a maturity beyond the author's years. If it is dismissed as being too difficult or too "Hegelian," then this is merely an evasion of the issues involved in accounting for Kierkegaard's (overall) writing strategy. And if Kierkegaard himself ignores it in his own personal appraisal of his production and cites *Either/Or* rather than *The Concept of Irony* as the beginning of his "authorship," then such a peculiar account must not be read lying down. On the contrary, one should note the omission of *The Concept of Irony* as being, in all likelihood, of very singular significance and question why the dissertation was not acknowledged, when it appears clearly to be, as the translators of the new English translation note, "the seedbed of the entire authorship" (KW II xviii). Of course, this last claim should not be uncritically accepted but, rather, be unveiled in its wonderful detail. This will mean nothing less than a holistic study of Kierkegaard's writings pivoting on *The Concept of Irony*.

Kierkegaard wrote his magisterial dissertation happily[12] in Danish, his mother tongue. That he should do so, however, was not a matter of course, for in Golden Age Denmark all academic dissertations were to be written and disputed in Latin, the official language of the schools. He was therefore required humbly to petition the king for permission to write in his native language. As Kierkegaard expressed it to the king, his wish to write in Danish was not based on any lack of ability in Latin. He had previously taught the subject and was fully prepared to defend his dissertation and the fifteen theses attached to it in Latin (theses which were later dropped upon commercial publication). As the candidate in theology[13] put the matter to His Majesty, "the concept of irony, to be sure, belongs in a sense to antiquity, but it essentially belongs to it only insofar as the modern age takes its beginning with it, so that the apprehension of this concept must in the strictest sense be claimed by modernity" (CI 350). Here Kierkegaard is claiming that, because irony is an historical concept, it must be grasped in a modern way in order to be fully (that is, dialectically) understood.

Furthermore, Kierkegaard pointed out how "impossible it would be to discuss the subject exhaustively in the language which has thus far been that of scholarship, not to mention that the free and personal presentation would suffer too much" (CI 350). Concerning the latter point, it is unquestionable that to have written the dissertation in Latin would have cramped the author's style. The former point is, however, more interesting. What is it about "the language of scholarship" that prohibits the complete unraveling of the concept of irony? Is it Latin per se or "scholarship" that has such a difficult time dealing with irony? Is it not a principle of the scholarly minded that the possibility of irony is either disregarded or flatly denied? Perhaps unaware of Kierkegaard's possibly ironic jab at the world of scholarship—and particularly the scholarship of (modern) philosophy, which had not, in that case, fully come to terms with the method of its master, Socrates—the king granted the petition, although I suspect more because two other magisterial candidates had been granted the same favor and the present applicant had demonstrated fluency in Latin than because the concept of irony is a modern concept that essentially belongs to the ancients only insofar as the modernists begin with it.

So be it. The work was written, and while Kierkegaard's faculty members could clearly see the intellectual merit of the work, they could also see the candidate's perspicuous—and, to their minds, reprehensible—personal style and individuality.[14] Kierkegaard's apparent rejoinder to the critics of his essay is found on a loose sheet of paper with this heading: "Preface. The significance of this is surely irrelevant for the dissertation, but is a necessary moment in my individuality." It reads:

> I have worked on this dissertation with fear and trembling, so that my dialectic would not devour too much.
>
> One will censure the abandon of style. One and another sciolist will say that the subjective element is too prominent. I would now, in the first place, request him not to plague me with a rehash of this new wisdom, which I must already regard as too old, and on the one hand, not to make such great demands on me—that the Idea's own movements should occur with me, that the Idea should come to expression in me, for most of the younger scholars rush forward like the lady in Ludlamshulen with the rural part of the country behind them—finally, on the other hand, that one cannot write about a negative concept except in this way and, instead of continually assuring that doubt is overcome, that irony is conquered, for once to permit it to speak. In general, I may have occasionally been too long-winded. When Hegel with his authority says that Spirit is the best epitomist (cf. Introduction to his Philosophy of History, p. 8), I humbly and without any demand allow myself to be judged, but by boys I will not be judged. [EP 283–4]

As to be expected, the dissertation stood as it was submitted, and on September 29, 1841, after seven and a half hours and nine opponents, young Severinus Aabye became Magister Kierkegaard, a master of irony.

To pose the question again: What is irony? It is often repeated in studies on irony that "we have known all along what irony is," but is this really so? Is irony primarily a classifiable, albeit difficult, concept of aesthetics, such as parody, sarcasm, and satire?[15] Might one not incredulously wonder whether it can actually be the object of a concept at all? How does one conceive of irony? How can it be grasped?[16] No doubt, similar questions stirred Kierkegaard, in which case his whole dissertation might be read as a great provocation for conceptual-minded, "modern philosophical" thinkers, for obviously irony does not lend itself to a straightforward, thetic exposition. It is a negative concept, a concept that cannot be conceived and cannot be put into words, for to do so would be to abrogate it. To try, nevertheless: irony (is) nothing, a nothingness attesting to the split between the ironist and the work, the world and the word, immediacy and language, and more.

Then, as glimpsed above, one may glance in an-other direction: irony as a philosophy of life, an ethical position, a religious point of view. When one looks away from the illusionary theoretical aspect of Kierkegaard's work, one finds that Kierkegaard treats of irony[17] as not a concept, not a category, not a principle; it appears, rather, "as a lived relationship to a totality."[18] This is impressed upon readers at every turn of Kierkegaard's consideration of Socrates, Schlegel, Tieck, Solger, and—ever so briefly in the final section—Goethe. The move to what one is tempted to call "existential irony" is enacted through a "qualitative leap," and here the relationship to the present totality of existence is wholly negative:

> Irony *sensu eminentiori* [in the eminent sense] directs itself not against this or that particular existent [*Tilværende*]; it directs itself against the whole given actuality of a certain time and under certain relations. It has, therefore, an apriority in itself, and it is not by successively destroying one segment of actuality after the other that it arrives at its total-view [*Total-Anskuelse*], but it is through the power of this that it destroys in the particular. It is not this or that phenomenon, but it is the totality of existence [*Tilværelsens Totale*] that it considers *sub specie ironiæ* [under the aspect of irony]. To this extent one sees the correctness of the Hegelian characterization of irony as *infinite absolute negativity* [CI 271; SV I 270].

Within such complex considerations also looms the question of the relationship between irony and subjectivity. Are they roughly synonymous terms or are they non-identical? Does one carry more weight than the other? How are they to be distinguished? Readers must encounter the all-important question about the relationship between irony and truth, and, ultimately, inquire into the significance of irony for their own lives.

That Kierkegaard was on to something leading to the existential relation between irony and truth can be gleaned in his writings from at least six years before his dissertation. Already in the famous Gilleleie letter of August 1, 1835, irony and Socrates are mentioned in the context of finding "a truth, that is truth for me, to find that idea for which I will live and die." Unfortunately for the Kierkegaardian community, this letter is seldom read in its entirety or discussed in its breadth. One often finds little more than this quote, which leaves the rather bad impression that Kierkegaard was bound to become an unhappy idealist. Kierkegaard makes clear, however, some twenty-eight lines later, that "to find that idea" is more properly expressed as "to find myself" (EP 46; P I A 75). This unambiguously opens up a whole new area of investigation, for the truth in question belongs to a deep aspect of the personal self and not to an idea per se.

Here, as to be expected, the development of the subjective value of truth dominates. The case for the subjective or living factor is powerfully expressed:

> Of what benefit would it be to me, if I discovered a so-called objective truth; if I worked my way through the philosophers' systems and could, when expected, give a review of them; if I could point out inconsistencies within every single system;—of what benefit would it be to me, if I could develop a theory of the State and of the particulars collected from many places combine a totality, construe a world, in which I nevertheless did not live, but simply held it out as a room for others;—of what benefit would it be to me to be able to develop the meaning of Christianity, to explain many singular phenomena, when it did not have any deeper meaning for myself and my life [EP 45–46]?

With a bit of healthy reasoning,[19] this passage makes a great deal of good sense. What utter foolishness for philosophers, scholars, or scientists to be so abstract and objective that their own lives are not affected by the knowledge they possess. But to read into this that Kierkegaard is mocking objective knowledge, as so very many Kierkegaardologists and even well-meaning philosophers do,[20] is to misread him badly. I do not read Kierkegaard to be the "great enemy of objectivity," and once one dispenses with this idea, his writing becomes much lighter. No more than seven lines following the above quote, Kierkegaard asserts: "I surely do not deny that I still accept *an imperative of knowledge* [*et Erkjendelsens Imperativ*]; and that this is also able to let itself work on human beings, *but then the living element must be taken up by me, and this is what* I now acknowledge to be the main thing" (EP 46).[21]

Kierkegaard nowhere condemns the acquisition and use of objective knowledge as long as it is appropriately related to a human being, such that through this knowledge the person comes to a deeper knowledge of him or herself. Kierkegaard formulates this into a "law" much later in *The Sickness Unto Death* (1849):

> The law for the development of the self with respect to knowing, insofar as it is the case that the self becomes itself, is that the increase of knowledge corresponds to the increase of self-knowledge, that the more the self knows, the more it knows itself. If this does not happen, the more knowledge increases, the more it becomes a kind of inhuman knowledge, in the obtaining of which a person's self is squandered, much the way men were squandered on building pyramids, or the way men in Russian brass bands are squandered on playing just one note, no more, no less [KW XIX 31].[22]

It is thus clear that Kierkegaard does not disparage the gathering of objective facts—be they about pyramids or brass bands. What is essential, however, is that human beings come to know themselves, and for this something other than objectivity alone is needed. Kierkegaard's concern is with self-knowledge that, although placing the emphasis elsewhere, does not seem to rid itself completely of objective knowledge.

At this juncture, it would help to find a word that would avoid the unnecessary and problematic dichotomy between objective and subjective knowledge. With this goal in mind, I need look no further than the text I am reading. It would be a great understatement to say that I am extremely surprised by what I have found. Within the famous Gilleleie letter of August 1, 1835, in a footnote to a footnote, printed in gothic letters is this: "*at netop den egenlige*

Philosoph er i høieste Grad subobjectiv" (that precisely the authentic philosopher is in the highest degree sub-objective) (EP 47; P I A 77).[23] For all I can tell, Kierkegaard has in this early letter made a most interesting coinage of a word, which he neither explains nor uses in later writings. I should consequently like to say that a "sub-objective" thinker is one who acquires and uses objective knowledge as a means for contributing to the end of developing a subjective knowledge of one's self.

The dialectical interplay of knowledge and irony is indispensable for the self-knower, and it is only by way of the one that the other assumes its rightful place within the life of a human being:

> One must first learn to know one's self, before one knows someone else. Thus, when a human being has first inwardly understood himself and now sees his course on track, only then does his life get peace and meaning, only then does he get rid of that troublesome, ominous traveling companion—that life-irony, which appears in the sphere of knowledge and commands the true knower to begin with a non-knower [Socrates], such as God created the world of nothing [EP 49–50].

Already at this early stage, the reader is alerted to the double meaning that Kierkegaard confers on the concept of irony, as he first refers to it as a troubling mentor, only to commend the "true knower" to begin with Socrates, the father of the ironic method. There are thus—and why not?—"good" and "bad" ironies, and Kierkegaard goes on to explore their differences in *The Concept of Irony*. Life-irony gives rise to "romantic irony"[24] and is likewise defined by its relationship to knowledge, whereas "Socratic irony" leads (indirectly) to "mastered irony" (although at this stage it is unclear as to whether Socrates has mastered irony himself in the Kierkegaardian sense) and is understood by its relationship to the knower's self.

In working toward an understanding of that concept of irony which "must in the strictest sense be claimed for modernity," one might begin somewhat unnaturally with Kierkegaard's developed view in "On the Concept of Irony," the title of Part Two of his dissertation.[25] Part One, "Socrates' Standpoint Conceived as Irony," which stands in its own right as a major contribution to ancient philosophical scholarship, comprises more than three-fourths of the entire text and serves as an overtly Hegelian means of motivating the conception of irony in its historical validity. Kierkegaard accomplishes this by taking the conception of Socratic irony—the original appearance of the phenomenon of irony—through the three Hegelian stages: possibility, actuality, and necessity.

To chart further the main moves made in this text, the consummative conception is repeated in Part Two of the dissertation under the heading "The World Historical Validity of Irony. The Irony of Socrates." Following this, Kierkegaard turns his attention to "Irony after Fichte." In this section, and this section alone, "irony" and "ironist" are synonymous with "romanticism" and "romanticist," for, as Kierkegaard notes, "both expressions designate the same thing. The one suggests more the name with which the movement christened itself, the other the name with which Hegel christened it" (CI 292). Here Kierkegaard takes a sparing look at Friedrich Schlegel's (1772–1829) *Lucinde*, a brief consideration of Ludwig Johann Tieck's (1773–1853) poetry, and a more philosophically interesting reading of Karl Wilhelm Ferdinand Solger's (1780–1819) *Vorlesungen über Aesthetik* (Lectures on Aesthetics) and posthumously published writings. Whereas the irony of Socrates was world-historically justified, the irony of the romanticists is viewed as a world-historically illegitimate manifestation of irony. As Kierkegaard appears to be following Hegel very closely on this point, an inconsistency within the Hegelian philosophy of history arises.

According to Hegel's interpretation, everything that appears in history must have a relative validity, such that to distinguish between valid or legitimate irony and invalid or illegitimate irony would be a mistake. "Thus it is only by an inconsistency that Hegel—and Kierkegaard with him—rejects, not Socratic, but romantic irony as illegitimate in an absolute, and not just in a relative sense."[26] Perhaps not seriously concerned about the problems an Hegelian philosopher of history gets himself into,[27] Kierkegaard moves from romantic to mastered irony, without directly explaining how the higher—and, as one would expect although it is not explicit in the text, mediative—conception of the concept is effected. In the final conception, mastered irony is defined as the truth of irony. How is one to understand this truth of irony?

In Kierkegaard's personal copy of his dissertation, used during the oral defense, he indicated page references for eight of his fifteen theses (SV I 342–43), the first seven, and the last thesis, which may now be translated, "As philosophy begins with doubt, so also that life which may be called worthy of a human being begins with irony." The page references Kierkegaard gives concerning this fifteenth thesis are to the final section of his dissertation, "Irony as a Mastered Moment. The Truth of Irony." Here in this brief concluding chapter he writes:

> In our time one has often heard much talk about doubt's meaning for "scholarship," but what doubt is for "scholarship," irony is for the personal life. Thus as scholars maintain that there is no true "scholarship" without doubt, so can one maintain with the same right that no genuine human life is possible without irony [SV I 328].[28]

In proportion to its size, "The Truth of Irony" is, in my view, the most pregnant segment of *On the Concept of Irony with Constant Reference to Socrates*, and yet it is not without wonder that one finds the name of Socrates written nowhere in this section. Here is a summarily glorious presentation of the concept in which Kierkegaard—as a true ironist—appears to be at his freest.

What is "mastered irony"? Following the dialectical method Kierkegaard appropriated from Hegel, should it be understood as the synthetic higher third that comes into existence through the differences of the thesis, irony as it was first expressed, Socratic irony—for as can hardly be forgotten, "Socrates primus ironiam introduxit"[29]—and the antithesis, "romantic irony," in which Kierkegaard follows Hegel in passing judgment on this phenomenon?

Or perhaps there is no mediation at all, but only the appearance of one, in which case Kierkegaard would only be feigning inconsistency in his criticism against the romantics. The transition is certainly lacking, as would be appropriate for a "qualitative leaper" who had earlier expressed his wariness at the mediation of absolute differences. In June 1839 he turns Hamlet against Hegel:

> That relative differences can be mediated, for that we do not really need Hegel. . . . That absolute differences should be able to be mediated, that personality, which will forever repeat its immortal dilemma: to be or not to be, that is the question [Hamlet] will forever protest [P II 173].

If this is the case, where does "mastered irony" fit? What is its relation to the preceding, its relation to Socrates? Kierkegaard is much too short-winded in his (un)concluding chapter.

Kierkegaard begins by saying that now, when discussing the poet relating himself ironically to his work, something else is meant than what was said in the foregoing. Kierkegaard does not mention Socrates but instead refers to the names Shakespeare and Goethe. On Shakespeare he writes:

> One has often enough praised Shakespeare as irony's great master, and there can hardly be any doubt that one has been correct in this respect. Shakespeare, however, by no means allows the substantial content to evaporate in an ever more fleeting sublimation, and insofar as his lyricism sometimes culminates in madness there is in this madness nevertheless an extraordinary degree of objectivity. When Shakespeare thus relates himself ironically to his poem, it is simply in order to let the objective prevail. Moreover, *Irony is now present everywhere*, it ratifies each particular feature, so that there will not be too much or too little, so that everything can receive its due, so that the true equilibrium can be established in the poem's microcosmic relation, whereby the poem gravitates in itself. The greater the oppositions there are in this movement, the more irony is needed in order to restrain and master those spirits which obstinately want to storm forth. The more irony there is, the more freely and poetically the poet hovers over his composition. Irony is therefore not present at some particular point in the poem, but is omnipresent in it so that the visible irony in the poem *is in turn ironically mastered*. Therefore, irony at once makes the poet and the poem free. But in order for this to be able to happen, the poet himself must be lord over irony [CI 336; SV I 326–27].

Here, too, one sees the validity of objectivity, and the extent to which the poet must become sub-objective, such that mastered irony may assert itself in its "attempt to mediate the discrete moments, not in a higher unity, but in a higher madness" (CI 274).[30]

Not only does the poet have to be a lord over irony; he also needs to be a kind of philosopher. Kierkegaard describes the mastered poetic work as something that must maintain an internal relationship to the poet because it serves as "a moment in his development." To illustrate his point he turns to "the German Shakespeare."

> Goethe's poet-existence [*Digter-Existents*] was so great, that he got his being-there as a poet [*Digter-Tilværelse*] to congrue with his actuality. *This again requires irony*, but note well, *mastered irony* [CI 274].

In a note of complete sympathy for Goethe, Kierkegaard rounds off his phenomenological description of the mastered irony of a poet, where the key to "the truth of irony" is that the individual poetic production is considered solely as a moment (*Moment*) within the life of the poet. He then turns his concern to *every single individual's life*, which is viewed as sharing a certain affinity with the existence of the poet. This brings the reader (back) to the relationship between irony and personal life.

Given Kierkegaard's attention to the great poets, the question quite naturally arises concerning Kierkegaard's silence on Socrates, or the irony of Socrates—earlier discussed as the world-historical validity of irony—when he writes, all too briefly for readers' contentment, about "mastered irony" or the truth of irony. Had Socrates not come this far? If he had not, what did he lack? Are Shakespeare and Goethe better personifications of "this" irony? Where is Socrates? Who is Socrates?

One possible and acceptable way to read *The Concept of Irony* would be to consider many, but not all, of Kierkegaard's pronouncements on Socrates as then doubly reflected back on himself and his writings. This way of proceeding would not be out of line with the oft-cited interpretation of Kierkegaard as the "gadfly of Copenhagen," for there is something to be said about this analogy. It becomes problematic, however, in light of the Nietzschean epithet for Socrates: "He who does not write."[31] (Might not Nietzsche's description help to answer the questions that arise concerning Shakespeare, Goethe, and Socrates? What is the difference between the existence of one who writes and the existence of one who does not? How is "mastered irony" related to both the writer and the non-writer?)

Still, one must inevitably realize that the only "Socrates" one can know is to be found in texts alone, even if they were written not by himself but rather by Xenophon, Plato, and Aristophanes. The same can be said with respect to the only "Kierkegaard" one can know, who, in a certain sense, did not consider himself as the writer of his texts. In wanting to go further, one inevitably bumps up against either "the Socrates Problem" or "the Kierkegaard Problem," both of which would seek to recover the actual, real individuals who were missing in their lives, who were lost through their deaths, and who live only through "their" texts. Concerning how Socrates is to be conceived, Kierkegaard writes:

> He was not like a philosopher lecturing upon his views [*Anskuelser*], wherein the very lecture itself constitutes the presence of the idea; on the contrary, what Socrates said meant something other [*Andet*]. The outer was not in the least in harmonious union with the inner, but rather the opposite of this, and only under this refracted angle is he to be comprehended. Thus, the question of a conception with reference to Socrates is quite another matter than with most other people [CI 50; SV I 71–72].

One could easily assert a similar view with respect to Kierkegaard. Indeed, Kierkegaard's proper names, both those pseudonymous and those his own, may function much like the different texts on Socrates by Xenophon, Plato, and Aristophanes.

Another way of reading Kierkegaard's writing on Socrates's contemporaries is to consider them as representative types of scholarly thinkers, for, following Kierkegaard's criticism, each writer may be personified into a certain type. This way of proceeding serves both to elucidate the text while also hoping to educate one or another Kierkegaardologist. Let me therefore do this in relation to Kierkegaardian scholarship.

Xenophon, Kierkegaard writes, held the preconceived objective of attempting to prove that Socrates was justifiable and that it was an error of the Athenians to condemn him. In a similarly methodical way, the "Xenophons" of Kierkegaard scholarship maintain the ready objective of trying to prove that Kierkegaard was an excellent sort of person, above all a Christian. Magister Kierkegaard points out that such a strategy is misguided, wrong, and ultimately boring. The "Xenophons" allow little room, if any at all, for the irony so immensely important for Kierkegaard's life-view.

> The more Socrates [read also: Kierkegaard] had undermined existence [*Existentsen*], the more deeply and necessarily each single expression [read also: work] had to gravitate towards that ironic totality, which as a spiritual condition was infinitely bottomless, invisible, and indivisible. Now Xenophon had no intimation whatsoever of this secret [CI 56; SV I 77–78].

Whether the "Xenophonic" thinkers lack a healthy suspicion for the hidden, or whether they harbor a fear of peering into the bottomless, they fail to approach their protagonist with the responsibility and respect that he inspires.

The "Platos" of Kierkegaardian research mark a definite advance over the "Xenophons." They question the Kierkegaardian corpus, but with a different intention from that of the "Aristophaneses" of Kierkegaard scholarship, who would appear to be the writers closest to Kierkegaard's actual position. To follow Kierkegaard's distinction between two types of questioning, the "Platos' " interest in asking questions lies in the answers in their fullness and significance. These writers, like Plato himself, presuppose a plentitude, and Kierkegaard calls this the speculative method. Such scholars stress the "positive philosophy" to be found, which with regard to Kierkegaard's writings would be seen hidden underneath the pile of pseudonyms—e.g., the dialectical theory of the stages and theories of the self, subjectivity, and truth—and explained by the author's direct report to history.

While there may be a strong resemblance between these two methods, the speculative and the ironic,[32] the "Aristophanic" thinkers ask questions with no interest in the answers. They presuppose an emptiness and wish merely to "suck out the apparent content" and leave the emptiness behind. But this emptiness, one is quick to note, like nothing or nothingness, is not emptiness in the usual sense of the word; it is, rather, an emptiness which is the content of life, a subjectivity that can never be made an object of knowledge, a non-knowledge if you will. As Kierkegaard will later write in answer to the questions "What was Socrates actually like?" and "What was the point of departure for his activity?": "Socrates's existence was irony." Are readers not at every bend and turn in the text(s) warranted in saying the same thing about Kierkegaard?

Have the "Aristophaneses" of Kierkegaardian scholarship made themselves known? If so, who are they? Do they provide the necessary contrast to the "Platonic" view and open up the possibility of a new approach and evaluation? Do they come closest to the actual Kierkegaard, a comic Kierkegaard? And if it is the case that Kierkegaard's whole activity was ironizing, like Socrates's, is it not then apparent that, in wanting to interpret him in a comic vein, the "Aristophaneses" are proceeding correctly, because "as soon as irony is related to a conclusion, it manifests itself as comic, even though in another sense it frees the individual from the comic" (KW II 145)? This other sense is immensely important, for if individuals are free from the comic, they would be able to relate themselves to the absolute as an absolute subject. But what is the absolute for the ironist (a rather uneasy juxtaposition)? Kierkegaard writes: "The ironist takes it obviously very easy even with the idea; he is in the highest degree free under it, for the absolute is to him nothingness" (CI 174; SV I 182). One must remember to read this "nothingness" very carefully, for "nothingness may be taken in several ways" (CI 275). Ironic nothingness is very spooky (cf. CI 275); it is an epitome of subjectivity, and if the God so chooses—the reasoning would go—something might become of it.

One can learn a great deal about Kierkegaard's understanding of Socrates' standpoint considered as irony by examining Kierkegaard's treatment of Aristophanes, for, of all his contemporaries, Aristophanes, according to Kierkegaard's reading, has the most accurate and correct portrayal of the actual Socrates. While both Plato and Aristophanes interpret Socrates ideally, "Plato has the tragic ideality, Aristophanes the comic" (CI 159). The comic conception is of the utmost importance for understanding the person of Socrates:

> As every development usually ends by parodying itself, and such a parody is a guarantee that this development has outlived itself, so the comic conception is also a moment, in many ways an infinitely correcting moment in the total illustration [*Anskueliggjørelse*] of a personality or tendency [CI 158].

Without a doubt, Socrates's personality and life present many comical aspects. His life also represented a new principle and a new standpoint. The clear exposition of this standpoint is a most urgent problem for Kierkegaard, who uses Aristophanes to argue against (the German Hegelian) H. Theodor Rötscher and his work *Aristophanes und sein Zeitalter: Eine philologisch-philosophische Abhandlung zur Alterthumsforschung* (Aristophanes and His Age: A Philological-Philosophical Dissertation in Antiquity Research) (Berlin, 1827). It is in this connection that Kierkegaard expresses a clear distinction between irony and subjectivity. He writes against Rötscher—apparently with greater Hegelian finesse—to argue (surprisingly?) that Socrates's standpoint was not subjectivity or inwardness but rather irony, which is the beginning of subjectivity but not subjectivity in its fullness. As is no doubt fitting, Kierkegaard states the case indirectly:

> If one will assume, however, that *irony* was the constitutive factor in Socrates's life, one will have to admit that this presents a much *more comic* aspect than when one lets the Socratic principle be *subjectivity*, inwardness, with the whole richness of thought which lies therein, and seeks Aristophanes' authority in the seriousness with which he, as an adherent of the old Hellenism, must strive to destroy this modern nuisance. For this seriousness oppresses too much, as it also limits the comic infinity, which as such knows no limit. By contrast, irony is at once a new standpoint, and as such absolutely polemical towards the old Hellenism, and in addition, a standpoint which continually cancels itself. It is a nothingness which consumes everything, and a something, which one can never get a hold of, which at once is and is not; but it is something in its deepest ground comical. As irony, therefore, conquers everything by seeing its misrelation to the idea, so it also succumbs to itself, in that it constantly goes beyond itself while it still remains in itself [CI 161; SV I 170–1].[33]

Here one hits upon the problem of the relationship between irony and subjectivity, for they are clearly related but distinguishable terms. The problem consists in adequately demarcating the two, but it is not easy to see exactly where one should draw the line.

Irony is "in its deepest ground comical," particularly when it gets related to a result, and "the comical must of course also have a truth" (CI 174; SV I 182). Had Socrates possessed an actual philosophical dialectic, "the subjective dialectic of Plato, it would have been completely untrue of Aristophanes to conceive of him in this way." Ostensibly, at this moment in Kierkegaard's development, Socrates is not considered to have reached the standpoint of subjectivity in all its glory. This follows from the above, as well as from theses six, eight, and nine, the eighth one reading: "*Ironia, ut infinita et absoluta negativitas, est levissima et maxime exigua subjectivitatis significatio*" ("Irony as infinite and absolute negativity is the lightest and weakest intimation of subjectivity") (CI 348–49). This thesis is found in the text in virtually the same form:

> But if irony is a determination of subjectivity, it must exhibit itself the first time subjectivity appears in world history. *Irony* is namely

> *the first and most abstract determination of subjectivity*. This points to the historical turning point at which subjectivity appeared for the first time, and with this we have arrived at Socrates [CI 281; SV I 278].

With Socrates subjectivity appeared, yet Socrates lacked subjectivity (inwardness) in the fullest sense of the word. To make matters clearer, it would be better to say he lacked "sub-objectivity":

> He lacked the objectivity wherein subjectivity in its freedom is free in itself, the objectivity which is not the constricting but the expanding limit of subjectivity. The point he arrived at was the internal self-consistency of ideal infinity itself, but in the form of an abstraction that was as much a metaphysical as an aesthetic and moral determination. The thesis so often propounded by Socrates that sin is ignorance already indicates this sufficiently. It is *subjectivity's* infinitely high-spirited *freedom* that we see in Socrates, but this is precisely *irony* [CI 233; SV I 236].

Kierkegaard's argument is that Socrates's standpoint is irony, that is, subjectivity insofar as the subject is negatively free. In this text, Kierkegaard reads Socrates as presenting neither a positive dialectic nor a positive freedom, which would seemingly result from the standpoint of sub-objectivity. On this point Kierkegaard's conception differs from Hegel's, and this provides an explanation as to why Socrates is missing from Kierkegaard's conclusion on mastered irony. Still, the personality of Socrates haunts in various forms: Is Kierkegaard correct in his conception? Was it impossible for Socrates to maintain the standpoint of sub(ob)jectivity without possessing a philosophical dialectic? Did this divine missionary lack the fullness of inwardness? Was he bound to lose the reward of blessedness?

If Socrates's entire activity consisted in irony and he maintained a wholly negative dialectic, this does not mean that he was completely dominated by the comical, even though the comical is considered to be the clearest portrayal of such an ironic dialectic. Kierkegaard is always quick to point out that "in another sense irony frees the individual from the comical" (CI 174; SV I 182). Irony, obviously, cannot be contained by the comical. Finitely understood, irony related to a result is comical (because existence is becoming itself), whereas infinitely understood—already a more proper characterization, since irony possesses a poetic infinity—it is emancipating and the individual "is completely free."

Aristophanes, then, is the one who has wittingly or unwittingly come closest to grasping the personality of Socrates and his non-philosophy, which was revealed in the symbol of the clouds. With Kierkegaard's use and description of this nebulous symbol one finds an early intimation that things are not always as they seem, and that thought and reality are not one. Implicitly, this undermines the silly idea that "the real is rational and the rational is real." The clouds provide an analogy to thoughts, or the

> directionless movement of thought, which with incessant fluctuation, without foothold, and without immanent laws of motion, configures itself in every which way with the same irregular variation as do the clouds, which now resemble mortal women, now a centaur, a leopard, a wolf, a bull, etc. But resemble them, be it noted, not *are* them . . . [CI 163].

The negative dialectic is characterized as a whirlwind which retains or holds fast to nothingness, and the ironic method, it is noted, is impotence; it can give birth to nothing other than its own likeness (CI 164–65).

As the clouds are first made to represent the shapes of women, one is reminded of Nietzsche's famous opening question to *Beyond Good and Evil*: "Supposing truth is a woman—what then?" Each is an expression for the unclarity and the ingraspability of truth, the Idea, which is oh so alluring, enticing, and fleeting. Unlike Nietzsche's Socrates,[34] however, Kierkegaard's exposition of Aristophanes's view presents a Socrates for whom the shapes of the clouds hold no validity. Thus, Socrates speaks of the shapes jokingly and worships rather the formless itself.

> What remains when one allows the various shapes assumed by the clouds to disappear is nebulosity itself, which is an excellent description of the Socratic Idea. The clouds always appear in a definite shape, but Socrates knows the shape is unessential and that the essential lies behind the shape. Similarly, the Idea is true, and the predicate as such has no significance. But what is true in this way never passes out into any predicate, it never *is* [CI 166].

The Socratic Idea is scarcely like the Platonic Idea, and one gets the impression from Kierkegaard's insightful writing that, already with the appearance of Socrates, metaphysics had met its master. It is thus scandalous that it took philosophy so long to come to this realization, and what Heidegger and Derrida do under erasure is not wholly irrelevant to the concerns of Kierkegaard, who seems to anticipate their erasures in his approximation to and appropriation of the Socratic Idea, which is essentially a non-Idea, the formless which can never take form, a formlessness which can never be signified, predicated, conceived, grasped, communicated, discussed, and so forth, because it never is (period).

It is, nevertheless, only in relation to this non-Idea, which is true in itself, that objective ideas, the clouds, can be formed into different shapes. The clouds then symbolize both the chorus and Socrates's thoughts viewed objectively, and between the clouds and the subject Socrates there exists "a very *profound harmony*":

> [T]he former as the objective power unable to find a permanent location upon the earth, and whose approximation to this always yields distance; and the latter, who, hovering above the earth in a basket, endeavors to elevate himself up into these regions because he fears the force of the earth will draw these thoughts away from him, or to dispense with the imagery, that actuality will absorb and crush his fragile subjectivity [CI 167; SV I 176].

Once again there is a congenial mingling of objectivity (of the clouds) and subjectivity (of Socrates). This new subjectivity, however, opposes the objectivity of the present actuality (i.e., the old Hellenism), which holds no validity for Socrates. Still, it fears the force of the present actuality, and therefore cannot be free for something but seeks rather only to become free from everything, and thus it floats away.

It was pointed out as early (or perhaps as late) as 1855, the year of Kierkegaard's death, that *The Concept of Irony* "not only treats of irony but is irony."[35] While this view is entirely correct, it is important to see (read) where Kierkegaard hints of the underlying ironic structure, and then to inquire into the problems or possibilities this irony opens up for the reading of this early work. I have already suggested that to read many of Kierkegaard's pronouncements on Socrates and irony as doubly reflected and therefore equally applicable to the "ironic" writer, who is always *ubique et nusquam* (everywhere and nowhere), provides a valuable hermeneutic insight. To read in this way is not to misread, nor does it require any great stretch of the imagination. (This would not, of course, apply to Kierkegaard's criticism of Socrates, which is actually quite marginal in relation to the bulk of a text that honors the father of irony. The slight distance Kierkegaard places between himself and Socrates will be removed throughout later writings, and, as a preview of coming attractions, it is interesting to note that it will be Kierkegaard who approaches Socrates's standpoint, not the other way around.)

For example, Kierkegaard considers it of the deepest irony that Aristophanes presents Socrates, the Sophists greatest enemy, as their teacher rather than as their antagonist, because for Socrates to undermine, destroy, and overcome the Sophists, he had to become a Sophist in the highest sense by carrying through their standpoint. Such is what Kierkegaard can be read as doing to the Hegelians, particularly those contemporaries of his in Denmark (i.e., Heiberg and Martensen). Kierkegaard proceeds and carries out his work in a heightened Hegelian fashion, and comes to a result or a conclusion that, on close inspection, stands in opposition to Hegelian philosophy.

On the one hand, while Hegel lets irony get under his skin, Kierkegaard mastered it in a momentous way that liberated him from (negative freedom) the fixed meanings that others might bring to this complicated work, and, simultaneously, made him free for (positive freedom) his own future creative meanings and readings of this work. In this sense, one sees the true nature of *The Concept of Irony* as omnipresent irony, and its author, a master of irony, is completely free in relation to his work. (That Kierkegaard scrapped the Latin theses is an early example of his positive freedom.)

On the other hand, what is characterized here both in the case of Socrates and in the case of Kierkegaard taken in a deeply ironic sense is that a purely negative dialectic produces nothing whatsoever. The "result" is in truth a "non-result" in that the simulacra of the standpoints of Socrates and Kierkegaard must be viewed as nothingness. They stand isolated and impotent. Thus, when Kierkegaard writes about

> the *curious confusion* that one who combats a particular movement may himself be conceived as its representative, since he himself to some extent partakes of it, conceals in itself so much intentional or unintentional irony that it should not *entirely* be lost sight of [CI 168]

it is read with self-conscious irony.

There is proof enough, Kierkegaard finds, to show that Aristophanes has not identified Socrates with the Sophists. The Sophist falls under the concept of species, genus, and so on, and need not be conceived in the singular. "Sophistry is the licentious and wild running around of selfish thought" (CI 176; SV I 183), which corresponds to the proliferation of the Sophists. By contrast, "*the ironist* falls under the determination of *personality* and is always singular" (CI 176; SV I 183). The determination of personality is first given through the ironist's act of leading the wild movement of thought back into him- or herself at every moment, unlike the Sophist, who is forever reaching for something that is outside and in front of him or her. Sophism can thereby serve irony, for the ironist takes up its initial wild grasping together with the moment when it is directed into him- or herself. Taking up both moments into consciousness is enjoyment, which is designated as the second determination of personality, although the ironist's enjoyment is the most abstract of all, and the weakest hint of the enjoyment that possesses absolute content, that is, *Salighed*, which could be translated as "happiness," "exhilaration," "blessedness," "salvation," or "bliss." Here again, irony is merely a hint, a beginning toward subjectivity and a fully developed personality, which does not as yet possess the richness of subjectivity. Although "*the ironist* is a prophecy about or an *abbreviation* of a *complete personality*" (CI 177; SV I 185), irony does come across as the only way toward one's blessed subjectivity.

As one seeks to focus on Kierkegaard's attitude toward Hegel in *The Concept of Irony*, this attitude shows itself as at once both critical and grateful. A single passage expresses both points of view:

> The fact that Hegel has become infatuated with the form of irony nearest him has naturally distorted his conception of the concept. And if the reader seldom gets a discussion, Schlegel, on the other hand, always gets a drubbing. But this does not mean that Hegel was wrong regarding the Schlegels or that the Schlegelian irony was not an extremely serious error. Nor does this deny that Hegel has certainly brought about much benefit through the seriousness with which he opposes every isolation, a seriousness which makes it possible to read many a Hegelian discussion with much edification and fortification. This does mean, on the other hand, that Hegel in one-sidedly focusing on post-Fichtian irony has *overlooked the truth of irony*, and as he identifies all irony with this, so he has done irony an injustice [CI 282; SV I 279–80].

Here, in a nutshell, one finds Kierkegaard's major complaint against the Hegelian view of irony, and it is worth calling attention to the fact that it is a complaint from within the system—that is, Hegel has not properly conceived the concept because he has not fully accounted for Socrates's irony in its formation. Notwithstanding this, Kierkegaard feels, ironically, that one can read Hegel with much edification. Rereading Hegel in this manner is to read him in a way quite opposed to the manner he himself would have expected to be read, for he was as wary of edification as he was of irony.[36]

What, then, about the question, Was Kierkegaard a Hegelian when he wrote *The Concept of Irony*? This question has been debated in the literature, and two important Danish scholars take broadly different views. In his *Søren Kierkegaards Opfattelse af Sokrates* (Søren Kierkegaard's Conception of Socrates), Jens Himmelstrup argues that Kierkegaard was basically an Hegelian at the time that he wrote *The Concept of Irony*. Niels Thulstrup, on the other hand, asserts that Kierkegaard was essentially anti-Hegelian, and argues that the author of the dissertation should be treated as a pseudonym who acted as an Hegelian historian of philosophy in order to undermine the Hegelian philosophy itself. Both scholars have extensive evidence on their sides, which makes one wonder whether either extreme view should be accepted. Kierkegaard's writing owes so much to the negative (ironic) dialectic that two honorable scholars have arrived at completely different results. This is hardly surprising, for if the dissertation is truly ironic, it is contradictory, following this simple logic:

> All ironies are contradictory.
> Kierkegaard's dissertation is irony.
> ....
> Kierkegaard's dissertation is contradictory.

The question, then, "Was Kierkegaard an Hegelian?" (and all others like it) is badly posed, for it presupposes a static Kierkegaard and a determinate set of beliefs that may be labeled "Hegelian." (In a similar vein, Kierkegaard will imply that the question, "Is so and so a Christian?" ignores the true nature of human existence as becoming.) Better scholarly questions are: "How much Hegel had Kierkegaard read?" and "How was he as a reader?" Thulstrup addresses the former question:

> Only a single book and a single article, which Hegel published himself, are identified and used by Kierkegaard, namely, *The Philosophy of Right* and the long review of Solger's writings.
>
> On the other hand, he used much more extensively Hegel's posthumously published lectures, *The Philosophy of History*, *The Philosophy of Fine Art*, and *The History of Philosophy*. In our own day these first editions of Hegel's lectures have been severely criticized for their unreliability, and rightly so.[37]

Kierkegaard's reading of Hegel was in a state of becoming. He was a developing writer, and, as such, the question of the label "Hegelian" holds no great interest.

In Part One of his dissertation, Kierkegaard unabashedly follows the Hegelian stages of development. He then supplies a "Supplement" (*Tillæg*, from *tillæge*, literally "to lay on") in which he writes about "Hegel's Conception of Socrates," and specifically asks, "In what sense is Socrates the founder of morality?" According to Kierkegaard, the treatment of this point will show his modification to the total Hegelian conception of Socrates. The term "modification" (the Danish is identical) itself may be understood dialectically, for, on the one hand, Kierkegaard recognizes and acknowledges his deep indebtedness to Hegel, and, on the other hand, he wishes to argue that, contra Hegel, Socrates was completely negative and did not possess any positivity at all. Such a "modification" leads to a totally different conception of Kierkegaard's "Hegelianism."

Kierkegaard's general criticism of Hegel has been given above—namely, that he failed to conceive the concept in its fullness because he became infatuated with the phenomenon closest him, romantic irony, and thereby slighted the original phenomenon of Socratic irony. He nevertheless finds in Hegel a sanction for his own conception. While not directly quoting Hegel, Kierkegaard refers a total of five times to Hegel's view that what was important for Socrates was not philosophical theorizing or speculation but, rather, individual life. Hegel's interesting remark concerning the philosophy of Socrates is as follows:

> Seine Philosophie, als das Wesen in das Bewusstseyn als ein Allgemeines setzte, ist als *seinem individuellen Leben* angehörig anzusehen; sie ist nicht eigentliche spekulative Philosophie, sondern *ein individuelles Thun* geblieben. Und ebenso ist ihr Inhalt die Wahrheit *des individuellen Thuns* selbst; das Wesen, der Zweck seiner Philosophie

> ist, *das individuelle Thuns* das Einzelnen als *ein allgemeingültiges Thun einzurichten.*[38]

> (His philosophy, as an essence placed in the consciousness as a universal, is to be seen as belonging to *his individual life*; it is not actually speculative philosophy, but rather remains *an individual action.* And as such its content is the truth of the *individual action* itself; the essence, (to discover) which is the purpose of his philosophy, is to establish *the individual action* of a particular person as *a universally valid action.*)

Mastered irony, to be sure, is a matter of individual action, and therein lies its truth. It may further be designated as imparting healthiness through the liberation of the individual, and providing the way to becoming a complete personality with a fullness of character. While readers may rightly assume that Kierkegaard himself sought the health bestowed by irony—in which case an ironic, holistic interpretation of his writings would also be a healthy one—he did, unsurprisingly for a dialectician, present its sick side as well.

> There are these two poles between which the ordinary human life moves somnolently and unclear: irony is a healthiness insofar as it rescues the soul from the snares of relativity; it is a sickness insofar as it is unable to tolerate the absolute except in the form of nothingness, and yet this sickness is an endemic fever which few individuals contract, and yet even fewer overcome [CI 113-14].

Might not irony be the sickness unto death? In the case of Socrates, who—it will be remembered—said that a philosopher's life-task is the preparation for death, one would have to answer in the affirmative. There is also a dialectical relationship involved here, since "in Christian terminology, death is the expression for the state of deepest spiritual wretchedness, and yet the cure is simply to die, to die to the world" (KW XIX 6). Irony awakens the individual to the possibility of this death. In short: Irony edifies.

This effect of irony is brought about through the infinite negativity that opposes serious-mindedness and is utterly polemical towards its "world-historical situation." Irony emancipates the individual from the snares of the finite, the chains of relativity, and sets the existential ironist free. Such a thinker maintains, with the philosopher from Ecclesiastes, that "all is vanity" and is thereby awakened to the possibility of establishing an absolute relationship with the absolute, for which any sensitive person continually longs. "But this longing must not hollow out actuality; on the contrary, the content of life must become a true and meaningful moment in the higher actuality whose fullness the soul desires" (CI 341; SV I 330). In such a way, practically considered, as Kierkegaard would say, the individual's life and its actuality acquire validity through self-purposive action.

A deep understanding of mastered irony, which is to say mastered infinite-absolute-negativity, ferries one to the coast of the ethical-religious standpoint. In fact, for Kierkegaard, the ironic standpoint and the religious standpoint express a similar point of view. Both "become conscious of the fact that existence [*Tilværelse*] has no reality," and through this "the lesser actuality, that is to say the relationship to the world, also loses its reality" (CI 274–75; SV I 273). According to Kierkegaard at this stage of his development, however, the ferryman Socrates seems never to have gotten off the boat. Social gadflies are not notorious for having achieved purity of heart or even the slightest degree of subjectivity that would eventually display itself as pure inwardness.

Yet, insofar as Kierkegaard was himself a master of irony, he was free to compose his own little modification to his description of Socrates's vocation, as he had modified the requirements of his dissertation by opting for the more pliant Danish over the stilted academic Latin of his own day. Changing his mind further, he will later call himself a "Hegelian fool" for not granting a certain subjective fullness to Socrates.[39]

And he is to go further still in developing his conception of Socrates's teaching by example. For, if it can be taken as established that the palpable thread of development throughout Kierkegaard's writings is the achievement of his own life-view—which shows itself *with constant reference to Socrates*—then one of the next steps in my demonstration must further consider the "individual action" of Socrates, the master of irony who served as teacher for all those who would master the art.

Specifically, it might be asked, if Socrates were truly the ironic master of Kierkegaard, How did Socrates become a Christian?[40]

Notes

1. My point is exemplified by a promising student of Kierkegaard, whom I met at the Kierkegaard Library at the University of Copenhagen. She had just made the happy purchase of Kierkegaard's *Samlede Værker,* but in order to do so tax-free, she had to have one of the volumes sent out of Denmark to her native land. Without a moment's hesitation, the work she chose to send home was *Om Begrebet Ironi,* which would be of no use for her in her investigation of Kierkegaard's writings.

2. Following common practice I shall refer to *Om Begrebet Ironi* as *The Concept of Irony* rather than *On the Concept of Irony.* Most scholars and translators find the "On" redundant, and therefore it is omitted.

3. *Kierkegaard's Relation to Hegel,* p. 257.

4. *Kierkegaard,* p. 187.

5. It is (perhaps) surprising that Louis Mackey, a usually very perceptive reader of Kierkegaard, gets confused about the relationship between irony and doubt. In *Points of View,* he writes: "It is true at the very least, if it is true at all, that philosophy in the modern age begins with (Descartes's) doubt. But the modern age also begins with irony. Therefore (perhaps) doubt equals irony and irony equals doubt.

On top of that, the only life worthy to be called human begins with irony, that is, with doubt. The beginning of philosophy is the beginning of modernity is the beginning of humanity equals irony equals doubt. The beginning begins with Socrates as well as with Descartes—and perhaps with the eternal" (p. 3). Mackey's own uncertainty resounds loudly in this passage. While irony and doubt are analogous, they are not equal (identical). One might say that their similarity consists in dissimilarity, as they mark different beginnings which engender different outcomes. In the next chapter I shall further discuss this beginning with doubt in an analysis of the incomplete narrative, *Johannes Climacus: Or, De Omnibus Dubitandum Est.*

6. Quoted from a transcript copy of a lecture given at Ohio State University on April 14, 1977 by Christopher Norris in "De Man Unfair to Kierkegaard?" p. 89.

Given *The Concept of Irony*'s special importance within the Kierkegaardian corpus and Kierkegaard's overall anticipation of postmodern thought and literary practice, Norris has rightly questioned, "Why has Kierkegaard so seldom been read or written about by deconstructionist literary critics who must surely realize that his work prefigures their own in many crucial respects?" This question will be considered more closely in my conclusion, "Rereading Kierkegaard as a Postmodern Philosopher."

7. For this insight into the etymological connection between "irony" and "word" I am indebted to David Stanley Randell and the "preface" of his dissertation, "Irony and Literary Criticism: Tropic Supplementarity in the Philosophy of Expressivism," which contains a slightly more detailed etymology of both words.

8. Since wayward personal pronouns have provoked violent intellectual debates, I shall take this opportunity to explain why I choose this slightly more cumbersome pronominal usage. Were I to only use feminine pronouns in general contexts, I could be accused of toadying to the politically correct crowd; and if this were my reason, it would certainly be non-Kierkegaardian. Still, I could appeal to Richard Rorty's example, or the deep view of Jacques Derrida, for whom the ironist (writer) is always (a) woman: "Human law, the law of the rational community that is instituted against the private law of the family, always suppresses the feminine, stands up against it, girds, squeezes, curbs, compresses it. But the masculine power has a limit—essential and eternal: the arm, the weapon, doubtless impotent, the all-powerful weapon of impotence, the inalienable wound of the woman, is irony. Woman, "(the community's) internal enemy," can always burst out laughing at the last moment; she knows, in tears and in death, how to pervert the power that represses. The power of irony—the ironic position rather—results—syllogistically—from what the master produces and proceeds from what he suppresses, needs, and returns to" (*Glas*, trans. J. P. Leavey and R. A. Rand [Lincoln: University of Nebraska Press, 1986], pp. 209–10). In light of Kierkegaard's ironic method, this appeal would appear to be quite Kierkegaardian.

Or, I could note that the Danish language usually avoids the problem when it refers to a human being, *et menneske*, because this word takes the neutral article and is replaced by the personal pronoun *det* ("it"). (Oddly enough, this is different from the Swedish, where a human being, *en människa*, is of common gender and takes the feminine pronoun *hon* ["she"].)

In an English-language context, however, if it were incorrect in the past to use masculine pronouns in a non-specific context, it is likewise incorrect to replace them with feminine pronouns in the present. I have therefore chosen, where it is possible, to write around the problem, and where it is not, to use both "he or she" and "his or her." I support this choice with the important—and in my opinion, Kierkegaardian—idea that a certain use of language engenders a certain way of thinking.

9. See Agacinski, *Aparté*, pp. 75–76.

10. This has become the accepted reading, and rightly so. This view was first expressed by Hans Friedrich Helweg, who in "Hegelianismen i Danmark," *Teologisk Tidskrift* 2 (December 16, 1855), states that

Kierkegaard's dissertation "not only treats of irony but is irony." Helweg also makes the perceptive comment that "Hegelianism ends with Kierkegaard, and nevertheless he did not entirely renounce Hegel."

11. The Danish *Intet* may be rendered as either "nothing" or "nothingness." While Capel oscillates between the two terms, I have modified the above quote by consistently translating it as "nothing."

12. In his journal he even went so far as to ask the reader to forgive him his gladness, for "I sometimes sing as I work in order to lighten my task" (P III B 2).

13. A theological candidate is one who has taken his first degree (equivalent to a Bachelor's degree) in theology.

14. For additional information on the Faculty of Philosophy's reaction to Kierkegaard's dissertation, see Capel's "Historical Introduction," CI 9–13.

15. Kierkegaard initially considered writing his dissertation on "the concept of satire among the ancients—the internal relationship between the various Roman satirists" (P II A 166).

16. The etymology of the Danish noun *begreb* (German *Begriff*) shows that the root *greb* means grasp, hold, or grip. One is thereby able to understand Kierkegaard's title *Om Begrebet Ironi* as an affront, for something defined by its negativity and singularity cannot be universalized into something one can grasp; it is in essence a false concept.

17. What is said here about irony might also be said about virtually all of Kierkegaard's important terms, e.g., angst, humor, faith, etc.

18. I am here indebted to Sartre's persuasive essay, "Kierkegaard: The Singular Universal," trans. John Mathews in *Between Existentialism and Marxism* (New York: Pantheon, 1974), p. 163. Sartre's paper was delivered to a UNESCO colloquium on Kierkegaard, entitled "The Living Kierkegaard," in April 1964.

19. A literal translation of the Danish expression for "common sense," i.e., *sund fornuft*.

20. An example of this overreaction is found in Mary Warnock's review of Alastair Hannay's *Kierkegaard* in "The Arguments of Philosophers" series (*Times Literary Supplement*, December 24, 1982). She writes: "In expounding his thought for this particular series, Professor Hannay has to face the question whether, thinking as he does, Kierkegaard was a philosopher at all. . . . For Kierkegaard the great enemy was objectivity, which he identified with scientific thought. . . ." I provide evidence to the contrary below.

21. The italics are found in the standard *Papirer* but not in Barfod's edition.

22. On the same page Anti-Climacus discusses the relationship between the imagination and knowledge. This passage is of interest in the

present context of self-knowledge, and will be of further interest later: "When all is said and done, whatever of feeling, knowing, and willing a person has depends upon what imagination he has, upon how that person reflects himself—that is, upon imagination. Imagination is infinitizing reflection, and therefore the elder Fichte quite correctly assumed that even in relation to knowledge the categories derive from the imagination" (KW XIX 31).

23. My initial impulse was that this had to be a typographical error. Of further interest is the sentence that follows this statement: "I simply need to mention Fichte."

24. This view also appears to be taken by Sanne Elisa Grunnet in her study *Ironi og Subjectivitet: En studie over S. Kierkegaards disputats "Om Begrebet Ironi"* (Irony and Subjectivity: A study of S. Kierkegaard's Dissertation "The Concept of Irony") (Copenhagen: C. A. Rietzel, 1987), p. 53.

25. While this might seem to go against the all-important order of thought noted by Kierkegaard, who is merely following Hegel in this regard, I am not actually suggesting that Part Two should be read before Part One. It is rather that in presenting the material it seems advantageous to form a preliminary grasp of the concept of irony in its full-blown sense—which has already been partially dispersed through the epigraphs to this chapter—and then to reread to see how this concept derives its meaning.

26. Thulstrup, *Kierkegaard's Relation to Hegel*, p. 224.

27. Thulstrup suggests that one should treat *The Concept of Irony* as an experiment in the indirect method and that the author, S. Kierkegaard, should be treated as "a pseudonym that represents a particular point of view on the basis of which the book was written, a pseudonym that plays the role as a Hegelian historian of philosophy" (ibid., p. 214). In like wise, one might argue that the author of *Works of Love* or *The Point of View* should be treated as a pseudonym.

28. When Kierkegaard writes about the importance of doubt for *Videnskab*, one must remember that he is referring to that philosophy which attempts to put itself on the secure path of science (or thinks that it has already succeeded in doing so); in other words, the idea may be expressed as "philosophy as a rigorous science." Thus, at the time Kierkegaard was writing, *Videnskab* could refer to both philosophy and science. Capel's translation (CI 338) chooses philosophy, while the Hongs (KW II 326) opt for science. The latter is a more literal translation, but may be misleading to someone who does not keep in mind that the concept of science was considerably different in the mid-nineteenth century. The former translation is equally appropriate when one considers that Kierkegaard uses *philosophia* in the Latin version of the statement

under discussion. I have chosen to translate *Videnskab* as "scholarship" in this context to alert readers to the difficulties involved, while at the same time hoping to avoid them.

29. Thesis X: "Socrates was the first to introduce irony" (CI 349; SV I 63).

30. At this point in the text Capel notes an interesting passage in Kierkegaard's journal from 1839 concerning "the category of the higher madness." Part of this amusing passage is worth repeating here: "I believe I would be doing philosophy a great service were it to adopt a category discovered by myself and utilized with great profit and success to exhaust and dry up a multitude of relations and determinations which have so far been unwilling to resolve themselves:—it is the category of the higher madness. I only ask that it not be named after me . . ." (P II A 808).

31. Derrida uses this epithet as an epigraph in his *Of Grammatology*, trans. Gayatri Chakravorty Spivak (Baltimore: The John Hopkins University Press, 1976), p. 6.

32. On this resemblance, think about Hegel and Kierkegaard, or Hegel and Derrida, and the latter's position that the former may be read as the first philosopher of writing.

33. A related passage, which occurs nearly twenty pages later in Kierkegaard's summary of Aristophanes's *The Clouds*, has given me considerable difficulty. Kierkegaard appears to contradict himself, for he says on the one hand, "Had the standpoint of Socrates been that of subjectivity, inwardness, it would have been comically incorrect to conceive him as Aristophanes has done." On the other hand, he writes, "It seems to me that if one agrees with Rötscher in characterizing Socrates's standpoint as subjectivity, one will find the conception of Aristophanes to be comically more true and hence more just. . . ." Here is the extended quote: "*The ironist*, to be sure, is lighter than the world, but he still belongs to the world; he hovers like the coffin of Mohammed between two magnets. Had the standpoint of Socrates been that of *subjectivity*, inwardness, it would have been comically incorrect to conceive him as Aristophanes has done. Subjectivity is hovering in relation to the substantiality of the older Hellenism, to be sure, yet it is infinitely hovering. Hence it would have been comically more correct to represent Socrates as infinitely vanishing and to have emphasized the comical in the fact that Strepsiades was unable to catch sight of him, than to represent him suspended in a basket. For the basket is the foundation of empirical activity which the ironist requires, whereas subjectivity in its infinity gravitates towards itself, i.e., is infinitely hovering.

"In summarizing this discussion of Aristophanes' *Clouds*, it seems to me that if one agrees with Rötscher in characterizing Socrates' *standpoint* as *subjectivity*, one will find the conception of Aristophanes to be comically more true and hence more just, as well as be able to remove some of the difficulties otherwise remaining with this Aristophanic work, than if he further determines this *standpoint* as *irony*, i.e., not let subjectivity overflow in its richness, but before this occurs allow it to egoistically close itself in irony" (CI 180–81; SV I 187–88).

34. Of course Nietzsche's view of Socrates is equally complex, if not more problematic than Kierkegaard's. Kierkegaard works to develop a consistency in his view, whereas Nietzsche is totally ambivalent. What I have in mind here, specifically, is Nietzsche's view that Socrates is the founder of a critical rationalism.

35. See note 10 above.

36. Hegel warned in the preface to *The Phenomenology of Mind*, trans. Baillie, that "philosophy must beware of wishing to be edifying" (p. 73).

Kierkegaard, like Derrida, expresses an ambivalent attitude toward Hegel, while also providing an alternative way of reading him. Consider the following entry in Kierkegaard's journal: "If Hegel had written his whole Logic and had written in the Preface that it was only a thought experiment, in which in many points he still steered clear of some things, he undoubtedly would have been the greatest thinker who has ever lived. As it is he is comic" (JP II 1605; P V A 73). Of course nothing prevents one from reading Hegel's writing as if it were a thought experiment, and in this sense one may better understand Derrida's description of Hegel as the first thinker of writing. It is also interesting to note that Hegel shares a point of comparison with Socrates in that they are both best regarded as comical. What about Kierkegaard himself?

Kierkegaard was surely aware that reading Hegel as edifying sounded an ironic note, for he was well aware of Hegel's mistrust of the edifying. On July 10, 1840, he wrote in his journal: "It is strange what hate, conspicuous everywhere, Hegel has for the edifying, but that which builds up is not an opiate which lulls to sleep; it is the Amen of the finite spirit and is an aspect of knowledge which ought not to be ignored" (JP II 214; P III A6). For Kierkegaard, then, not only has Hegel misunderstood irony, he has misunderstood edification as well.

37. Thulstrup, *Kierkegaard's Relation to Hegel*, p. 216.

38. Hegel, *Vorlesungen über die Geschichte der Philosophie* (Jubiläumsausgabe), XVIII, 53. Capel provides this quote in the original in his notes (see CI 390*nn*30 and 16 for a clarification of the edition of Hegel's *Vorlesungen* that Kierkegaard used). The translation that follows is my own.

39. The passage referred to was written in the Fall of 1850, some nine years after Kierkegaard's dissertation: "A Place in my Dissertation: Influenced as I was by Hegel and all that was modern, and without the

maturity enough to rightly understand greatness, I have somewhere in my dissertation not been able to let matters be, and shown that it was a shortcoming of Socrates that he did not have an eye for the totality, but only numerically considered the particulars.

"Oh, what a Hegelian fool I was,—this is precisely the principal evidence for how great an ethicist Socrates was" (EP 284).

40. I first raised this question in my essay, "How Did Socrates Become a Christian? Irony and a Postmodern Christian (Non)-Ethic," *Philosophy Today*, 36 (May 1992), 256–65. In the present work, however, a more thorough discussion of the problem appears.

3

Johannes Climacus's Meditations on First Philosophy*

> I have, alas, studied philosophy,
> Jurisprudence and medicine, too,
> And, worst of all, theology
> With keen endeavor, through and through—
> And here I am, for all my lore,
> The wretched fool I was before.
> Called Master of Arts, and Doctor to boot,
> For ten years almost I confute
> And up and down, wherever it goes,
> I drag my students by the nose—
> And see for all our science and art
> We can know nothing. It burns my heart.
>
> Goethe, *Faust*[1]

> The possibility of doubt is essential to existence, is the secret of human existence.
>
> Søren Kierkegaard, P IV B 10:11

THE CHARACTERIZATION OF THE LIFE-VIEW (*Livsanskuelse*) sought after by Kierkegaard in his writings may be more closely determined through the consideration of a life-view gone wrong. For, as Kierkegaard reasons,

> In order to see one light determinately, we always need another light. For if we imagined ourselves in total darkness and then a single spot of light appeared, we would be unable to determine the position of this light without a relation to another [P I A 1; JP 2240].

*This chapter was first published as "Kierkegaardian Meditations on First Philosophy: A Reading of *Johannes Climacus*," in the *Journal of the History of Philosophy*, 32 (October 1994), 623–43.

Through the difference doubt presents to irony, readers may gain a deeper insight into the conditions that make for a valid or authentic life-view. As the last chapter disclosed, irony ultimately entails consequences that would provide the foundations for one to be led beyond the clouds to the only genuine human life. No matter what criticisms Kierkegaard makes of his beloved Socrates, it is clear that both thinkers are united in the pursuit of a similar goal. This is expressed in Kierkegaard's fifteenth thesis to *The Concept of Irony*: "As philosophy begins with doubt, so also that life which may be called worthy of a human being begins with irony." This thesis constitutes the original analogy between the concepts of irony and doubt, and, what is more, appears to be Kierkegaard's unmistakable appropriation and rewriting of the famous Socratic maxim, "The unexamined life is not worth living."[2] Thus, one may argue that, although irony invokes dialectical ramifications, insofar as it is mastered, it conditions the production of positive fruits in the individual.[3] To put the matter in other words—words that I shall only state at present—edification presupposes irony.

By contrast, doubt, which looks deceptively like irony, operates in the conceptual realm of "scholarship," and, unlike irony, holds no practical or personal consequences for an individual (KW II 257). This is to say, it is purely theoretical. Kierkegaard, however, being the cunning dialectician that he is, allows himself a way around this position, for, strictly speaking, he deals with doubt insofar as it is appropriated and understood by the modern philosophizers of his day. With the few exceptions of when he refers to the Greeks, when Kierkegaard writes "doubt" he intends the specific designation of "modernist, systematic, or objective doubt."

Early on in his writing, Kierkegaard devotes considerable attention to the study of doubt's importance for "scholarship." He even goes so far as to project a writing on this alternative beginning from the beginning, the modern beginning with doubt, and sketches out a substantial portion of this work. For apparently unknown reasons, however, these meditations are never fully developed, and thus Kierkegaard does not finish or publish the philosophical narrative entitled *Johannes Climacus, Or, De omnibus dubitandum est.* As this chapter endeavors to extend my philosophical reading of Kierkegaard's writings, and since this work is strictly philosophical, it warrants a critical reading.

In addition to delineating the difference involved in the life-view begun with doubt, the question concerning the reasons behind *Johannes Climacus*'s incompletion is of more than passing interest to readers, who can be sure that Kierkegaard had both the time and the ability needed to execute this work, a work that might very well have been the most philosophically detailed of his writings had he followed the design he had sketched, and a work whose unfinished totality may make it that much easier for readers to focus attention primarily on the reading of this writing, which is not so much a finished book as it is a propaedeutic text.

With regard to the placement of *Johannes Climacus, Or, De omnibus dubitandum est* in Kierkegaard's corpus, my sympathies lie with the French editors and translators, who include this work alongside *Le Concept d'ironie constamment rapporté à Socrate* in volume 2 of *Oeuvres complètes de Søren Kierkegaard.*[4] Let me begin by explaining in more detail why I find the French organization to be both fortunate and beneficial.

With regard to the strict chronology of Kierkegaard's writings, it is perhaps only fitting that the dates of the composition of *Johannes Climacus* remain in doubt. The general consensus of 1842–1843 is concluded by the early editors of Kierkegaard's collected works (Heiberg and Kuhr), Niels Thulstrup, and the English translators Howard and Edna Hong. The usual evidence for this dating, more precisely given as from November 1842 to early 1843, is a passage from Kierkegaard's journal of 1844, where he writes: "A year and a half ago I began a little essay, *De omnibus dubitandum*, in which I made my first attempt at a little speculative development" (P V A 98; JP III 3300).[5] No one, of course, can pinpoint exactly when this entry was written, and even if one could, its possible deceptiveness—or, if you prefer, idiosyncrasy—could then be interrogated. The Danish scrivener Henning Fenger, who has argued in the first chapter of his *Kierkegaard-Myter og Kierkegaard-Kilder* (Kierkegaard Myths and Kierkegaard Sources) that Kierkegaard was guilty of falsifying history,[6] raises his own critical doubts concerning the "traditional" dating of *Johannes Climacus*. For Fenger, the passage from Kierkegaard's journal quite simply does not prove a thing.[7] He raises the question, When would Kierkegaard have had time to start *Johannes Climacus* while the monstrous *Either/Or* was in the works up until its publication on February 18, 1843? In other words, to pose the question more directly: Was *Johannes Climacus* written before or after *Either/Or*?

While the answer to this last question cannot be definitely determined since portions of this work were in great likelihood written both before and after the working on *Either/Or*, there is more important evidence that weighs in favor of the view that *Johannes Climacus* should be read in connection with the early academic writings (i.e., *From the Papers of One Still Living*, *The Battle Between the Old and the New Soap-Cellars*, and *The Concept of Irony*) and not with the pseudonymous works after and including *Either/Or*.

Furthermore, that *Johannes Climacus* should be placed after *Philosophical Fragments* (1844) in the definitive English translation (KW VII[8]) may give rise to certain misconceptions that would find their source in the understandable, but unfortunately mistaken, way of reading *Johannes Climacus, Or, De omnibus dubitandum est* as if it were written by the pseudonymous author Johannes Climacus, the pseudonymous author of *Philosophical Fragments* and *Concluding Unscientific Postscript*. The fact of the matter is that the manuscript title page of *Johannes Climacus* (reproduced in KW VII 228-29) does not include any designation of an author. This third-person narrative is, strictly speaking, not pseudonymous, and I consider it highly unlikely that Kierkegaard would have made the Caesarean move of signing "Johannes Climacus" to a work entitled *Johannes Climacus*. He would have either created some other "Simon Stylita" or—and, had the philosophical details of this writing been worked out to the extent that they were in *The Concept of Irony*, this would appear the more likely alternative—signed his own name.

In their "Historical Introduction," the Hongs write that "although *Philosophical Fragments* is also by Johannes Climacus [*sic*] and was written after *De omnibus dubitandum est*, it is not in direct continuity in substance, tone, and form" (KW VII xv–xvi). Assuming that Kierkegaard took great care in his choice of pseudonyms, this sound impression should have alerted them to the possibility that *De omnibus dubitandum est* was not written by Johannes Climacus.[9] While they search for the differentiae in drafts of *Philosophical Fragments* rather than in the content of *Johannes Climacus*, it is easier to see that the latter work's continuity lies with the early academic writings and Kierkegaard's timely meditations on the need to find a life-view or philosophy of life.

That *Johannes Climacus* has firm roots in Kierkegaard's early philosophical ruminations and in Copenhagen University's academic climate in the 1830s can be textually demonstrated. While Fenger casually remarks without supporting evidence that "there is an unmistakable sign of solidarity between the book on Andersen and the unfinished, philosophical novel *Johannes Climacus, Or, De omnibus dubitandum est*,"[10] I find the relatedness to be more conspicuous between *Johannes Climacus* and Kierkegaard's unfinished play, *The Battle between the Old and the New Soap-Cellars*.[11] There exists a certain affinity between the young Willibald, who "had not found himself much edified or satisfied by von Jumping-Jack's philosophical lectures" (KW I 119; P II B[19] 301), and the young Johannes Climacus, who, "if he encountered a recent philosophical work, he of course did not lay it aside before he had read it, but when he had read it, he often felt dissatisfied and discouraged" (KW VII 129; P IV B I 112). As these two quotes indicate, both young men found that a consideration of the claims of the (modern speculative) philosophizers filled their consciousnesses with unhappiness. Who were the philosophers who vexed these poor young men?

Without wandering outside of the primary source material, the answer may be found in the final paragraph of *The Concept of Irony*, although there it is given an ironic twist as Kierkegaard commends where he would also condemn. He refers the reader who would like "food for afterthought" to Professor Martensen's review of Heiberg's *New Poems* (1841).[12] The careful reader, however, would hardly suspect this food to be high in nutritional value (cf. CI 342, 426–29). (The reader might even also suppose that if a man filled his mouth so full with this food, he would thereby be prevented from eating and likely to starve in the consequence, such that someone would be needed to remove some of the food [CUP 245].) Magister Kierkegaard thus refers ironically to those who are only indirectly implicated in *The Soap-Cellars* and *Johannes Climacus*: the Danish Hegelians Johan Ludvig Heiberg (1791–1860) and Hans Lassen Martensen (1808–1884).

In Kierkegaard's day, Heiberg was a cultural leader in Copenhagen, Heiberg's wife was the prima donna in the theater, and Heiberg's mother was a recognized author whom Kierkegaard would review in *A Literary Review*. Heiberg was convinced of the truth of Hegel's speculative philosophy, and he had personally gotten to know the philosophical master in Berlin. Although Kierkegaard would protest against Heiberg's views, he had more than a modicum of respect for the man. The same cannot be said of Martensen, who is the thinker Kierkegaard continually alluded to with the words "Privatdocent" and "Professor."[13]

Fenger explains the academic/cultural situation as follows:

> At any rate, *De omnibus dubitandum est* has roots back in the 1830s, or, more closely designated, to the intellectual situation in Copenhagen in 1838 after Martensen's Hegelian lectures and the ensuing commotion in the academic duck pond. These lectures, which with support from Hegel sketched the contemporary time's philosophical development from Descartes [in Kierkegaard always *Cartesius*] to Hegel threw Kierkegaard into a fit, or rather a fury. The two expressions that he bit into and sucked the blood out of like a leech were Martensen's phrase on the necessity of "going beyond Hegel" and the one borrowed from Hegel on *De omnibus dubitandum est*. This is found in Kierkegaard's account of Martensen's lecture of 29 November 1837, but in general it goes back to Martensen's review of Heiberg's *Logic Course* in the December 1836 issue of the *Monthly Journal*.[14]

As Fenger vividly expresses it in this passage, Kierkegaard is very polemical about the academic situation at the University of Copenhagen, whereof his play is a fine example. His polemic is not without humor, however. Consider Kierkegaard's description of the *World-Historical College*, the academic institution founded by the prytaneum:

> This, however, was not yet completed, and only the atrium could be used, but this was so large that four professors lectured there simultaneously without disturbing one another. Indeed, it was so large that the audience could not even hear what the lecturers were expounding, although these were incessantly wiping the sweat from brows softened by their efforts. Two of these four professors were saying the same thing verbatim, and when finished they turned round with an air as if no one in the world could say anything like it [KW I 119–20].

One can be sure that at least two of the professors were lecturing on the modern movement in philosophy: from Descartes, "who said *cogito ergo sum* and *de omnibus dubitandum est*," to Spinoza, who "carried through this standpoint purely objectively, so that all existence became undulations of the absolute," to Kant, who "carried through this skepticism only to a certain extent," to Fichte, who looked "this Medusa in the face in the night of criticism and abstraction," to, finally, Hegel, "who speculatively drew together the previous systems" (KW I 118-19).

Through the narration of the life of Johannes Climacus, Kierkegaard attempted to remedy the misguided Danish philosophy of his day by taking it back through the movements of modern philosophy, so that the errors of its ways would clearly come to light. This theme was projected for "Pars tertia" of *Johannes Climacus*, where the heading would have read: "Johannes philosophizes with the help of traditional philosophical studies." Kierkegaard intended to begin with Danish philosophy and the traditional concepts and then move backwards toward the source of modern philosophy. He outlined this development as follows:

Para. 1. Hegel
Para. 2. Kant
Para. 3. Spinoza
Para. 4. Cartesius [P IV B 13:16; cf. P IV B 2:18; KW VII 238, 264]

Unfortunately, what might have become Kierkegaard's most focused writing on (modern) philosophy—which, it is interesting to note, did not contain the slightest trace of or reference to Anglo-Saxon ideas—remained unwritten.

The parallel between *The Soap-Cellars*[15] and *Johannes Climacus* can be made explicit by considering two passages which find their origin in Kierkegaard's notes on Martensen's lecture of November 29, 1837, although Martensen's first mention of the thesis that "philosophy begins with doubt" is found in his review of Heiberg's *Indledningsforedrag til det i November 1834 begyndte logiske Cursus paa den kongelige militaire Høiskole* (Introductory Lecture for the Logic Course begun in November 1834 at the Royal Military High School).[16] According to Kierkegaard's notes, Martensen professed that by "*de omnibus dubitandum est*" Descartes "denoted a doubt not about this or that but about everything" (P II C 18; cf. KW VII 324, n. 13). As in the final paragraphs of *The Concept of Irony*, where Kierkegaard plays with another one of Martensen's reviews, he rewords part of the review under discussion and puts it into the mouth of von Jumping-Jack:

> Yes, that's all very fine with the popular, but my doubt is by no means popular; it is not a doubt about this, that, or the other, about this thing or that thing; no, it is an infinite doubt [KW I 114].

The same view is also cited in *Johannes Climacus*, where Johannes heard one of the philosophizers express it:

> To doubt everything is no easy matter; it is, namely, not doubt about one thing or another, about this or that, about something and something else, but is a speculative doubt about everything, which is by no means an easy matter [KW VII 165].

There can be no doubt, then, that *Johannes Climacus* essentially belongs to Kierkegaard's early academic writings, which are characterized by an inquiry into the ways of philosophy and a meditation on the search for a philosophical method.

As I now turn to the Faustian problem that became the sum and substance of Johannes Climacus's life, as narrated by Søren Kierkegaard, it is clear that from the word Go the author intends this work as an attack on modern speculative philosophy. The method of attack is given in the narrative form through which Kierkegaard will show that a life-view founded on doubt must ultimately lead one to despair and emptiness. Doubt, in contrast to practical irony, cannot show the way to a full life, because it is strictly contemplative. Kierkegaard impresses upon readers that doubt, "real doubt existing in the mind," is "anti-life," for, with regard to Johannes, "life has not acquired any meaning for him, and all this is the fault of philosophy" [KW VII 235; P IV B 16].

Thus, Kierkegaard wants to counteract this (modern) philosophy that, unlike ancient philosophy, preaches ideas that it does not itself deem worthy of practice. Johannes had heard "*de omnibus dubitandum est*" uttered repeatedly. Indeed, it was cited as the all-important beginning for philosophy. He therefore chose to make it the object of his thinking, "even though it were to cost him his life" (KW VII 131; P IV B 1 115).

Johannes Climacus is divided in two: "Pars prima" and "Pars secunda." The first part presents a close scrutiny of the three main theses that were asserted by the prominent philosophizers of the day: "(1) philosophy begins with doubt; (2) one must have doubted in order to philosophize; (3) modern philosophy begins with doubt" (KW VII 132; P IV B 1115–16). This part forms the bulk of Kierkegaard's closely argued polemic against modern philosophy, whereas in the second part, the examination takes a more profound, quasi-metaphysical turn, as the author inquires into the ontological and existential conditions that make doubt possible. As usual, readers find a juxtaposition of destructive polemics and constructive "philosophy"—although even this latter term may be understood in an ultimately negative sense—both of which are important for charting the edifying and ironic polemics of Kierkegaard's life-view.

Kierkegaard begins his narration of the meta-philosophical meditations of Johannes Climacus with a strictly grammatical look at the thesis: modern philosophy begins with doubt. Initially, he focuses on the adjective "modern," which when applied to the subject "philosophy" implies that all previous philosophy originated in some other way. The question that follows asks whether the same adjective might be applied to the same substantive if this philosophy had not begun with doubt. If not, would this modern philosophy in turn "have a retroactive power, so that the extent to which that older philosophy can be called philosophy would become dubious" (KW VII 134; P IV B 1 117)? If this were the case, then it would imply that doubt is more than a historical beginning for modern philosophy, it would be the essential beginning for philosophy proper. And if *this* were the case, then essential (modern) philosophy would invoke the same annoying difficulty that it found in Christianity, that is, a beginning that is both historical and eternal.

Climacus then proceeds to take note of the eternal present tense involved in the thesis "Modern philosophy begins with doubt." "It does not use a historical tense or a present in the historical style such as one uses in saying 'Descartes begins with doubt'" (KW VII 135; P IV B 1 118). This latter thesis does not present Johannes with any problems, for it is something quite different to refer to a particular philosopher, and I suspect that he was a true admirer of Descartes, like his contemporary Johannes de Silentio, who in *Fear and Trembling* writes that Descartes was

> a venerable, humble, honest thinker, whose writings no one can read without being profoundly affected—he did what he said and said what he did. Alas! Alas! Alas! That is a great rarity in our day [KW VI 5].

So much for the modern philosophizers of Kierkegaard's day, who apparently did not do what they said and said what they did not do. Despite this attack on modern philosophizers, however, the impression one gets from many a Kierkegaardian text is that the author has a great respect for unique, individual thinkers of rank, of which the Danes had none at all (cf. P X 19). While he does not, of course, hesitate to offer his corrections to their views, he is thankful for their insights—and this is equally true for the mighty Hegel. So, in general, it is a common misperception that Kierkegaard attacked "philosophers" per se. It was rather the "philosophizers" he loathed, in which case one draws an important distinction between unique, honest thinkers and the unoriginal ones who merely jump on the bandwagon and form schools, fashion trends, and movements that provoke wholesale excitement for crowds of people but leave reflective individuals troubled and empty.[17]

Johannes's reflections on the grammar of the third thesis continue to weave a carefully woven snare for world-historical thinkers. Since modern philosophy is understood in the present tense, it must be considered as being in a process of becoming, and if it is not yet complete, how can it be judged to provide the essential beginning for philosophy? If it is finished in its entirety and does provide the essential beginning, then the adjective "modern" is obscure and unnecessary, and this thesis reduces to the first thesis, "Philosophy begins with doubt."

When Johannes turns to consider the first thesis he finds that, like the third thesis, it is neither as straightforward nor so precise as the utterances of the philosophizers would make it seem. Whereas an analysis of the third thesis yielded its transformation from a historical to an essential thesis, an examination of the first thesis produces the exact opposite result. To say that philosophy begins with a negative principle such as doubt presupposes an antecedent, because this negative principle "implies a polemic against not only this or that which lies outside of philosophy but also against a principle in philosophy" (KW VII 144; P IV B 1127). If there were not a principle prior to doubt, it would hardly make sense as a beginning. Moreover, it is the nature of doubt that for it to occur a dichotomy must present itself to the mind. Kierkegaard writes in a sketch that "Doubt arises when I become a relation between two (objects)," and he is well aware of the conspicuous etymological connection between the words "doubt" and "two" in several languages: in Latin, *dubito/duo*; in German, *zweifeln/zwei*; in Danish, *tvivle/ tve* (P IV B 10:2 & 13:2; KW VII 258). The thesis that claims that essential philosophy begins with doubt thus "admits an antecedent philosophical principle," which transforms it into a properly historical proposition.

Such a difficulty would not be encountered if the thesis were to state that philosophy begins with a positive principle, such as wonder, which is what the Greeks had taught.

> For wonder is an immediate determination and does not reflect upon itself. Doubt, on the other hand, is a determination of reflection [*Reflexions-Bestemmelse*]. When a later philosopher said: Philosophy begins with wonder—he was straightway in continuity with the Greeks. They had wondered, he had wondered too; they had perhaps wondered about one thing, while he wondered about something else. But every time a later philosopher repeats or says these words: Philosophy begins with doubt—the continuity is broken, for doubt is precisely a polemic against the foregoing. [KW VII 145; P IV B 1 127].

In order to flush out the deepest ramifications of doubt, it will be necessary to develop it as a determination of reflection and "search out *doubt's ideal possibility in consciousness*," which is what Kierkegaard aims to do in "Pars secunda." Before this, however, he sustains his polemic through a consideration of the single individual in relation to the thesis "Philosophy begins with doubt."

The humble Johannes is a shy and careful thinker who wonders about the possibility of doubting doubt.

> He was well able to comprehend that an individual could take it into his head to doubt, but he could not understand how it could occur to him to say this to another person, least of all as advice (it would be another matter if it were said to deter), for if the other person was not too slow, he might very well say, "Thank you, but please forgive me for also doubting the correctness of that statement." [KW VII 146; P IV B 1128].

Johannes could have raised many more critical questions about this thesis, but he was far more interested in the existential aspect of successfully relating himself to it. His goal was nothing less than to embrace philosophy, so that perhaps he, too, could become a philosopher.

Johannes heard from one of the philosophizers, who had assuredly found support in Hegel, that the beginning of philosophy is threefold.[18] This observation sat well with Johannes, for he was always delighted with a clear thought from which he could derive the consequences, "to climb step by step to a higher one, because to him coherent thinking [*Consequentsen*] was a *scala paradisi* [ladder of paradise]" (KW VII 118; P B 1105).[19] To think in this way filled Johannes with an indescribable pleasure and happiness, that is, insofar as he could draw the simple thought through all of its logical consequences in order to conclude with the same simple thought, although now with the slight addition of the majestic expression *quod erat demonstrandum*.

This Climacian method shares much with the thinking of Hegel, and one could derive a lot from the fact that it is Hegel whom Kierkegaard calls a Johannes Climacus in his first written reference to the monk on January 20, 1839.

> Hegel is a Johannes *Climacus* who does not storm the heavens as do the giants—by setting mountain upon mountain—but *climbs up* to them by means of his syllogisms [JP II 1575; P II A 335].

Since both thinkers seem to hold that there is reality in thought, one ought not to be too hasty in wanting to oppose Hegel to Climacus.[20]

On the other hand, when Climacus was unable to reach his beloved Q.E.D., he became sad and melancholic, verging on the suicidal. This state befell him all too frequently when he reflected on the claims of the philosophizers, who paid little attention to their logical consequences. Johannes could not understand how the threefold nature of the beginning of philosophy—defined as the absolute, the objective, and the subjective beginning—could help to elucidate the thesis that philosophy begins with doubt. Yet the philosophizers proposed that this was the case, so Johannes assumed that this thesis was included under the subjective beginning, which was defined as "the work of consciousness by which this (i.e., consciousness) elevates (*opløfter*) itself to the thought or to positing the abstraction." This leads Kierkegaard to canvass the "up-lifting" nature of the subjective beginning, and he proceeds to play on the alternative meanings of the Danish verb *opløfte*. He writes that Johannes found the subjective beginning to be very beautiful, "particularly very uplifting (*opløftende*), but his consciousness still was not lifted up (*løftet op*) by it" (KW VII 150; P V B 132).

The "lifting up" of consciousness involves a positive principle in contrast to the negative doubt. Still, it is possible that these two methods might lead one to the same place, but the movements would be different, and the movement is what mattered to the climber, Johannes. It is readily apparent that to uplift oneself (*at opløfte sig*) and to doubt are not identical. The former presents continuity, whereas the latter does not. And "does not the negative specifically lack continuity, without which no communication and no reception is conceivable?"[21]

Johannes found it impossible to relate himself to the thesis "Philosophy begins with doubt," for he perceived that it broke off all continuity with past philosophy and could not be seriously considered to offer the way into philosophy or the way to becoming a philosopher. The bottom line, then, of Johannes's meditations on this thesis is that such a beginning keeps one outside of philosophy (KW VII 156; P IV B 1 138), which is surely an original and valid criticism of modern philosophy. Doubt must be viewed as providing a false beginning for philosophy, for insofar as I suspend judgment on something, I cannot philosophize about it. If this is the case, Johannes must now be prepared for the possibility that doubt, which he has determined lies outside of philosophy, serves not as philosophy's beginning but as a preparation for this beginning.

Johannes's thoughts lead him in this direction, as he turns to the third thesis: "In order to philosophize, one must have doubted." Johannes considers that perhaps his earlier investigations were not a complete waste, since they may serve as background to his later becoming a philosopher. This investigation is unusually brief. Readers are reminded that the proposition *de omnibus dubitandum est* was the original object of Johannes's meditations, and it is to this thesis that he intends to devote himself in "Pars secunda."

With the end of "Pars prima" Johannes gravely decides to take leave of the deceitful philosophizers forever. He chooses—rather like Descartes—to follow the method of making "everything as simple as possible." The seven pages that follow, however, are not so few by virtue of the simplicity of the subject matter, for Kierkegaard abandons this onerous project—perhaps for other, more pliant ones—just as it was getting really good.

It is generally agreed that the understanding of human existence as a synthesis is one of Kierkegaard's central aims. This synthesis is expressed in various ways in the Kierkegaardian corpus, however. One can argue that it is the driving thought behind Kierkegaard's philosophical search, which—as I have suggested above—essentially follows the call of the Socratic maxims "Know thyself!" and "The unexamined life is not worth living." *The Concept of Irony with Constant Reference to Socrates* is Kierkegaard's first full-scale attempt to come to terms with this synthesis of thought (or language) and being, and here the synthesis is decidedly described *sub specie ironiæ*, an inherently contradictory concept. The contradictory nature of this synthesis is not lost in *Johannes Climacus*, however, and this writing marks Kierkegaard's second philosophical attempt to bridge the gap between reflection and immediacy, the two "terms" that are contradicted in the non-simple synthesis of human existence.[22]

Thus, in turning to the chapter entitled "What is it to doubt?" the reader should be alerted to the fact that this text exhibits perhaps the densest philosophical exposition of the source problem for Kierkegaard. While it is frequently recognized that Kierkegaard's philosophical ideas are based on the rupture between language and the world, the concrete textual ground for this common assumption is seldom identified. My argument is that Kierkegaard's early writings, primarily *The Concept of Irony* and *Johannes Climacus*, fulfill the conditions for his "indirect communication," the methodology of which is thereby largely worked out prior to the use of the pseudonyms and the discussions of absurdity and the paradox—but more on this shortly.

In order to begin at the root of the problem of this chapter, Kierkegaard poses the pointed existential question: "How must existence be constituted for it to be possible to doubt?" He is well aware of the shortcomings of the empirical method, so he has Johannes proceed in a phenomenological manner by isolating consciousness "as it is in itself, as that which explains every specific consciousness, yet without being itself a specific consciousness" (KW VII 167–8; P IV B 1145). Thus, with the exception of the small child, when Kierkegaard explains the contradiction of consciousness, it holds for every human being.

In a rich draft of *Johannes Climacus,* Kierkegaard concisely states what he more gradually develops in the text.

> Immediately, then, everything is true; but can consciousness not remain in this immediacy? If this immediacy and that of animals

were identical, then the question of consciousness would be canceled; but the consequence of that would be that a human being was an animal or that a human being was inarticulate. That which therefore cancels immediacy is language, if a person could not speak, he or she would remain in immediacy.

This, he thought, could be expressed thusly: immediacy is reality, language is ideality, as I speak I produce the contradiction. Thus when I want to express sense perception, the contradiction is there, for what I say is something rather different than what I want to say. I cannot express reality in language, since to characterize it I use ideality, which is a contradiction, an untruth.

The possibility of doubt, then, lies in the duplicity of consciousness [KW VII 255; JP III 2320; P IV B 14:6].

Here Kierkegaard broaches the problem of language, and his analysis may be interpreted as providing grounds for the rejection of a purely phenomenological language. "Consciousness is contradiction" (KW VII 168; P IV B 1 146). The word (i.e., mediacy) stands not in mere opposition to the world (i.e., immediacy), but rather in contradiction to it. Contradiction is thus more than mere opposition; it is the third needed to posit oppositions (i.e., consciousness). As Kierkegaard had read Hegel on the nature of consciousness and contradiction, it is not irrelevant to quote the latter here:

This contradiction and the removal of it will become more definite if, to begin with, we call to mind the abstract determinations of knowledge and of truth as they are found in consciousness. Consciousness, we find, distinguishes from itself something, to which at the same time it relates itself; or, to use the current expression, there is something for consciousness; and the determinate form of this process of relating, or of there being something for a consciousness, is knowledge. But from this being for another we distinguish being in itself or per se; what is related to knowledge is likewise distinguished from it, and posited as also existing outside this relation; the aspect of being per se or in itself is called Truth.[23]

For Kierkegaard, however, the notion that "contradiction resolves itself"[24] is impenetrable. Therefore, although he is obviously indebted to Hegel for his exposition of consciousness in *The Phenomenology of Mind*, he quite emphatically opposes the identification of thought (or language) and being found in this work and others.[25] In addition, in a note to *Johannes Climacus*, Kierkegaard alludes to *The Phenomenology of Mind* and rightly criticizes Hegel for not explaining the transition from consciousness to self-consciousness and from self-consciousness to reason: "When the transition consists merely of a heading, it is easy enough" (KW VII 169; P IV B 1 148).

Kierkegaard therefore concludes early in his development—before his so-called proper production begins—that there can be no solution to the problem of language. This provides the necessary philosophical background to understanding why Kierkegaard embarked on the sea of "indirect communication." When one reads Kierkegaard's early writings closely, one finds that the pseudonymous writings were born of Kierkegaard's reflections on the problem of language, and not of a need to rid himself of inauthentic perspectives. Thus, Kierkegaard's early philosophical period yields methodological insight into his entire production; for the later writings—veronymous and pseudonymous alike—presuppose the philosophical reflections of *The Concept of Irony* and *Johannes Climacus*.[26]

Consequently, readers will not be surprised to find that there is an intrinsic tension in all of Kierkegaard's writings based on the nature of the contradiction, and this cannot be removed by naïve ontologies of language. In this tension, in the "dialectical knot" (KW XX 133) of Kierkegaard's writings, in the thoughts of Johannes Climacus, readers familiar with the difference of otherness may recognize a kinship to what Derrida or de Man has to say on the subject. Christopher Norris explains the point of contact between deconstruction and Kierkegaard:

> Deconstruction sets out to demonstrate that meaning can never coincide with its object in a moment of pure, unimpeded union; that language always intervenes to deflect, defer or differentially complicate the relation between manifest sense and expressive intent . . . . Mediation—or "reflection" in Kierkegaard's terminology—is the inescapable predicament of language, whatever those pretences to the contrary maintained by poets, philosophers or the normal run of commonplace metaphysicians.[27]

Norris goes wrong, however, in writing that "Kierkegaard, of course, entertains this outlook under cover of a pseudonym ('Johannes Climacus'), intended to mark it as a strictly 'aesthetic' and hence inauthentic standpoint." It is now apparent that this view is mistaken for two reasons. First, Kierkegaard never found the time to append a signature to this writing, so, strictly speaking, it cannot be read as pseudonymous. Second, if I am correct in arguing that Kierkegaard's use of pseudonyms grew out of his ruminations on the problem of language, then the mere pseudonymity of a given work does not make it inauthentic, just as the sheer fact of its veronymity would not make it authentic. The question of authenticity/inauthenticity refers to the life-view portrayed—though, be it noted, as lived, not as written—and not to the text itself. For example, in consideration of *Johannes Climacus*, one may argue that the life-view of speculative doubt is inauthentic, but this by no means renders the text inauthentic or null and void.

For Kierkegaard, then, the only way to get readers to focus on their own life-views is to communicate with them indirectly, because direct communication[28] ignores the contradiction of consciousness and the problem of language, which is certainly more than just one problem among others; it forgets the lost origin of the word and proceeds in the manner of a modern, systematic philosophizer. If one admits that Kierkegaard maintained the eternal discrepancy between language and immediacy throughout his short life, then one would, by the same token, be obliged to admit that any attempted direct communication would be an ironic incognito calculated to draw attention elsewhere.

The next point of interest is Johannes's definition of "reflection," which is given lucid philosophical expression by Kierkegaard. "Reflection is the *possibility of the relation*; consciousness is *the relation, the first form of which is contradiction*. . . . Reflection's categories are always *dichotomous*" (KW VII 169; P IV B 1 147). In reflection, in ideality, ideas are always dichotomous (KW VII 252; P IV B 10a; JP V 5620). This only introduces the possibility of doubt, however; it does not establish doubt's existence. Despite its etymology, doubt requires a third to come into existence. Without this third there would be nothing but sheer oppositions without relation.

> For example, ideality and reality, soul and body, to know the true, to will the good, to love the beautiful, God and the world, etc. are categories of reflection. In reflection, they touch each other in such a way that a relation becomes possible. The categories of

> consciousness, however, are *trichotomous*, as language also demonstrates, for when I say, I am conscious of *this sensory impression*, I am expressing a triad. Consciousness is mind,[29] and it is remarkable that when one is divided in the world of mind, there are three, never two. Consciousness, therefore, presupposes reflection. [KW VII 169; P IV B 1 147–48].

Consciousness is the third that establishes the relation between ideality and reality, or thinking and being. This relation has the form of contradiction, for to maintain that thinking and being are held in opposition by consciousness is to state the philosophically contradictory. Ideality and reality collide in consciousness and have nothing to say to each other.

To rewrite the Cartesian maxim in a Kierkegaardian fashion, "I think, therefore I do not exist."[30] In other words, thought cannot prove existence, and consciousness is such that it presupposes itself (KW VII 255; P IV B 10:14). This often forgotten presupposition merges itself between each and every dichotomy. Kierkegaard, then, shares in the tripartite understanding of the creation of meaning based on his further characterizations of reflection and consciousness as disinterested and interested, respectively.[31] Consciousness is interest, which expresses both the literal meaning of "being between" (*inter-esse*) and the general meaning of "concern." What the philosophizers lack is interest, and therefore they have misunderstood doubt.

> [A]ll disinterested knowledge (mathematics, aesthetics, metaphysics) is only the presupposition of doubt. As soon as the interest is canceled, doubt is not conquered but is neutralized, and all such knowledge is simply a retrogression. Thus it would be a misunderstanding for someone to think that doubt can be overcome by so-called objective thinking [KW VII 170; P IV B 1 149].

For this reason, the doubt spoken about by the modernist philosophizers is very dangerous, if not suicidal, for they have attempted to rid themselves of doubt through the systematic destruction of their own personal interests and wills. Kierkegaard notes elsewhere that doubting involves an act of the will, for otherwise it "would become identical with being uncertain" (KW VII 259; P IV B 5:8). Doubt can never be stopped through reflection or knowledge.

Such folly would never have happened in ancient Greece, where the genuine skeptics "considered that the trick was to preserve doubt despite all the inveiglements of thinking" (KW VII 259; P IV B 5:15). Thus, insofar as true doubt involves interest and invokes an act of the will, it begins what Kierkegaard calls "the highest form of existence, because it can have everything else as its presupposition" (KW VII 170; P IV B 1 149). This is a recognizably different form of doubt, one that perhaps would have allowed Kierkegaard the possibility of discussing "Mastered Doubt. The Truth of Doubt." Shortly after this point, Kierkegaard mentions "the question of a repetition in consciousness," and with that his narration breaks off.

Kierkegaard does not explain why he never finished *Johannes Climacus*, which was intended to "strike a blow at modern philosophy" through the conscious use of form. The conclusion that may be drawn is that, in effect, the incomplete form achieves Kierkegaard's purpose, in that the life-doubt of Johannes Climacus cannot be concluded; it cannot be stopped through thinking or knowledge. The only way to halt forever the mind's wheels of contemplation would be for the thinker to take his or her own life.[32] Another Johannes Climacus—the writer, in contrast to the pure thinker—explicitly unfolds the suicidal nature of pure thought.

> If philosophical reflection had not in our time become something queer, highly artificial, and capable of being learned by rote, thinkers would make quite a different impression upon people, as was the case in Greece, where a thinker was an existing individual stimulated by his reflection to a passionate enthusiasm; and as was also once the case in Christendom, when the thinker was a believer who strove enthusiastically to understand himself in the existence of faith. If anything of this sort held true of the thinkers of our own age, the enterprise of pure thought would have led to one suicide after the other. For suicide is the only tolerable existential consequence of pure thought, when this type of abstraction is not conceived as something merely partial in relation to being human, willing to strike an agreement with an ethical and religious form of personal existence, but assumes to be all and highest. This is not to praise the suicide, but to respect the passion. Nowadays a thinker is a curious creature who during certain hours of the day exhibits a very remarkable ingenuity, but has otherwise nothing in common with a human being [CUP 273].

Again, one must not forget that the point of this attack is the speculative philosophizer par excellence, and that the writer begins this passage conditionally in order to leave himself open for the possibility of original philosophical reflection, such as the kind found among the ancients.

The philosophy that would take itself seriously as beginning with infinite, speculative doubt—*Johannes Climacus, Or, De omnibus dubitandum est* arguably shows—could never begin a philosophy, let alone a life worth living. Besides, as everyone knows, Descartes's doubt was hyperbolic, and he concealed more than one faith-induced presupposition in his *Meditations on First Philosophy*.[33]

Through this metaphilosophical text, then, Kierkegaard shows by way of an indirect narration that the claims of modern philosophy are contradictory and that the term itself, when taken as signifying more than mere historical differences, is a misnomer. He accordingly finds that modern philosophy has little to offer in terms of substance and life; it simply keeps the wheels of thought and knowledge spinning without any possibility of closure.

But what is more important for a holistic interpretation of Kierkegaard's writings is this: Readers find that the problem of language lies coiled and tense at the heart of his writing. It ties the dialectical knot, which cannot be unraveled. Thus, the general conclusion that emerges from this study so far is that the nature of consciousness and the determinations of language make up the philosophical grounds behind Kierkegaard's method of indirect communication, and that this method structures the ensuing authorship, both pseudonymous and veronymous writings included.

Notes

1. Johann Wolfgang von Goethe, *Faust*, bilingual edition, trans. Walter Kaufmann (New York: Doubleday, 1961), p. 93.

2. Plato, *Apology*, in *Dialogues of Plato*, trans. B. Jowett (New York: Scribner's, 1871), 38a.

3. Certainly, this argument may appear problematic when one considers that since Kierkegaard actually rejects doubt as the beginning of philosophy, would it not then be likely for him to reject irony as the

beginning of a worthy human life? In this case his fifteenth thesis and concluding section of *The Concept of Irony*, "Irony as a Controlled Element: The Truth of Irony," could themselves be interpreted as ironic.

To sort out this complexity, one would have to explain first how Kierkegaard uses the term "irony" dialectically, and then how his conception of irony, which cannot be separated from his conception of Socrates, undergoes profound changes throughout his development as a writer. For Kierkegaard, irony marks the beginning of subjectivity, but insofar as he did not perceive the "fullness" of Socrates's subjectivity in his dissertation, it is fair to read the passages alluded to above as ironic. However, Kierkegaard embraces Socrates (and irony) much more warmly in his later writings, and as we shall see, his view culminates in the certainty that Socrates has become a Christian.

4. Trans. Paul-Henri Tisseau and Else-Marie Jacquet Tisseau (Paris: Éditions de L'Orante, 1975).

5. The following sentence reads: "The motivating concept I used was error. Aristotle does the same." This reflection is puzzling and casts a rather dubious shadow on Kierkegaard's reference to *Johannes Climacus* in general, since not once in the text does he mention "error." The relation between error, particularly Descartes's explanation of it, and doubt is not made explicit, but I gather that what Kierkegaard has in mind is that both error and doubt are products of the will.

6. That Kierkegaard would agree with this position is, I think, given through his understanding of the contradictory nature of consciousness, which will be explained below.

7. *Kierkegaard-Myter og Kierkegaard-Kilder*, p. 117. Although my references will be to the original, this work has been translated into English. See Kierkegaard, *The Myths and Their Origins*, trans. George C. Schoolfield (New Haven, Conn.: Yale University Press, 1980).

8. This edition follows the earlier German translation of Kierkegaard's collected works. See *Gesammelte Werke* 10. *Philosophische Brocken und De Omnibus Dubitandum Est*, trans. Emanuel Hirsch (Düsseldorf: Diederichs, 1952).

This arrangement at least yields the benefit of having located *Johannes Climacus* in the collected writings, unlike the original Danish which assigns it to the *Papirer*, which could be taken as assigning it a somewhat inferior status. Additionally, the Hongs' translation of *Johannes Climacus* obviously improves on the first English one by T. H. Croxall (Stanford: Stanford University Press, 1958), which would seem to insult the intelligence of readers by appending a religious writing, *A Sermon*, to the philosophical one for the purpose of "clarification."

9. Perhaps the Hongs could have argued for the more natural possibility that *Johannes Climacus* is a philosophical narrative about the student

who would become the author of *Philosophical Fragments* and *Concluding Unscientific Postscript*. This could account for the discontinuity in "substance, tone, and form." Still, there is little evidence to support this, except perhaps that Johannes Climacus, the writer, says he is from Copenhagen and Johnannes Climacus, the young thinker, is presumably also from Copenhagen (H. . ., i.e., Hafnia, the Latin name for Copenhagen). That two men with the same unusual name were contemporary Copenhageners seems very unlikely indeed.

10. *Kierkegaard-Myter og Kierkegaard-Kilder*, p. 116.

11. The actual date of this work is also unknown. At least three possibilities have been advanced, ranging from 1838 to 1840. For a detailed discussion of the dating of this play, see Thulstrup's *Kierkegaards Forhold til Hegel*, pp. 156–71; *Kierkegaard's Relation to Hegel*, trans. George L. Stengren (Princeton, N.J.: Princeton University Press, 1980), pp. 180–200.

12. These included four poems: "Divine Service," "A Soul after Death," "The Newly-Weds," and "Protestantism in Nature."

13. Søren Holm, *Filosofien i Norden før 1900* (Philosophy in the Nordic Countries before 1900) (Copenhagen: Munksgaard, 1967), pp. 81–89.

14. *Kierkegaard-Myter og Kierkegaard-Kilder*, p. 117.

15. In addition, if Carl Roos is correct in his study, *Kierkegaard og Goethe* (Copenhagen: Gad, 1955), that the "satirical, quasi-Aristophanic comedy" *The Soap-Cellars* was intended as a parody of Faust, then this work would share an even closer affinity with *Johannes Climacus*, since the deep subject matter of each work would be the problem of doubt.

From the mid 1830s onward, Kierkegaard was preoccupied with the idea of Faust, which he viewed as "personified doubt." It permeated his consciousness as he felt a troubling uncertainty concerning his life's vocation. In a letter from Kierkegaard's journal dated June 1, 1835, he writes: "It is this Faustian element which in part asserts itself more or less in every intellectual development, which is why it has always seemed to me that one ought to allow the idea of Faust world-significance" (EP I 39; P I A 72). For a thorough discussion, see Roos's section "Kierkegaard og Faust," pp. 56–157.

16. Martensen's review appeared in *Maanedsskrift for Litteratur* (Monthly Journal for Literature), 16 (1836), 518–19.

17. To offer another example of an original philosopher whom Kierkegaard esteemed, I cite the elder Fichte. It has often intrigued me how Fichte's name appears in important contexts (see, for example, p. 58 above, notes 22 and 23), and always without the slightest trace of criticism.

While Kierkegaard esteems Descartes, he points out in his journal that "Descartes's philosophy has a birthmark," and he subsequently accepts the elder Fichte's criticism of *cogito ergo sum* without further ado: ". . . I act *ergo sum*, for this *cogito* is something derived or it is identical with 'I act'; either it is the consciousness of freedom in the action, and then it should not read *cogito ergo sum*, or it is the subsequent consciousness" (P IV C 11; JP III 2338). The Fichtean position that Kierkegaard embraces is that freedom, not thought, is absolute.

18. The Danish editors of the *Papirer* and the English translators cite two textual sources for this observation: Johan Ludvig Heiberg, *Perseus*, 1 (1837), and Peter Michael Stilling, *Philosophiske Betragtninger over den spekulative Logiks Betydning for Videnskaben* (Philosophical Observations on Speculative Logic's Significance for Science) (1842).

19. As previously noted, the name Johannes Climacus belongs to a sixth-century monk who wrote a work entitled *Ladder of Paradise*.

20. As is well known, Johannes Climacus will later be transformed into the writer of *Philosophical Fragments* and *Concluding Unscientific Postscript* and a reader of much philosophical literature, while the present Johannes is, strictly speaking, a mere thinker "who does not like to read"—let alone write—especially not philosophical books (KW VII 238; P IV B 4). Johannes the writer (and here readers see why it is important not to read *Johannes Climacus* as though it were authored by Johannes Climacus) will take great pains to distinguish thought from existence, with the latter term designating the written trace that cannot be thought. In other words, action (of writing, for example) is primary and thought (of meanings) is secondary. If this is correct, then it is not difficult to perceive how Kierkegaard, in general, may be read as a philosopher of writing.

21. This question serves to highlight the intrinsically contradictory nature of ironic (i.e., negative) communication.

22. Cf. Pat Bigelow's challenging study, *Kierkegaard and the Problem of Writing*, for an interesting elucidation of the term "reflection" in Kierkegaard's writings. It bears repetition: "*Reflection*, as Kierkegaard's principal catagory, has all the ambiguity of human existence, for he invokes multiple uses. Sometimes reflection means the reflected image and effect of the age in private, domestic, and public life (the Danish *Reflex*), sometimes deliberation (the Danish *Reflexion*, meaning *Besindelse*, akin to Heidegger's *Besinnung*). Kierkegaard's category of reflection, then, designates the unwitting conflation of specularity with speculation—the source problem for Husserl" (p. 56).

23. Hegel, *Phenomenology of Mind*, trans. Baillie, p. 139.

24. Hegel, *Science of Logic*, trans. A. V. Miller (New York: Humanities Press, 1969), p. 433.

25. That Kierkegaard rejects the resolution of thought (language) and being (immediacy) often leads to the interpretation of Kierkegaard as

an irrationalist. But this romantic interpretation ignores too much, particularly the fact that Kierkegaard will later speak of a "second immediacy" (i.e., faith), an immediacy after reflection. Kierkegaard harbors no false desires to return to a state of being before language. Rather, he leads readers in the direction beyond language, which is to say that when fully self-conscious and committed one must acknowledge that the depth of his or her being is not amenable to any explicit or direct account. It seems that for Kierkegaard—to put the matter into Hegelian terms—the move is from reason to self-consciousness, and this transition is performed by a leap.

26. Thus I can agree with Lars Bejerholm, who writes: "The Kierkegaardian statements concerning his pseudonymity have been used as a justification for methodological principles in the study of Kierkegaard by certain researchers. In this investigation, however, it will be maintained that these remarks by Kierkegaard can be given a plausible interpretation if one considers the age's literary conventions, and that therefore, Kierkegaard's own remarks on his pseudonymity do not give Kierkegaardian research methodological principles" ("*Meddelelsens Dialektik*": *Studier i Sören Kierkegaards teorier om språk, kommunikation och pseudonymitet* ("The Dialectic of Communication": Studies in Søren Kierkegaard's Theories of Language, Communication and Pseudonymity) (Copenhagen: Munksgaard, 1962), p. 24. However, I find my own reasons in Kierkegaard's earliest writings.

27. *The Deconstructive Turn: Essays in the Rhetoric of Philosophy* (London: Methuen, 1983), p. 102.

28. Thus I have coined the term "veronymous," so that I could distinguish between "direct communication" and Kierkegaard's veronymous works, for it is arguable that all Kierkegaard's writings are indirect, even the ones to which he signed his own name, e.g., *From the Papers of One Still Living, The Concept of Irony, Edifying Discourses, Works of Love,* etc. That the specifically religious writings face the contradiction and that Christian discourse takes the problem of language seriously are recognized by Kierkegaard, who wrote that "everything Christian is ambiguous, redoubling" (P XI 2 A 65).

29. Here the Danish is *Aand*, which—like its German equivalent *Geist*—signifies both "mind" and "spirit."

30. Adi Shmuëli, *Kierkegaard and Consciousness*, trans. Naomi Handelman (Princeton, N.J.: Princeton University Press, 1971), p. 12. This follows from the opposition Kierkegaard posits between thought (reflection, ideality) and existence (action, immediacy). For Kierkegaard, one can neither think existence nor "exist" in one's own thought.

31. This point should play a significant role in any focused discussion of Kierkegaard and postmodernism.

32. This is also evidence that freedom, i.e., free action, is absolute, and not thought. Similarly, the existentialist Jean-Paul Sartre will embrace this conclusion based on the possibility of suicide.

33. While teaching "modern philosophy" I got the distinct impression that things might have gone otherwise for Descartes, who had, after all, admired Horace's line: "Who has hidden himself well has lived well" (Quoted by Berel Lang in *The Anatomy of Philosophical Style* [Oxford: Basil Blackwell, 1990], p. 27.) Had "the father of modern philosophy" continued in the spirit of his *Discours de la Méthode* (1637)—a work written in French to counteract the scholasticism of his day, and one that reads quite differently from the *Meditationes de prima philosophia* (1641), which was written in a conciliatory Latin—the landscape of modern philosophy might have been irrevocably changed.

PART TWO

A Look at the Pseudonymous Writings

4

The Problem of Pseudonymity

> Precisely in the degree to which I understand a thinker I become indifferent to his reality; that is, to his existence as a particular individual, to his having realized his teaching, and so forth.
>
> Johannes Climacus, CUP 289

WERE THE READER to cast a look back over the distance traveled, it might not be without a certain happy surprise that he or she reflects on the unusual and fecund islands visited. Although making the acquaintance of many new personae such as S. Kjerkegaard, an Echo, Willibald, Severinus Kierkegaard, and Johannes Climacus, one must readily acknowledge that, of all the works treated thus far—*From the Papers of One Still Living*, *The Battle Between the Old and the New Soap-Cellars* (although briefly), *The Concept of Irony with Constant Reference to Socrates*, and *Johannes Climacus, Or, De omnibus dubitandum est*—not one contains a pseudonym. Consequently, up to this point, the reader has had no occasion to grapple with the complicated problem of pseudonymity, a problem that is usually cited as a prerequisite for reading Kierkegaard.

This does not mean, however, that readers have been freed from "the problem of reading": the somewhat mysterious way in which meaning arises through the interaction of a person and a text. One may even see that this problem shares a certain relatedness to the problem of pseudonymity—for both problems are raised in order to avoid material extraneous to the text, such as an actual author. Indeed, the problem of reading is that of appropriation, and it is generally conceded that perhaps the most important reason for the pseudonyms is to facilitate the personal appropriation of whatever a reader makes of a given text. Still, as I see it, the problem of pseudonymity remains little more than shorthand for the problem of indirect communication, and invites the question: What meaning can be made (up) from a text that is only accidentally related to its author?

But if one desires to respect Kierkegaard's own rather ad hoc assertions regarding the authoritativeness of the veronymous writings, then the early writings that have been discussed must, by the same token, be granted the identical literary force accorded the works of so-called direct communication, works considered to be direct merely because the author was predisposed to signing his own name, 'Søren Kierkegaard.' And to grant this is to raise in a roundabout way the question of irony with respect to the veronymous discourses.

It is Kierkegaard's first attempt to explain his production that may be at fault in leading contemporary readers into misreading him. Despite his deep, heartfelt reverence for divine governance, Kierkegaard apparently had to take matters into his own hands midway through his productivity in order to prevent being greatly misunderstood by readers who evidently disregarded the pseudonymous authors and talked about the odd books by Søren Kierkegaard. To clear up the confusion, he appended "A First and Last Explanation" to an appendix, "An Understanding with the Reader," at the end of *Afsluttende uvidenskabelig Efterskrift til de philosophiske Smuler* (Concluding Unscientific Postscript to the Philosophical Fragments [1846]). The sole appearance of this confession creates the sharpest of interpretative problems, for in distinguishing himself from the pseudonyms, Kierkegaard makes possible yet another mask, another persona. The distance he seeks to diminish through this revelation becomes all the greater.

Contrary to Kierkegaard's own specific intentions to clarify and conclude his activity as an author with the "Explanation" sent to the typesetter at the last minute before the setting of the bulky *Concluding Unscientific Postscript* was completed, this would not be his final word on his production. It could not present the ultimate interpretation of his writings. Nor would it be the final work of his production, as the word "concluding" in the title would lead one to believe. Instead, here one finds a clear example of how an author's (good) intentions serve to obstruct the meaning of a text, a meaning that must be created in the act of reading. It reads:

> Therefore, whereas surely everyone who has felt the least concern about such things has as a matter of course hitherto regarded me as

> the author of the pseudonmous books . . . I, who after all must know best, am the only one that very doubtfully and ambiguously regards me as author, for the reason that I am figuratively the author, whereas on the contrary I am quite literally the author of the Edifying Discourses, and of every word in them [CUP 552 (unnumbered)].

By a strange twist of logic, Kierkegaard seems to be saying that because he is the "real" author of the pseudonymous books he must assuredly know what's what regarding them. Consequently, he can tell you that he is not really the author of them. In my reading, this is a rather uncharacteristic passage by one who comes across more frequently as a "Socratic writer," maintaining that what he knows best or what he knows deepest is of little or no importance to readers, who should, after all, be intersted in their own reading and not in the author's.

When one rereads this unconcluding declaration, matters become even more confusing.

> A single word by me personally in my own name would be an arrogating self-forgetfulness that, regarded dialectically, would be guilty of having essentially annihilated the pseudonymous authors by this one little word. [KW XII 1 (626)]

Now, if I am to understand Kierkegaard as literally the author of this "Explanation" since his own name is attached to it, then this sentence, this single word, presents a paradox for readers. For in this pseudonymous work, one finds at the end several self-forgetting personal words by Kierkegaard which, regarded dialectically, undermine the thoughts of Johannes Climacus. Climacus needs no help in revoking his massive treatise, however, for he undermines himself with the greatest irony and humor. Perhaps Kierkegaard had better stick to the earlier passage:

> I have no opinion about them (the pseudonymous works) except as a third party, no knowldege of their meaning except as a reader, not the remotest private relation to them, since it is impossible to have that in a doubly reflected communication [KW XII 1 (626)].

There is a sharp contrast of perspectives between this passage and the quote on the preceding page where Kierkegaard declares his authorial sovereignty. Only as a reader can one approach the meaning of the text; simply being the author of a writing is no guarantee that the meaning one ascribes to it is the best. To write a text does not necessarily mean that one understands it, just as to experience an event does not necessarily mean that one knows it. To have an experience is no guarantee that one can put it into words; and even if one could, the question of understanding these words could then be raised.

Kierkegaard's exercises in pseudonymity can undoubtedly be understood as a reaction to the way that the cultured public of Copenhagen read philosophical books. The practice of consistently separating a book from its author was not understood by the general reading public, and even if it were, it would not have been without some difficulty for readers to successfully perform the operation.[1] Kierkegaard relates in his journal, "I cannot quite make myself intelligible to others, for whatever I write they promptly categorize as pertaining to me" (P X^2 A 163; JP VI 6523). Therefore, in this respect, Kierkegaard tried to make it easier for readers by resorting to the pseudonyms. He would most likely have little need for the pseudonyms in the present age, however, since postmodern readers have only a trivial regard for an author's intentions, if any at all.

To return to the idea of a "third party": in *The Concept of Irony* Kierkegaard described himself as "the third" in relation to the source material on Socrates (CI 183), and I should like to suggest that the idea of Kierkegaard—the reader/writer—as a third party, or "the third," is one that may be profitably carried throughout the literature. The writer remains outside the text and can enter into its possible meaning only as a reader. (Of course, practically speaking, writers should be better readers of their own texts, but this is not necessarily the case, for they may be blinded by their prejudices like any other reader.) While in the example of *Concluding Unscientific Postscript* Kierkegaard wants to pin the duplicitous communication onto the fact of the work's pseudonymity, it was seen earlier in *Johannes Climacus* that the duplicity essentially belongs to the nature of language (reflection) and the nature of writing. In this respect, then, Kierkegaard, qua author, must remain a third in relation to all his writings. Upon this consideration, it is not surprising that in his journal Kierkegaard wrote that concerning his activity as a writer in general, "a third person, the author, was constituted, which was the unity of myself and the pseudonyms, and he spoke directly about that" (P

X^1 A 300). In a sense, then, the writer is a "mediator,"[2] and writing is a "mediation" of the problem of language that does not solve the contradiction between thought and immediacy but rather carries it further and, in so doing, preserves it.

A marginal addition to a draft of "A First and Last Explanation" may help to elucidate further this notion of the third or mediator.

> I am only an unknown person who is the author's author, which still is distinguished from the impropriety that an actual author has someone else behind his back, who actually is the author's author; for the book's author is not the second one, but it is the first one who through the book became an author, thus the other person is the author of the author. This relation between the two in reality is improper, my relation in possibility is ideally innocent when I, dialectically-reduplicated, may be called the authors' author, not in the eminent sense as foremost, but in the philosophical sense as the ground that falls to the ground [P VII^1 B 76].

Kierkegaard is the ground, the third, the consciousness, that mediates between his self and his other in the act of writing, for when I claim that "he is the author's author," there are three parts to be considered: the author, say Johannes Climacus; the author's author, S. Kierkegaard; and the third, "he," that is, the consciousness that makes the dialectical reduplication possible.

In the preceding chapters I have wanted to suggest that what is encountered in the early Kierkegaard is a literary-philosophical pursuit that is anything but inauthentic. So I have avoided the thorny problem of pseudonymity, which is ushered in with the reading of the "Explanation" above. This explanation is not an argument, however, as it does not present evidence for its acceptance or denial. In content and tone it is closer to a "declaration," which is how the first translators took it, although the Hongs are correct in translating *Forklaring* as "explanation." I suspect that Kierkegaard became aware that his supposedly thorough explanation was lacking detailed argumentation, and consequently was forced to return to the defense of its thesis. Thus, he took the initial concern underlying "A First and Last Explanation" and extended and eventually argued for it in the posthumously published *The Point of View for My Work as an Author*, a writing that he withheld from publication during his lifetime and—what is more interesting and more surprising—a writing that he at one point considered signing with a pseudonym, specifically Johannes de Silentio (P X[1] A 78). At the very least, this indicates that Kierkegaard was quite unsure how to relate himself to the argument in *The Point of View*, but more on this in a later chapter.

The problem of pseudonymity is quite frequently one of the first things discussed in studies on Kierkegaard. This is because most discussions begin with *Either/Or*, Kierkegaard's first pseudonymous work, though not, as common opinion would have it, his first major or important work. If they do not begin with this work, it is still more likely than not that authors of studies on Kierkegaard have their earliest deep reading of Kierkegaard in *Either/Or*. Because I have structured this study so as to begin from the beginning with the philosophical seedbed of the early academic and polemical writings, the problem of pseudonymity qua pseudonymity has not emerged with the same importance that one or another Kierkegaardologist has given it. In my view, a Kierkegaardian pseudonym is a humorous signification that a particular work is infected with the problem of language, which is, admittedly, not so easily grasped, if it is graspable at all. The pseudonyms portray the problem in a dramatic and forcefully creative way and make it easier for readers to proceed without initially having to set their focus on this cumbersome problem (the problem of reading = the problem of pseudonymity = the problem of indirect communication = the problem of language), which may be conceptualized through the dialectic of the non-concept of irony.

One aspect of the argument I am developing is that the early writings need figure heavily in the interpretation of Kierkegaard's literature. They present a genuine aspect of Kierkegaard's developing *Livsanskuelse*, and perhaps it is not going too far to say that deep within *The Concept of Irony* lies a buried treasure map for "Kierkegaard Island." The early Kierkegaard appears as a profound philosophical ironist whose views cannot be easily discredited or dismissed through a consideration of pseudonymity. Even by granting that *The Soap-Cellars* and *Johannes Climacus* were unfinished, unpublished writings, which therefore cannot be said to represent complete viewpoints, one would be extremely hard put to refute the fact that the writer of *The Concept of Irony* was a philosophical seeker who had decidedly taken irony under his wing in the search for a methodology that would enable him to approach the truth. Since *The Concept of Irony* discloses the thesis that "the possibility of writing is also the possibility of irony,"[3] it would be anything but a trivialization[4] to focus on the possibility of irony. Therefore, in order to read Kierkegaard seriously, one must develop an ear for the echoes of irony.

The problem of pseudonymity refers readers to the problem of language (reflection/ideality as distinct from immediacy). This is, in turn, a cross-reference to existence, which has been defined by Kierkegaard as a synthesis of ideality and immediacy (more on this in a later chapter). It is important to notice that Kierkegaard's veronymous writings are also marked by the problem of language,[5] although there his concerns lie elsewhere so that he chooses (again) to sign his own name—as if this should make some difference in the reading. It would seem to make a difference only to someone who holds that authors possess some sort of privileged interpretative authority in relation to their works—an idea that conflicts with Kierkegaard's repeated classification of himself as one who is "without authority" (and this consideration is what makes the above quote from "one who knows best" strikingly uncharacteristic)—or to someone who has a biographical or historical interest in wanting to know which views Kierkegaard held personally—an interest that could never get beyond the status of an approximation and has little place in a philosophical study.

A similar perspective is expressed by C. Stephen Evans in his study *Kierkegaard's "Fragments" and "Postscript": The Religious Philosophy of Johannes Climacus*. In the chapter entitled "Reading Kierkegaard's Pseudonymous Literature," he writes:

> But if our purposes are essentially personal and philosophical—if we are interested in the truth of the views presented, in understanding (reading) more profoundly some basic existential concepts, and thereby understanding (reading) ourselves and our existence more deeply—then it really does not matter very much whether Kierkegaard personally held these views. For from the fact that he held a view, nothing follows as to the truth, profundity, or value of the view. If we accepted a view simply on the basis of our respect for Kierkegaard's authority, we would be deceiving ourselves and would certainly have missed the point he was trying to make. Thus there is great value in taking his advice and simply thinking of the *Fragments* and *Postscript* as the work of Johannes Climacus. In so

> doing our admiration for S.K. (or our distaste for him) will not get in the way of our understanding (reading).[6]

Moreover, Evans also sees that there is "an intimate coherence between the concepts of indirect communication . . . and Kierkegaard's employment of the pseudonyms."[7] As I have suggested, both the concept of indirect communication and the use of the pseudonyms have their ground in the problem of language; which is to say that they are grounded in a contradiction, namely, in life, for "life is a contradiction" (KW V 15). The talk of the pseudonyms in this context does not entail that indirect communication, "the maieutic method" (i.e., irony), is abandoned by Kierkegaard in the veronymous writings, however, for "even here the essential ideal embodied in the maieutic method remains valid: There is no understanding of existential truth apart from the process of personal appropriation."[8] As I indicated above, it is clear that the joyful play between the veronym and the pseudonyms can be accounted for by the Copenhagen reading public's inability to read Kierkegaard. His pseudonymous writings were undoubtedly read largely out of context, so that after several of these ill-received publications a turning point was inevitable. Although the ironic method makes it possible to discuss Christianity without ever mentioning God, Kierkegaard came to realize that readers just did not get it—or, what is worse, just did not care—and so he fashioned a direct (in the grammatical sense) approach. I shall consider this approach more fully in a later chapter.

What has been encountered in Part One of this study is plainly and unequivocally a "substantial Kierkegaardian life-view" that, as yet, has little to do with what is (was) to follow. But this life-view has the nature of a non-view, which is to say that it is not didactic; it is not something that may be straightforwardly set forth and learned; it is not something that may be deduced in a scholarly treatise. Kierkegaard's "life-view" revolves around the ineffable heart of existence, and this is a good reason why it makes sense to affix the "non." As Kierkegaard—the third, the reader/writer—is a mediator of sorts,[9] so, too, is the existing individual who must hold the reins and steer a carriage drawn by the two horses of time and eternity. For

> this is just what it means to exist, if one is to become conscious of it. Eternity is the winged horse, infinitely fast, and time is a worn-out jade; the existing individual is the driver [CUP 276].[10]

It is well known that Kierkegaard repeatedly stresses the incomplete character of existence that makes it impossible for an individual to rest at any given moment. To take an example from *Philosophical Fragments*—one that finds an echo in Kierkegaard's first upbuilding discourse, "The Expectancy of Faith"—"with regard to faith, one never celebrates triumphantly ahead of time, that is never in time" (KW VII 108). If readers take this consideration seriously, they must acknowledge that it is of little avail to try to pin down "Kierkegaard's views." Nevertheless, one may suspect that he shared some general characteristics with the thinker Johannes Climacus, who

> did not express his views, never betrayed what was going on inside him—the erotic in him was too deep for that. He felt that he might blush if he talked about it; he was afraid of learning too much or learning too little. He was always attentive, however, when others were speaking. Just as a young girl deeply in love prefers not to speak about her love but with almost painful tension listens when other girls talk about theirs, in order to test in silence whether or not she is just as happy or even happier, to snatch every important clue—just so did Johannes silently pay attention to everything. Then, when he came home, he reflected on what the philosophizers had said, for it was their company, of course, that he sought [KW VII 123].

Kierkegaard, that historical person with certain views, cannot be found, and, as I shall argue, neither can the ultimate view or reading of Kierkegaard's writings.

Not overly concerned, then, with the fact of pseudonymity, we can proceed to read the writings of Johannes Climacus in order to follow the application of Kierkegaard's ironic methodology and evaluate its results. The aim of this "look at the pseudonymous writings" is to show that these works are rooted in an ironic dialectic and that this prevents them from developing a positive philosophy. A positive philosophy that may be exposed, espoused, and explained lies far from Kierkegaard's dialectic which seeks to come to terms with human existence and continually finds that it runs up against the limits of language and into the wall of contradiction. Moreover, it is outrageous to treat "Kierkegaard's stages or existence-spheres," to take a single example, as if they were a positive theoretical construction as well defined and rigid as Piaget's stages of learning development. Yet this is what a great many scholars have done—from shortly after Kierkegaard's demise down to the present day.

On the other hand, to read Kierkegaard's pseudonymous literature as pervaded by the negative dialectic of irony which cannot lay claim to a positive philosophy does not mean that what emerges from the reading is wholly nothing, for of course there is something—something that belongs to the individual reader alone. When one is in touch with the irony—defined above as the being-for-itself of subjectivity—the possibility of learning and growing is at its most evident. Consequently, to read the pseudonymous writings as rooted in irony does not render them purposeless or without benefit, just as, in an analogous way, "to write a book and revoke it is something else than not writing it at all" (CUP 548). If anything, the presence of irony increases the benefits, since irony is essentially a practical determination of existence and not a theoretical one.

In order to illuminate this view of the pseudonymous production—a view that understands the irony of these writings as "mastered" and not "romantic"—it would be helpful at this point to analyze a suspect reading of Kierkegaard's pseudonymous works, one that takes irony all too seriously and, therefore, warrants close attention. The following chapter contains a review of a failed recent attempt to understand "the nature and meaning of the pseudonymous works." It will thus contribute to the constitution of my argument in a negative fashion.

Notes

1. In a preface intended but never included in *Christian Discourses* Kierkegaard admits to being so difficult for his contemporaries: "it is part of my task to employ about two-thirds of my strength in confusing, in working against myself and weakening the impression—which is precisely what makes me difficult for the contemporaries" (CD 2).

2. In this context when one considers that the Danish *Tredie* (third) is a straightforward translation of Hegel's quasi-technical term *der Dritte*, which signifies the mediator, then a further description is apparently given to Derrida's designation of Hegel as "the first philosopher of writing." But if one considers that Hegel wanted to settle the contradiction, and that for Kierkegaard mediation can mean little more than being in the middle of two contradictory terms—unless one wants to talk

about non-mediation—then it is more readily conceivable that Kierkegaard should be dubbed with the prestigious title "the first philosopher of writing."

3. Agacinski, *Aparté*, p. 78.

4. This is what Sylvia Walsh argues about Agacinski's approach in an at times intentionally ludicrous critical review essay. See "Kierkegaard and Postmodernism," *International Journal for Philosophy of Religion*, 29 (1991), 113–22.

5. Obviously the scriptural language Kierkegaard quotes and writes about is often metaphorical and indirect. Consider his first biblical quotation in *Works of Love*: "For each tree is known by its own fruit. For figs are not gathered from thorns, nor are grapes picked from a bramble bush" (Luke 6:44). Quite clearly, what is said is not what is meant, which is a basic characteristic of all ironic speech. Since for Kierkegaard "everything Christian is ambiguous, redoubling" (P XI 2 A 37), ironic speech is undoubtedly also pervasive in Kierkegaard's religious writings, but in a more subtle way. The "indirectness" of the veronymous writings will be the theme of chapter 8 below.

6. (Atlantic Highlands, N.J.: Humanities Press, 1983), pp. 8–9.

7. Ibid., p. 14. Evans adds that the spheres of existence share in this intimate coherence.

8. Ibid., p. 11.

9. See note 2 above.

10. Behind this passage lie the Greeks, as Eugene Webb explains in *Philosophers of Consciousness* (Seattle: University of Washington Press, 1988), p. 244: "Kierkegaard is alluding to the episode in Plato's *Phaedrus* (246a–248c) where Socrates says that it is impossible for a man to know *psyche* by direct vision, one may perhaps speak truly of it in a philosophical myth. Then he takes up the myth of the soul as a chariot driven by a horseman who has to guide the energies of two steeds, one of noble stock and the other of base, so that the noble steed's upward motion, countering the tendency of the other to seek solid ground, will carry the chariot toward the region where 'true being dwells, without color or shape, that cannot be touched.'"

5

Are the Pseudonymous Views Completely Bogus? On Hartshorne's *Kierkegaard: Godly Deceiver**

N. B. N. B.

As yet I have not said a direct word about myself: the postscript to *CP* contains nothing of the sort; all I did was to assume responsibility for the pseudonymous authors and speak *hypothetically* ("according to what I have understood") about their ideas. The information given in *CP* about the character of the pseudonymous authors is by a third party.

S. Kierkegaard, JP VI 6366

A Godly Deceiver—the oxymoronic title[1] would make Descartes shiver and the author of the equally oxymoronic *Philosophical Fragments* smile. M. Holmes Hartshorne (1910–1988) has hit upon a title that is sufficiently attention-getting, and he manages to keep the reader's attention throughout this relatively slim work. Despite his brevity, Hartshorne develops a comprehensive interpretation of the pseudonymous writings as well as a consideration of two of the religious works, *Works of Love* and *The Sickness Unto Death*. He also exhibits a knowledgeable acquaintance with Kierkegaard's journals and papers.

Is there anything in Kierkegaard's pseudonymous literature that can be ostensibly ascribed to Kierkegaard? Anything at all? This

*An earlier version of this chapter appeared in the *Søren Kierkegaard Newsletter*, 26 (1992), 10–14.

is the question with which Hartshorne's study concerns itself, and his answer is a resounding "No!" His thesis is straightforward: to take literally Kierkegaard's statement in "A First and Last Declaration" that "in the pseudonymous books there is not a single word by me" (KW XII 1 [626]). It is a curious idea to take a single statement by Kierkegaard absolutely literally, which is perhaps why not a few scholars have—implicitly or explicitly—read the irony behind it.

The good news is that Hartshorne rightly emphasizes "the pervasiveness of irony in Kierkegaard's pseudonymous writings."[2] The bad news is that he offers an all-too-terse look at Kierkegaard's magisterial dissertation, *The Concept of Irony*, which would certainly have helped in unpacking the loaded concept of irony that, as I see it, runs throughout the entire Kierkegaardian corpus. This omission is even more surprising when we consider that, in an appendix devoted largely to criticizing the most well known interpretations of the pseudonymous writings, Hartshorne chides Mark C. Taylor for virtually ignoring Kierkegaard's concept of irony in his study *Kierkegaard's Pseudonymous Authorship*. Although Taylor's study contains more references to *The Concept of Irony* than does Hartshorne's, it is true that he provides a more positive, non-ironic reading of the pseudonymous literature than does Hartshorne. In light of all the secondary literature, it seems clear that we are still lacking a work that, first, sets forth the conceptual methodology of irony found in Kierkegaard's dissertation of 1841, and then, second, explores the application of this methodology throughout Kierkegaard's varied writings. Readers may agree, as I do, that "the key to understanding Kierkegaard's pseudonymous authorship is his use of irony,"[3] but they are still left at least partially in the dark with regard to the conditions, conceptions, and ends irony entails—ones that would ultimately bring it into close association with edification and change Socrates into a Christian.

Hartshorne does have an ear for the echoes of irony, but it is perhaps overly sensitive. He presents an interesting illustration of the use of irony in *Fear and Trembling*,[4] a work held to be "ironic to the core." The interpretation is controversial, for it would prevent readers from labeling as Kierkegaardian such famous notions as "the absurd," "infinite resignation," "the leap of faith," "the teleological suspension of the ethical," and others. These are, strictly speaking, the "absurd, if not blasphemous views" of Johannes de Silentio. According to Hartshorne, Kierkegaard, by contrast,

> is ironically showing the ultimate absurdity of attempting to reach faith by a mighty effort. Good Lutheran that he was, he believed that faith is a matter of grace, not of spiritual heroics. It is a gift to be accepted, not a task to be performed by spiritual gymnastics. The biblical witness is clear: God spoke to Abraham, and Abraham believed. The miracle of faith does not yield to intellectual dissection that would lay bare its human movements. The grace of God in Christ is received by faith, not achieved by spiritual movements.[5]

Here is the emergence of an "old-fashioned orthodoxy in its rightful severity," which is what Kierkegaard (excuse me—Climacus) sought to express (cf. KW XII 1 275). Blind faith without reflection would appear an acceptable substitution for "the miracle of faith" that "does not yield to intellectual dissection." But whose thesis is it that faith cannot be penetrated? Does it not belong to Johannes de Silentio—he who, ultimately, could not understand Abraham's faith—and not to Kierkegaard? In which case Kierkegaard might ironically be saying that faith is not blind but hyperopic, and that reflection can, if not must, lay bare some general human movements with regard to faith.[6] But what, then, would these look like if they do not resemble the notions of Johannes de Silentio?

In chapter 2 Hartshorne turns his attention to *Either/Or*. Initially, however, he mentions that the necessary starting point for any study of Kierkegaard is essentially the claim made in *The Point of View* that Kierkegaard was a religious author from start to finish. At one time, *nota bene*, Kierkegaard considered publishing this work under the pseudonym Johannes de Silentio (P X^1 A 78). Instead of doing this, however, he chose not to publish it at all. Furthermore, recent critics such as Christopher Norris and Joakim Garff[7] have presented argumentative evidence that raises serious doubts concerning whether *The Point of View* contains the ultimate point of view for reading Kierkegaard. Regardless, it is self-evident that *Either/Or* may be read apart from *The Point of View*.

According to Hartshorne, Kierkegaard's purpose in writing *Either/Or* was to force the "Philistines" of his day to take notice of their lives and, ultimately, to show them that "there is only one escape from philistine existence, only one true salvation,"[8] namely, to become a Christian through the grace of God. It is perhaps not without irony that a thoroughly indirect communication yields such a simple, direct message when given a secondhand report. Kierkegaard had no thought of actually "nudging" readers to become Christians, however. That was beyond his ability. Nor did he construct a "theory of the stages" by which he conceived "of individuals as passing through the aesthetical stage to the ethical and then on to the religious."[9] Hartshorne points out that both "A" and "B" are abstractions from existence, since no one's life is either wholly aesthetic or entirely ethical. On these last two points Hartshorne has found something important to say, especially considering that the "theory of the stages" has been positively blown out of proportion in Kierkegaardian scholarship. So Hartshorne's negative approach is not unwelcome, although in general, as I am suggesting, his overall interpretation is not without some serious problems.

Chapter 3 presents an undoubtedly original reading of *Philosophical Fragments* and *Concluding "Unscholarly" Postscript* (to use Hartshorne's justifiable preference in translation). In short, he argues that Johannes Climacus's philosophical view is not Søren Kierkegaard's. Given this thesis, a regrettable omission is found in Hartshorne's not discussing the significance of Kierkegaard's name as editor of these two works. If Kierkegaard wanted to divorce himself completely from Climacus's views, why did he include his name as editor? Moreover, both an original draft and the final copy of *Fragments* had "S. Kierkegaard" as author, and the three-part question on the title page was originally written in the first person (see KW VII xvi, 176–77). Hartshorne, however, views these writings as aesthetic works on a par with the earlier ones (thus he makes no mention of Kierkegaard's direct discussion of the nature of the turning point in his authorship), and agrees with Josiah Thompson that all the pseudonymous writings "ring false to the core."[10]

That *Fragments* and *Postscript* are both ironic communications is true enough, but the dialectic of irony does not seem to have been fully grasped by Hartshorne. His logic seems to run thus: If a work is ironic, then it is altogether false (i.e., Kierkegaard does not personally believe what is written); *Fragments* is ironic; hence, *Fragments* is false. This logic runs the other way as well. For

Hartshorne, *The Sickness Unto Death* contains no irony (and was written by the pseudonym Anti-Climacus!) and is, therefore, a true work—that is, a work in which what is written is what Kierkegaard himself believes. The confusion here revolves around the nature of ironic communication. Hartshorne believes that if irony is present, then there cannot be seriousness, and he cites the *Fragments* in his defense: "an author of pieces such as I (Johannes Climacus) has no seriousness of purpose."[11] One should not forget to consider the possible irony of this statement, however, which was later explained dialectically by Climacus in a lengthy footnote in the *Postscript*. (And I would dare say that Kierkegaard agrees with Climacus on this note.)

> The presence of irony does not necessarily mean that the earnestness is excluded. Only associate professors assume that. . . . [T]hey make an exception of irony; they are unable to mediate that [KW XII 1 277].

The point, then, is to see both the irony and the seriousness present in the pseudonymous writings, for if we take Kierkegaard's emphatic remark—that not a single word in the pseudonymous writings is his own—as an absolute hermeneutical postulate, then it does not seem at all likely that one could form any idea of his "purpose" in such a writing (assuming that one is interested in the search for purposes). The best that one who accepts Hartshorne's argument could say is: "This work is by Johannes Climacus. I have no idea how Kierkegaard reads it or what he might mean by it." Hartshorne wants to go beyond this statement, however.

Of course, interpreting Kierkegaard is less complicated when one has a fundamental axiom that can be taken didactically. One tends to forget that in this context 'Kierkegaard' is a metonym for "Kierkegaard's writings" (i.e., the texts). These are all readers should really be concerned with if their intentions are personal or philosophical and not biographical. That Kierkegaard personally held a view is of little importance to someone interested in the truth value of the view, and we would surely be deceiving ourselves to accept something solely on Kierkegaard's authority. As cited above, C. Stephen Evans has made this point in his book *Kierkegaard's "Fragments" and "Postscript."* It is odd that Evans's view is given a brief, slightly more congenial appraisal by Hartshorne in his appendix.

Hartshorne's problem seems to be that certain well-known, generally-taken-to-be-Kierkegaardian views found in the pseudonymous writings turn out to be idolatrous after his close inspection and do not "properly" account for the miraculous grace of God. Consequently, he wants to save Kierkegaard by arguing that he did not mean a single word of the pseudonymous works. For example, "truth as subjectivity," according to Hartshorne, "is the essence of all fanaticism and idolatry."[12] He sees faith as not solely a subjective matter of "the passion of inwardness intensified to the utmost degree." It is, rather, a matter of the grace of God and the work of the Holy Spirit. Thus, Hartshorne takes a bold step in writing: "*Truth as objectivity and truth as subjectivity are equally removed from Christian truth—from the miracle of grace that is received through faith in Christ.*"[13] Now, if it was Kierkegaard's hope to deceive readers into taking notice of the (Christian) truth, then he could hardly be considered wise or a genius when one acknowledges that most of Kierkegaard's most careful readers have been deceived into a gross error.

Chapters 4 and 5 present a less problematic defense of Hartshorne's thesis. There one finds a critical contrast between two religious writings and *Either/Or.* In general, this is intended to show that although Kierkegaard uses language similar to the aesthete and Judge Wilhelm, the words do not share a common meaning, for the contexts have changed. In *Works of Love* and *The Sickness Unto Death,* "one moves in an atmosphere entirely different from that of the pseudonymous works. The irony of the pseudonyms is absent."[14] If "the irony of the pseudonyms" is absent, however, this does not entail that irony altogether is absent. In my view, Hartshorne's argument must be taken further to show that irony is pervasive throughout the Kierkegaardian corpus; but, again, so is that earnestness. Together they form "a dialectical knot" (see KW XX 133) that cannot be untied. But whether the different manifestations of irony share a common meaning and goal—as perhaps set forth in *The Concept of Irony*—remains at present an open question.

Nevertheless, Hartshorne is on solid ground when he demonstrates that the concept of love in *Works of Love* is different from that encountered in both volumes of *Either/Or.* There can be little doubt that Johannes the Seducer's love is self-centered, but it is also crucial to see that Judge Wilhelm's love is, in like manner, based on self-interest. Hartshorne expresses the difference between eros and agape clearly:

> Marriage is a commitment made by husband and wife in the interests of giving permanence to their romantic love. There is no "Thou shalt," because the commandment is irrelevant where interest dictates the moral act. And there is no need for commandment because, in the world of Judge William, there is no sin. . . . [I]n the last analysis both views are aesthetical: both appeal to the self-interest of those concerned. Neighbor love has no place in either.[15]

It is clear that, for Hartshorne, the "ethical stage" ultimately reduces to the "aesthetical stage." There is never any question of the former being superior to the latter. I find this way of reading Kierkegaard to be particularly interesting and refreshing.

Chapter 5 contrasts the discussion of despair in *The Sickness Unto Death*—a book that expresses Kierkegaard's deepest Christian convictions, although he refrained from signing his own name out of "a decent humility"[16]—with Judge Wilhelm's writing on the subject. This involves the two key concepts of the self and sin, and Hartshorne succeeds in showing the difference between Wilhelm's and Anti-Climacus's—that is, Kierkegaard's—views. Wilhelm's "atheism" posits the self as an absolute that is responsible for the creation of good and evil and is not aware of the reality of sin. According to Hartshorne, this is an elaboration of Kant's position, which shares no kinship with the Christian faith of Anti-Climacus.

Anti-Climacus does not argue for his position, however. It is, rather, a "confessional statement" asserting that the self is posited by an-Other and can in no way eradicate its despair on its own. "There is but one possibility by which despair can be eradicated—the Possibility that is God, for whom all things are possible."[17] Thus, Judge Wilhelm's discussion of "choosing oneself in one's eternal validity" leads, for Hartshorne, down the road of atheism, which was taken by both Sartre and Camus. It seems that this presents the deeper explanation for why Hartshorne wants to argue that Kierkegaard is not Judge Wilhelm.

In the final chapter, Hartshorne returns to question his basic premise by arguing that *The Point of View* is, indeed, correct and should be accepted as the authoritative reading of Kierkegaard's authorship. This thesis has come under serious attack in recent years, but I shall not get into an explication of the criticism here. I should like, rather, to speak of a general confusion underlying Hartshorne's interpretative strategy.

Rather than simply wanting to find which views are worthy of Kierkegaard qua Christian, Hartshorne harbors a biographical interest in wanting to uncover what Kierkegaard actually believed personally. Consequently, confusion arises when he belatedly brings up the broken engagement to Regine Olsen and wants to read it back into Kierkegaard's pseudonymous works—works that purportedly do not contain a single word by Kierkegaard. It seems contradictory to argue that *Fear and Trembling* is ironic to the core and does not contain a single view of Kierkegaard and then to speak of it as "implicitly addressed to Regine" and concerned with "Kierkegaard's problem in breaking the engagement."[18] It seems contradictory to say that *Either/Or* does not contain a single word by Kierkegaard and then to write that "his (Kierkegaard's) dilemma is also set forth in *Either/Or*." Otherwise a bad slip-up occurs when Hartshorne quotes part of the first diapsalmata and then adds: "That Kierkegaard was speaking of his own life is obvious."[19] If this were the case, then it would be quite obvious that these words were personally his. These few examples highlight the problems involved in psychologizing an author, and show that any biographical/psychological reading of Kierkegaard is ultimately subject to confusion and contradiction. One had better stick to philosophical readings.

Here, then, I take leave of Hartshorne's study, which serves as a counter to my own reading. While several of Hartshorne's considerations invite further investigation, his attempt to construct a comprehensive, negative hermeneutical hypothesis fails in its implicit intent to develop a straightforward method for interpreting Kierkegaard; and, thus, a sufficiently cogent reading of the so-called first productivity is not forthcoming.

Notes

1. M. Holmes Hartshorne, *Kierkegaard, Godly Deceiver: The Nature and Meaning of His Pseudonymous Writings* (New York: Columbia University Press, 1990).
2. Hartshorne, *Kierkegaard, Godly Deceiver*, p. 6.

3. Ibid., p. 74.

4. Ibid., pp. 7–12.

5. Ibid., p. 11.

6. In this way Kierkegaard presents a contrast to the Hegelian school which understood faith as "the immediate" which must be surpassed by reason. In *Fear and Trembling* he writes: "Recent philosophy has allowed itself simply to substitute the immediate for 'faith.' If that is done, then it is ridiculous to deny that there has always been faith. This puts faith in the rather commonplace company of feelings, moods, idiosyncrasies, *vapeurs* (vagaries), etc. If so, philosophy may be correct in saying that one ought not to stop there. But nothing justifies philosophy in using this language. Faith is preceded by a movement of infinity; only then does faith commence, *nec opinate* [unexpected], by the power of the absurd. This I can certainly understand without consequently maintaining that I have faith. If faith is nothing more than philosophy makes it out to be, then even Socrates went further, much further, instead of the reverse—that he did not attain it" (KW VI 69). Thus, following Socrates's example, Kierkegaard goes further to let his understanding of "faith" embrace reflection. He defines it as "immediacy after reflection," a definition that is found in many a diverse Kierkegaardian writing, e.g., *Stages on Life's Way, Concluding Unscientific Postscript, Works of Love*, and the *Journals and Papers* (see KW VI 350).

7. For Garff's intriguing reading see "The Eyes of Argus: The Point of View and Points of View with Respect to Kierkegaard's 'Activity as an Author,' " trans. Bruce Kirmmse, *Kierkegaardiana*, 15 (1991). 29–54.

8. *Kierkegaard, Godly Deceiver*, p. 27.

9. Ibid., p. 22.

10. Ibid., p. 33. Hartshorne considers Thompson's work, *Kierkegaard* (New York: Alfred Knopf, 1973), to be the most accurate of the secondary literature. Here is a sample of Thompson's view: ". . . to paraphrase them (the pseudonymous writings), to earnestly elucidate the philosophy expounded or the metaphysics presupposed in this or that work, is to miss the point that ultimately they seek to show the vanity of all philosophy and metaphysics" (p. 146). Unless one substitutes "speculative philosophy" for "all philosophy," I think I have provided evidence to show that Kierkegaard was not so disparaging toward philosophy or philosophers as commonly considered.

11. Hartshorne, *Kierkegaard, Godly Deceiver*, p. 35.

12. Ibid., p. 42. This is an important criticism and will be considered in the next chapter.

13. Ibid., p. 43. The italics are Hartshorne's.

14. Ibid., p. 46.

15. Ibid., p. 61.

16. Ibid., p. 66.
17. Ibid., p. 70.
18. Ibid., p. 75.
19. Ibid., p. 76.

6

The Non-Philosophy of Truth

The true philosopher makes light of philosophy.

Blaise Pascal, *Pensées*

True philosophy is non-philosophy.

Maurice Merleau-Ponty[1]

To speak dialectically, it is not the negative which constitutes an encroachment, but the positive. How strange!

Johannes Climacus, CUP 5 and 547

To GET ON NOW with my reading of the pseudonymous writings: This can be little more than a look at a few select works, for a detailed analysis of each individual pseudonymous text would fill volumes. What is more important, however, is that the focus has been changed in this part of the study. In contrast to Part One, where it was necessary to provide thorough readings of the early academic writings because (1) these works are less familiar and (2) their methodology and their total-view set the stage for the writings that follow, the pseudonymous writings are by far the most familiar of Kierkegaard's texts; so the question is now one of reading the application of the ironic methodology. Moreover, most of the secondary literature has been devoted to the pseudonymous writings, so there is no urgent need to carry out a critical reading of each pseudonymous work, no matter how enjoyable this would be. Therefore, I consider it justifiable to leave out a consideration of the writings of any one of Kierkegaard's pseudonyms.

Those I choose to focus on are the writings of Johannes Climacus (in the present chapter) and Anti-Climacus (in the following chapter), two closely related pseudonyms whose views share a number of similarities. The former is easily the most philosophical of the pseudonyms and the most productive in terms of number of pages written; the latter is the most theological. In addition, these are the only pseudonyms to write two books each, which may be taken as a sign of their relative importance.

I turn now to Johannes Climacus's first writing, which, unsurprisingly, has its point of departure in Magister Kierkegaard's seminal dissertation.

On the Concept of Truth with Constant Reference to Socrates

Similitudo Christum inter et Socratem in dissimilitudine præcipue est posita.

Severinus Kierkegaard[2]

In 1844, less than three short years after Kierkegaard successfully defended and published his doctoral dissertation, he returned to experiment with its first thesis in *Philosophiske Smuler* (Philosophical Fragments). While his dissertation is an exercise in developing a methodology to be used in approaching the truth, this pamphlet is a thought experiment using the established methodology, which now endeavors to examine the presuppositions behind any answer to Pontius Pilate's infamous question, "What is truth?" Appropriately, then, Climacus/Kierkegaard emphasizes "the indefatigable activity of irony" practiced throughout the *Philosophical Fragments* when in the *Concluding Unscientific Postscript* he reviews its one and only contemporaneous review in a German periodical (see KW XII 1 275).[3] This reaction to the review is interesting and helpful in gaining an insight into how Kierkegaard[4] ought not be read.

On the one hand, the reviewer is esteemed, and his report is judged as "accurate and on the whole dialectically reliable." On the other hand, in relation to the text itself, the review is considered to be foolish. To read the review would not give one an accurate impression of the book, for the review is didactic, and this is its greatest fault, insofar as it should correctly represent the pamphlet under review. For Climacus, it holds that if the review is didactic, then the book will be considered didactic also—and this would present the grossest misreading possible.

Despite the obvious uncertainty disclosed in the reviewer's closing statement—"we leave it to each person to consider whether he wants to look for earnestness or possibly for irony in this apologetical dialectic"—he does not, as Climacus sees it, present the slightest hint of the ironic play that underlies "the contrastive form of the communication" (KW XII 1 276). Consequently, it does not make good sense to leave it up to the reader to look for irony or earnestness in the pamphlet, because there actually is irony there, and the reviewer has not accounted for it. Obviously, for Kierkegaard there are some natural limits to what may be considered good criticism, and granting that this work is given to ironic play by no means entails that "everything is permitted." Nor does it necessarily exclude the possibility that earnestness is also present. This point Climacus succeeds in illustrating quite well:

> Suppose that someone had been present at one of Socrates' ironic conversations; suppose that he later gives an account of it to someone but leaves out the irony and says: God knows whether talk like that is irony or earnestness—then he is satirizing himself. But the presence of irony does not necessarily mean that the earnestness is excluded. Only associate professors assume that. That is, while they otherwise do away with the disjunctive *aut* [or] and fear neither God nor the devil, since they mediate everything—they make an exception of irony; they are unable to mediate that [KW XII 1 277].

To begin, then, with the irony: where does it lie in *Philosophical Fragments*?

As is the case with most of Kierkegaard's writings, the irony is pervasive throughout both the form and the content of the work. (And even if it were not, as some scholars want to argue with respect to the veronymous writings, this does not prevent readers from reading the works ironically.) Consider first the (in its day) oxymoronic title: *Philosophical Fragments, Or a Fragment of Philosophy*. As the leading philosophizers of Kierkegaard's time were occupied with the systematic construction of the Hegelian whole—for philosophy was by definition a whole and could be understood only as such—Kierkegaard's title smacks of contradiction. Perhaps it would be like writing in our day "Deconstructive Books, Or a Book of Deconstruction" or "Postmodern Philosophy, Or a Philosophy of Postmodernism."[5]

While it is the ironic dialectician Johannes Climacus who authors the *Fragments* and its sequel, he was fortunate enough to have S. Kierkegaard (Magister of Irony) edit his work. This duplicity signals Kierkegaard's awareness of the nature of writing (and the problem of language) and his nature as a writer. So, in the process of writing, Kierkegaard carefully edits himself out of the text, and he thereby creates a more powerful product.

Kierkegaard's involvement with the text on a personal level is, however, given in a draft of the title page which includes his own name as author.[6] This draft also contains a personal expression of the tripartite question posed at the outset of this work in which all references to the first person were deleted and changed (see KW VII 176). Without the changes the translation reads:

Philosophical Pamphlets
or
A Bit of Philosophy
by
S. Kierkegaard

No. 1

> How do I obtain a historical point of departure for my eternal consciousness; how can such a point of departure be of more than historical interest to me; how can I build my eternal happiness on historical knowledge [KW VII 177]?

Kierkegaard's own name appears on the final copy as well (KW VII xvi), which indicates that he had not considered the use of a pseudonym until the last moment. The pseudonym represents a new perspective from which Kierkegaard read his writing, but it does not thereby erase his earliest reading. On the published title page, however, readers encounter both an author and an editor. As an editor is not responsible for the author's meaning, Kierkegaard is no longer responsible for the meaning of the text. But qua editor he is free to read the text and appropriate it as any other.

Johannes Climacus is such a crafty dialectical trickster that he would even nudge readers into thinking that his ironic construction is entirely without seriousness. In an imaginary dialogue with an imaginary reader, he drops the hint that a follow-up to this pamphlet might be written, but quickly adds that to promise a sequel would be feigning a seriousness that a pamphlet writer such as he is completely lacking (KW VII 109). In retrospect, one knows from his *Postscript* of more than six hundred pages (in the new English translation) that Climacus's irony was in earnest, or that he was not serious in claiming the absence of seriousness, and that, to refer again to the passage quoted above, "the presence of irony does not necessarily mean that the earnestness is excluded." Readers are thus implicitly instructed to become good dialecticians in following a thought-project that will require them to distinguish between irony and seriousness and between philosophy and Christianity.

That this work is a "bit of philosophy" is doubly ironic. As explained above, it was not "philosophical" in the sense that Kierkegaard's contemporaries used the word, but, supposing that they were wrong in their assumptions, might it not be philosophical in another sense? Might not this new "ironic philosophy" explain Christianity in a profound, novel way? Not by any means. For Kierkegaard the reader, no philosophy could ever think Christianity (which is the [for the most part] unnamed new understanding of truth), could ever begin in explaining its relation to Christianity, or could ever begin to approach what has never entered into a human heart (cf. KW VII 109–10). Since these ideas are found at the end of this writing, it is plausible to think that Kierkegaard came to consider the possibility that what he had just written might be read as the development of a new philosophical approach to Christianity. As any philosophical approach to Christianity would be a grave mistake, Kierkegaard chose to make Johannes Climacus the author, and changed his own status to editor. This should suggest, however, not that he thereby devalued the many important details of the text but rather that he reevaluated the work's total impression and saw that it was not philosophical in any positive sense. To put it another way, it was not philosophy but writing.

Nevertheless, this writing ironically appears in a philosophical guise. Climacus develops his thought-project with a deductive logic that, when a different situation is contrasted with the Socratic-Platonic one, would seem to deduce entirely new terms in its climbing "the ladder of divine ascent"[7] to the truth; for example, the moment, sin, a savior, the fullness of time, conversion, rebirth, repentance, the absolute paradox, offense, and faith are all central concepts in this climbing of the heights.

Climacus is not all logician, however. He is also a poet—not a writer of verse, but a creator in general—who has ventured into the fantastic. He is a whimsical metaphysician who posits the absolute paradox, which no philosopher or metaphysician can honestly hope to resolve. And he also appears as an illusionist who would seemingly try somehow to trick readers into noticing the eternal truth of the new hypothesis, which is not yet dressed in the historical gown called Christianity. If this were Climacus's intention, however, it would blatantly conflict with the "Moral" of the *Fragments*.[8] Here Climacus explains that the preceding experiment was not given to deciding whether the Socratic (Platonic) position, which understands truth as outside time, is truer than the Christian proposition that the (eternal) truth has made itself known in time. In this context, it is curious that Climacus chose the adjective "truer" (*sandere*), for this does not fit the nature of the eternal truth as absolute, and it also grants a relative truth-value to the Socratic in its comparison to Christianity. But, for the most part, this appears as a minor problem of expression, for it is clear throughout Climacus's discussion that the two conceptions of truth are qualitatively different. They are therefore fundamentally incompatible with each other, and this leads readers indirectly to the choice between the truth of the one situation and the falsity of the other.

Robert C. Roberts puts the matter in more doctrinal terms:

> The point of Climacus's discourse is to force upon his reader some fundamental exclusive disjunctions that will inoculate him against a certain kind of heretical understanding of Jesus and thus free him to come into the correct kind of relationship with Christ.[9]

Yet concerning the ultimate disjunction—either the moment is a mere occasion, or the moment has decisive significance—Climacus has not the slightest opinion (cf. KW VII 7).

Climacus's tangled web of vague logic and hidden presuppositions has prompted a considerable amount of scholarly investigation.[10] When reduced to rigorous logical analysis, however, it is not incorrect to maintain that "Climacus's argument is so full of holes that no careful reader will trust it as a vessel for its precious contents."[11] But while Climacus's deductive thought experiment may appear as the ostensible purpose of his writing, it is his "poetical venture" toward faith that makes up the book's serious purpose.

An example of the slippery logical moves is found in Climacus's deduction of the state of sin. It is clear that he must presuppose the ontological definition of "god"[12] to make the argument work.

> But insofar as the moment is to have decisive significance (and if this is not assumed, then we do in fact remain with the Socratic), he must lack the condition, consequently be deprived of it. This cannot be due to an act of the god (for this is a contradiction) or to an accident (for it is a contradiction that something inferior would be able to vanquish something superior); it must therefore have been due to himself [KW VII 15].

The concept of the god must include the attributes of omnipotence and benevolence to make the statement "an act of the god deprives a person of the condition for learning the truth" entail a contradiction. Climacus's later criticism of Spinoza's version of the ontological argument casts a considerable doubt on how far he himself would be willing to accept his own reasoning in reality, that is, beyond the realms of a thought experiment.

In his discussion in "The Absolute Paradox (A Metaphysical Caprice)," he sharply distinguishes between the definition of a concept of god and the existence of god. God's existence—or its non-existence—cannot be demonstrated, for "factual being is indifferent to the differentiation of all essence-determinations" (KW VII 41). Ideally, which is also to say in language, the situation is quite different: "*But as soon as I speak ideally about being, I am speaking no longer about being but about essence*" (KW VII 42). One cannot capture existence in language, in ideality. Therefore Climacus concludes:

> Spinoza's thesis is quite correct and the tautology is in order, but it is also certain that he completely circumvents the difficulty, for the difficulty is to grasp factual being and to bring god's ideality into factual being [KW VII 42].

It would seem that a related difficulty is involved in my factually being in a state of sin or untruth as determined ideally. Both difficulties must continually collide with the understanding and can be transcended only by a leap.

To put the matter into other words, the paradoxical passion of the understanding collides with the unknown. But what is this passion, and what is the unknown? Climacus explains the former:

> The paradox is the passion of thought, and the thinker without the paradox is like the lover without passion: a mediocre fellow. But the ultimate potentiation of every passion is always to will its own downfall, and so it is also the ultimate passion of the understanding to will the collision, although in one way or another the collision must become its downfall. This, then, is the ultimate paradox of thought: to want to discover something that thought itself cannot think [KW VII 37].

The axiom—"the ultimate potentiation of every passion is always to will its own downfall"—is an interesting one. According to Roberts, it evokes "a pressing doubt" and "as a general principle . . . is outrageous."

> Instantiating the principle a few times, we get "The highest potentiation of the desire for wealth is the desire for poverty," "The highest potentiation of the desire for fame is the desire of obscurity," "The highest potentiation of gourmandism is the desire to taste something really revolting," and so forth.[13]

But here Roberts does not fully take into consideration the power of the passion. What Climacus wants to say is that when the power of the passion is at its ultimate strength, it may inadvertently, unintentionally will its own collapse. (Remember that the state of error or untruth is brought about through an act of the will.) Consider, for example, that I take my passion to protect my daughter to its highest potentiation. Is it not likely that, taken to its greatest intensity, my untempered passion would lead to a strict overprotectiveness that could ultimately destroy the very relationship I am so passionate about? The Danish scholar Poul Lübcke presents a similar criticism when he writes that Climacus may mean that "every passion drives itself to higher challenges and therefore to a point of higher risk." His counter-example is this: "it is the highest potentiation of the desire for wealth to go into a risky business—which in most cases will lead to poverty."[14] For Climacus, then, to respect the passion is to respect the risk involved in taking it to its limits.

The limit of the passion of the understanding is the unknown. The unknown is characterized, though not understood, as

> the absolutely different in which there is no distinguishing mark. Defined as the absolutely different, it seems to be at the point of being disclosed, but not so, because the understanding cannot even think the absolutely different; it cannot absolutely negate itself but uses itself for that purpose and consequently thinks the difference in itself, which it thinks by itself (KW VII 45).

The unknown, the god, the truth, is itself the absolute difference that cannot be conceived or grasped. As absolute difference, any attempt to approach the god (truth) will be arbitrary and false in the sense that the god that is approached is, inevitably, a god produced by the understanding and not the god that is absolutely different. Such a god cannot be known at all.

All this discourse about absolute difference verges on a paradox, or what Climacus discusses under the heading of "the absolute paradox." At this point in the text, the absolute paradox is set forth as, strictly speaking, the intractable epistemological problem involved in understanding the unknown (the god) as the absolutely different. Human beings could not come to know this by themselves, for a contradiction is involved in saying that the understanding can come to know that the god is absolutely different from itself. Consequently, it must be through the god that the understanding comes to know the absolute difference. But is it? Here Climacus writes that:

> if it does come to know this, it cannot understand this and consequently cannot come to know this, for how could it understand the absolutely different? If this is not immediately clear, then it will become more clear from the corollary, for if the god is absolutely different from a human being, then a human being is absolutely different from the god—but how is the understanding to grasp this [KW VII 46]?

Between a human being and the god there is an absolute qualitative difference that cannot be conceived, grasped, known, thought, or understood. The absolute paradox lies in the knowledge that there is this absolute qualitative difference, for I do seem to know it in a certain sense. But how can I have this knowledge? Where did it come from? This is precisely the pinch of the absolute paradox. It cannot be resolved.

With this as the situation, how does one respect the absolute difference and the absolute paradox? Moreover, how is one properly supposed to act in light of all these unresolved quandaries? Who can show the way?

Who else but the ironist Socrates? The Christian author Anti-Climacus—who shares many things in common with Johannes Climacus and is not "against" but "before" him, that is, "higher in rank" (KW XIX xxii)—explicitly identifies the absolute paradox with Christianity. He writes:

> So let others admire and praise him who pretends to be able to comprehend Christianity. I consider it an outright ethical task, perhaps requiring not a little self-denial . . . when all "the others" are busy comprehending, to admit that one is neither able nor obliged to comprehend it. Precisely this is . . . what Christendom needs: a little Socratic ignorance with respect to Christianity—but please note, a little "Socratic" ignorance. Let us never forget that Socrates's ignorance was a kind of fear and worship of god, that his ignorance was the Greek version of the Jewish saying: The fear of god is the beginning of wisdom. Let us never forget that it was out of fear of veneration for god that he was ignorant, that as far as it was possible for a pagan he was on guard duty as a judge on the frontier between a human being and god, keeping watch so that the deep gulf of qualitative difference between them was maintained . . . That is why Socrates was the ignorant one, and that is why the deity found him to be the wisest of men.—Christianity teaches that everything essentially Christian depends solely upon faith; therefore it wants to be precisely a Socratic, god-fearing ignorance, which by means of ignorance guards faith against speculation, keeping watch so that the gulf of qualitative difference between a human being and god may be maintained as it is in the paradox and faith [KW XIX 99].

Whether one be a humorist or a Christian on an extraordinarily high level, when you respect the qualitative difference between a human being and god, Socrates comes across as a better Christian than the Christians in Christendom. And behind his ignorance there lies irony, there lies faith, through which he becomes engaged with the absolute difference that is separated from him. This is, however, precisely the absolute paradox which cannot be penetrated.

Given the nature of the epistemological situation described by

Climacus as the absolute paradox, what reason could be adduced for his proceeding to write a sequel five times the length of the *Fragments*? Is it not clear from the above that it could not be to further what is necessarily an arbitrary, ambiguous attempt toward the ultimate, eternal truth—toward god? The sequel is, of course, a diversion, a surplus, a supplement, and any reason for its being would have to be referred to the mad momentary strength of Kierkegaard's ability to write.[15] It is thus with the greatest irony that the same author assisted by the same editor added *Concluding Unscientific Postscript to the "Philosophical Fragments"* to the world.

The Madness of Faith, or, Truth Is Subjectivity

> I believe I would be doing philosophy a great service were it to adopt a category discovered by myself and utilized with great profit and success to exhaust and dry up a multitude of relations and determinations which have so far been unwilling to resolve themselves: it is the category of the higher madness. I only ask that it not be named after me. . . .
>
> S. Kierkegaard, P II A 808

> The irony of Socrates makes use . . . of a form of speech which sounds in the first instance like the speech of a madman.
>
> Johannes Climacus, CUP 77

By virtue of the nature of a *Postscript*, Johannes Climacus admits that if there is any salient point to the whole matter at hand, or any most important part in his presentation, it lies essentially in the *Fragments*. Here the problem of placing the god in relation to the single individual was formulated with the highest regard for dialectical clarity. Here the absolute absurdity involved in basing an eternal happiness (or sadness) on historical knowledge was brought forth, but without an actual historical costume. Thus the task (or the diversion) of Climacus in the *Postscript* is to invest the problem in its elaborate historical costume, such that, rather than speaking of "historical knowledge," Climacus speaks of "Christianity" or, better, Christ.

But Climacus does not consider himself a Christian.[16] Nor is he concerned with evaluating the truth of Christianity, although he does show in Book One that this objective problem could never result in more than an uncertain approximation. Instead, his work is "an existential contribution," since the treatment of the problem posed in the *Fragments* "merely deals with the question of the individual's relationship to Christianity" (CUP 19). This is now termed the subjective problem, and it is clear that Climacus thinks that if the promised eternal happiness of Christianity may be acquired, then the proper individual relationship to Christianity must be established.

Climacus wants to try a new approach to the problem of the *Fragments*. But why? Perhaps the answer lies in his introduction.

> The problem concerns myself alone; partly because, if it is properly posed, it will concern everyone else in the same manner; and partly because all the others already have faith as something given, as a triviality of little value, or as a triviality which amounts to something only when tricked out with a few proofs. So that the posing of the problem cannot be regarded as presumption on my part, but only as a special kind of madness [CUP 20].

How can readers approach this madness? Is there some method to it? Shall they, too, try the experiment—that is, test the difficulty of becoming a Christian—that has been solely and simply addressed to Climacus himself? Of course, concerning this Climacus can have no opinion, and to help his readers understand that he has no doctrine either, he writes the appendix, "For an Understanding with the Reader." Here he abolishes any possible pretense of a philosophical doctrine by stating that "the book is superfluous; let no one therefore take the pains to appeal to it as an authority; for the one who thus appeals to it has *eo ipso* misunderstood it" (CUP 546). Consequently, the worst impression one could have of the *Postscript* is that, like its companion piece, the *Fragments*, it is scholarship. In the deepest sense it is an "unscholarly" (*uvidenskabelig*) protest against scientific scholarship. Kierkegaard saw this as a crucial point, and in an unpublished reply to Rasmus Nielsen's[17] review of the *Postscript*, he condemned the positive reading of his work. For Kierkegaard, his own text offers no "new scientific principle that is now supposed to be made into the science that there is no science." It contains "no didacticizing that there must be no didacticizing in any way; everything is transposed into the existential, and the author himself is an existing humorist" (P X^6 B 114).

In a manner similar to that of the *Fragments*, in order for Climacus's dialectical analysis of the essential truth to reach individual readers, the total impression of his communication must be ironic and negative so as to maintain the personal freedom of all potential readers. That Climacus is a mere pseudonym serves to accentuate the negativity involved in the writing. In the text, Kierkegaard attempts to mimic the midwifery of Socrates,[18] one who performed his examinations ironically "not because he 'did not have the positive,' but because he perceived that this relation is the highest relation a human being can have to another" (KW VII 10).

No didacticism: for, strictly speaking, there can be no human teacher in how to exist. Though this would conflict with the common sensibilities of the majority of people—Do parents not teach their children how to exist?—Socrates and Kierkegaard most certainly regard the sane and sober majority opinion as sheer human madness. Although they do have a certain respect for madness, theirs is of another species.

For Socrates, it is the "madness which is heaven-sent" that brings the greatest blessings and is superior to human sanity.[19] And for Kierkegaard, a schoolmaster in the art of existing cannot exist, for the following reason:

> With respect to existing, there is only the learner, for anyone who fancies that he is in this respect finished, that he can teach others and on top of that himself forgets to exist and to learn, is a fool. In relation to existing there is for all existing persons one schoolmaster—existence itself [P VI A 140].

Neither Kierkegaard nor Climacus has any desire to teach others. Their works are written as acts of learning the art of existence. Let other learners be as thoughtful.

It is apparent that the use of the method of "indirect communication" avoids the charge of didacticism. The notion of "indirect communication," however, is an ambiguous and ironic one. The reasoning behind it might seem simple enough—that truth understood as inwardness or subjectivity cannot be communicated directly—but this misses the great complexity and subtlety involved. One finds an indication of the complexity when Climacus addresses the reflection of inwardness early on in the *Postscript*.

> The reflection of inwardness gives to the subjective thinker a double reflection. In thinking he thinks the universal; but as existing in this thought and as assimilating it in his inwardness, he becomes more and more subjectively isolated [CUP 68].

There is a tension between one's becoming highly isolated in one's inwardness and in wanting to communicate this inwardness to others. Climacus is well aware of this tension, and actually cites it as the contradiction[20] that marks the impossibility of direct communication. In the example of a lover, Climacus remarks that it is not difficult to imagine that someone should want to communicate one's inwardness, since it is one's dearest possession. But as this inwardness is what one is "essentially occupied constantly in acquiring and reacquiring," no result or finality can be imposed on it. Thus, a direct form of communication could not be used to express it, "because such a form presupposes results and finality." Certainty is also presupposed by direct communication, "but certainty is impossible for anyone in process of becoming, and the semblance of certainty constitutes for such an individual a deception." Climacus uses the example of an erotic relationship to explain the deception of certainty.

> If a loving maiden were to long for her wedding day on account of the assured certainty that it would give her; if she as "pure and lofty-wedded wife" wanted to make herself comfortable in the legal security of marriage, exchanging maidenly longing for wifely yawning, her lover would have the right to complain of her unfaithfulness, notwithstanding that she did not love another, but because she had lost the idea, and did not really love him [CUP 68; SV IX 64].

One other example of the inwardness spoken of here is a god-relationship. This could never be expressed directly, and to think otherwise would be a deception, for the movement involved in the inwardness of a god-relationship precludes all results and certainty.

This insight into the nature of inwardness lies very far from the majority of "religious" individuals or individuals who have their ultimate concerns elsewhere. It is exceedingly difficult to live in uncertainty and without coming to any closure as a human being. Yet this is what the character of existence dictates to the reflective individual. Climacus wants to make individuals aware of this difficulty. In a telling personal passage, he writes:

> "You are going on," I said to myself, "to become an old man, without being anything, and without really undertaking to do anything. On the other hand, wherever you look about you, in literature and in life, you see the celebrated names and figures, the precious and much heralded men who are coming into prominence and are much talked about, the many benefactors of the age who know how to benefit mankind by making life easier and easier. . . . And what are you doing?" Here my soliloquy was interrupted, for my cigar was smoked out and a new one had to be lit. So I smoked again, and then suddenly this thought flashed through my mind: "You must do something, but inasmuch as with your limited capacities it will be impossible to make anything easier than it has become, you must, with the same humanitarian enthusiasm as the others, undertake to make something harder." This notion pleased me immensely, and at the same time it flattered me to think that I, like the rest of them, would be loved and esteemed by the whole community [CUP 165–66].

This "gadfly of Copenhagen" wants to make individuals aware of the serious difficulty involved in existing as a human being. With advances in rationality and science, life has become easier and easier, quick results abound, and, particularly with increased knowledge, individuals have overlooked or forgotten what is essential to existing (becoming) as a human being, namely, in a word, pathos.

A deeper difficulty in Climacus's dialectical (conceptual) analysis resides in his wanting to analyze that which cannot be thought, namely, existence itself. The category of existence, according to Climacus, cannot properly be thought, for to think it abrogates it, because thinking involves reflection which cancels existence (CUP 274, 292). But is thinking not a part of existence? For Kierkegaard, it is that part which contradicts the immediacy of existence.

That existence, life, involves a contradiction between thought (language) and reality has already been discussed, and in the *Postscript* one finds it again at the heart of understanding what it means to be a human being.

> Existing is ordinarily regarded as no very complex matter, much less an art, since we all exist; but abstract thinking takes rank as an accomplishment. But really to exist, so as to interpenetrate one's existence with consciousness, at one and the same time external and as if far removed from existence, and yet also present in existence and in the process of becoming: that is truly difficult [CUP 272].

The second sentence of this quote is the important and perhaps obscure one. While not explicit, this passage seems to witness to what has been considered Kierkegaard's fundamental presupposition, the basis for his "theory of the stages," and the basic premise of his entire authorship.[21] The premise is this: a human being is a synthesis. According to Climacus, a human being is a synthesis of the finite and the infinite, the temporal and the eternal, and the material and the spiritual.[22] The difficulty involved in reality, therefore, is how to hold "these two factors together, infinitely interested in existing" (CUP 268).

This last quote is significant, for it may help to clarify the potentially misleading equation of a human being with a synthesis. Since Climacus and Kierkegaard understand existence as a contradiction that may not be mediated—in contrast to the prevailing "Hegelian" notion[23]—that a human being is a synthesis seems almost to imply a result of the merger between the contradictory factors. But as existence involves holding the finite and the infinite factors together throughout the process of becoming, a better expression of "Kierkegaard's fundamental presupposition" is that a human being is not a synthesis but a synthesizing. Anti-Climacus appears to make this distinction in the opening to *The Sickness Unto Death* when he writes: "the self is not the relation but is the relation's relating itself to itself" (KW XIX 13).

Because of the great accumulation of knowledge that has obstructed the difficulty of existing, Climacus struggles, in effect, to take knowledge away. The *Postscript* is to be read not as a rational communication intent on imparting new knowledge to the reader (again, no didacticism, in different words) but rather as an attempt to remove knowledge, for with the overabundance of knowledge[24] much that is essential has become trivial. In the age of our author, individuals could hardly begin to assimilate what was needed in order to be able to exist as genuinely as they possibly could. Climacus thinks that he has succeeded in explaining this curious and ironic approach through raising an analogous question:

> When a man has his mouth so full of food that he is prevented from eating, and is likely to starve in consequence, does giving him food consist of stuffing still more in his mouth, or does it consist of taking some of it away, so that he can begin to eat [CUP 245]?

The vital food that Climacus would have his readers digest concerns the essential truth pertaining to existence. Consequently, he takes pains to direct readers' attention to a consideration of what it means to exist. He does this metaphorically and ironically, however, for when the question of truth is raised by an existing individual, it will involve personal assimilation and appropriation, and these are actions lying outside the text and within the subject.

Hence, the commentators and writers "after" Climacus face what may be termed a Kierkegaardian dilemma: if they endeavor to impart unambiguously to readers what they need to understand concerning the essential truth of existence, and which has presumably been discovered through their own experience, then readers cannot really come to understand this, for the only way one can truly come to understand something concerning essential truth is through self-discovery. Alternatively, if commentators do not endeavor to explain what readers need to understand, they run the risk that readers may never discover the essential truth for themselves. Clearly, the latter alternative is the only proper choice, as it allows for the only possible successful outcome. Furthermore, who could ever be certain that he or she fully understands the essential truth? Certainly not this commentator. Only a doctrinizing didactic would make such a claim, something that lies very far indeed from any point of view of Climacus or Kierkegaard.

In *The Point of View for My Work as an Author* one reads repeatedly that the *Concluding Unscientific Postscript* is the turning point in Kierkegaard's entire production. This is properly read as a backward-looking attempt by Kierkegaard to understand his authorship in its entirety, and it should be taken as such. In his journal he writes:

> Strangely enough I always understand best afterwards. . . . I manage to do things the entire significance of which I do not understand until later. This I have seen again and again. For that reason I cannot become serious in the trivial sense in which serious people are serious, for I realize that I am nothing [P X^2 A 163; JP VI 6523].

Thus, while Kierkegaard may have later found an insightful way to read his writings, it is clear that his does not provide the only way, or necessarily the best. Notwithstanding, these comments ought not to suggest that it should be ignored.

In *The Point of View*—a so-called direct communication and report to history—the *Postscript* is said to define the problem of the whole authorship, which is to answer the questions: What does it mean to become a Christian, and how does one do so? These are the problems that Johannes Climacus sets for himself, and the methodology he uses in his inquiry is an ironic conceptual analysis of the central notions of existence and truth. Ironic because in their purest form these notions repel conception.

Although Climacus's text can assuredly not be reduced to a report on its central thesis that "truth is subjectivity," such a moment is bound to occur.[25] To acknowledge this is to regain one's bearings, and the effort to proceed becomes possible.

How is truth subjectivity? What is meant by the proposition that "truth is subjectivity"? Can this thesis be philosophically defended? Kierkegaard felt that it could be defended, but was indifferent to the matter and disregarded it entirely, for it had not found anyone who had sufficient skill to read it and then attack it (P VII[1] B 87). The defense, it seems, is still unwarranted today.

It is important to remember that Climacus is raising the question of truth for an existing individual, such that the individual can appropriately relate himself to it. "Existing" itself must be understood before the question of truth can even be raised. The description of existence is thus essential to Climacus's argument, for if what it means to be an existing individual is agreed upon, then the claim that "truth is subjectivity" should be easily conceded. In other words, the cogency of the answer depends upon correctly setting up the problem.

Climacus's explication is carried on "pen in cheek," for, strictly speaking, what it means to exist cannot properly be thought, spoken, or written in language. The ruminations of Kierkegaard in *Johannes Climacus* are not out of place here: existence is immediacy and language/thought is mediacy. The two cannot meet, so Climacus is forced to stretch the limits of language to describe existence. An essential feature of existing is given in a word. That word is *pathos* (passion).

In order to bring a person into a passionate state Climacus would

> get him seated on a horse and the horse made to take fright and gallop wildly, or better still, for the sake of bringing the passion out, if I could take a man who wanted to arrive at a place as quickly as possible, and hence already had some passion, and could set him astride a horse that could scarcely walk—and yet this is what existence is like if one is to become consciously aware of it. Or if a driver were otherwise not especially inclined toward passion, if someone hitched a team of horses to a wagon for him, one of them a Pegasus and the other a worn-out jade, and told him to drive—I think one might succeed. And it is just this that it means to exist, if one is to become conscious of it. Eternity is the winged horse, infinitely fast, and time is a worn-out jade; the existing individual is the driver [CUP 276].

Usually, we would agree that a person in innocence asking the age-old question "What is the truth?" has an active interest in the answer to the question. An answer such as "The truth is that the world we live in is round, and you are composed of flesh, bones, and blood" will undoubtedly receive the response "I did not mean that kind of truth." Objective, scientific thinkers will always try to be disinterested, as far as they are capable, when they raise the question "What is the truth?" It is a well-known fact that scientists try, as far as it is possible, to keep their own personal concerns outside the search for truth. But subjective thinkers do exactly the opposite. They have a passionate interest in striving to discover the truth as it relates to their personal concerns. They accept as true only the truth that is related to their respective individual existences.[26]

Again, one must beware. Is it possible to come to a conclusion on the meaning of truth as subjectivity when one raises the question in an objective, scholarly fashion? Obviously, any attempt to explicate the meaning of "truth is subjectivity" will ultimately fail as it is surrounded by the perimeters of language. If it was Climacus's deepest private experience that "truth is subjectivity," then how can this be made public? The proposition itself is an abstraction from the experience, and it is Kierkegaard's considered opinion that the inner, private world of experience cannot be outwardly or publicly expressed.[27] The way around the impasse is "indirect communication."

Perhaps, then, I would stand a better chance of successfully explaining "truth is subjectivity"—to myself, the subject interested in the answer—if I could explain the "parable of the wig," which Climacus repeats in closing his work in order to emphasize its importance. The parable is worth repeating here.

> It is said to have chanced in England that a man was attacked on the highway by a robber who had made himself unrecognizable by wearing a big wig. He falls upon the traveller, seizes him by the throat and shouts, "Your purse!" He gets the purse and keeps it, but the wig he throws away. A poor man comes along the same road, puts it on and arrives at the next town where the traveller has already denounced the crime, he is arrested, is recognized by the traveller, who takes his oath that he is the man. By chance, the robber is present in the courtroom, sees that misunderstanding, turns to the judge and says, "It seems to me that the traveller has regard to the wig rather than to the man," and he asks permission to make a trial. He puts on the wig, seizes the traveller by the throat, crying, "Your purse!"—and the traveller recognizes the robber and offers to swear to it—the only trouble is that already he has taken an oath. So it is, in one way or another, with every man who has a "what" and is not attentive to the "how": he swears, he takes his oath, he runs errands, he ventures life and blood, he is executed—all on account of the wig [CUP 544].

The moral of this parable is powerful, for it insinuates—by all accounts rightly—that people generally focus not on their experiences as they are actually lived but on the external, incidental aspects (i.e., on the "wigs").

Much earlier in his work, in the section entitled "Truth Is Subjectivity," Climacus relates that "*The objective accent falls on WHAT is said, the subjective accent on HOW it is said*" (CUP 181). When the question of truth is raised objectively, what is most commonly meant is that the questioner wants a description of the world as it is; reflection is directed outward toward the object, but the truth in this sense cannot be fully apprehended, for the world is perpetually changing. Climacus defines this empirical way of approaching truth as the agreement of thought with being. He is following Heraclitus; concrete empirical being is in constant flux so that the best one can hope for is an approximation. The traveler in the parable seems to think that the empirical being of the robber will not undergo any important future change. There are many rather realistic philosophers like this traveler.

Climacus also discusses an idealistic approach to truth. This is defined as the agreement of being with thought. But this approach gets one nowhere when being is understood purely conceptually, for this leads to a meaningless tautology.

A third way to approach the truth is existentially. This approach does not try to describe the world with scientific precision. It does not dwell solely in the realm of concepts and does not involve sitting down at a word processor and trying to organize one's jumbled thoughts. For an existing individual—that is, a person always in the process of becoming—the highest truth attainable is "*an objective uncertainty held fast in an appropriation-process of the most passionate inwardness*" (CUP 182). This "definition for truth is an equivalent expression for faith," which is "the contradiction between the infinite passion of the individual's inwardness and the objective uncertainty" (CUP 182). That one's infinite passion is objectively uncertain means that faith is essentially a risky venture.

The claim that essential truth is subjectivity means that the individual is in a passionate state, ready to risk his or her entire life for whatever is of the utmost inward concern. To risk one's life does not necessarily mean that the life is cut short by an early martyrized death; it means, rather, that one risks striving to maintain an inwardness devoted to something that is unsure. And this is precisely what must be decided upon by the individual. "Only in subjectivity is there decisiveness" (CUP 181), and only the truth that is subjectivity necessarily involves action on the part of the subject.[28] In short, the truth or faith that Climacus is describing involves these elements: active striving, decisiveness, infinite passion, and risk.

Readers can gain a better insight into the claim that "truth is subjectivity" when considering that within this principle "there is comprehended the Socratic wisdom" (CUP 183). This refers to the fact that Socrates recognized "the knower as an existing individual." He was, consequently, a non-knower who maintained an ironic ignorance, while many around him claimed to know so much. On the importance of Socrates, Climacus and Kierkegaard are undoubtedly of the same persuasion as Anti-Climacus:

> Socrates, Socrates, Socrates! Yes, we may well call your name three times; it would not be too much to call it ten times, if it would be

> of any help. Popular opinion maintains that the world needs a republic, needs a new social order and a new religion—but no one considers that what the world, confused simply by too much knowledge, needs is a Socrates [KW XIX 92].

For Climacus, the Socratic wisdom, which may also be called the life-view of irony, serves as the point of departure for ethico-religious activity. For Kierkegaard, as for Socrates, this life-view marks the only life worth living as a human being, which is now given expression in that the ethico-religious life is the only one that cultivates the essential, eternal truth in an existing individual. Socratic irony, which I understand as comprehending Socratic ignorance, shows that, objectively, truth is uncertain, such that the inwardness of existing in the truth is the important factor.

But, the Socratic-Platonic understanding that the truth resides within all individuals and may be obtained through recollection is not embraced by Climacus. To explain "truth is subjectivity" as quite simply meaning that a "man tries to act in accordance with the eternal truth which he finds in his innermost being"[29] is to turn Climacus into a Platonist and miss the import of his contrasting the Socratic-Platonic conception of truth with the Christian. While Climacus claims that "the Socratic inwardness in existing is an analogue to faith" (CUP 184) and yet dismisses the proposition that all knowledge is recollection, this does not lead to an inconsistency.

> This proposition is not for Socrates a cue to the speculative enterprise, and hence he does not follow it up; essentially it becomes a Platonic principle. Here the way swings off; Socrates concentrates essentially upon accentuating existence, while Plato forgets this and loses himself in speculation. Socrates' infinite merit is to have been an *existing* thinker, not a speculative philosopher who forgets what it means to exist [CUP 184].

For this reason, Climacus does not think one should "hold Socrates down to the proposition that all knowledge is recollection" (CUP 184). By explaining in a note that "the Socratic position is to accentuate existence, which also involves the qualification of inwardness" (CUP 184), Climacus has prevented any possible objections to his referring the paradoxical and faith to Socrates. The point is that Socrates expresses what it takes to become a Christian; Plato does not.

But, if the truth is not within us, so the thought experiment runs, then not only must the teacher present it to us, but he also must give us the condition to recognize it as such. As was seen above, this scenario leads one to the absolute paradox and the category of the absurd, that is, "the negative criterion of the divine or of relationship to the divine . . . of that which is higher than human understanding and knowledge" (JP 1 10–11). The power of the absurd enables the leap of faith, the leap into divine madness.[30]

One must recognize that there is madness, and then there is madness. It is apparent that the dialectically minded Climacus and Kierkegaard use "madness" to refer to several different conditions. There is the higher or divine madness, which invokes the logic of the absurd and entails a passionate inwardness or faith in the objectively uncertain. Socrates and the Christian partake of this madness, which is deemed such from the human vantage point but not from the divine. Thus, when Climacus says that truth understood as subjectivity is indistinguishable from madness (CUP 174), he is referring to the higher madness. But Climacus does attempt to qualify this claim in a note. In the example of Don Quixote's madness, inwardness and passion are directed toward a fixed idea that is finite. This lower expression might be called simple "human madness," which is opposite the inwardness of truth that is directed toward the infinite, that is, potentiality. And, for Climacus, a human being is potentially spirit.

Although madness and fanaticism might seem to resemble each other, to claim, as Hartshorne does, that "truth is subjectivity" is "the essence of all fanaticism and idolatry"[31] is to do Kierkegaard a rather grave injustice. On Climacus's account, the subjective individual would appear as the complete opposite of the fanatic. This passionate individual recognizes the impossibility of disclosing his or her inwardness, and therefore rarely tries. If it is disclosed, it is done so ironically or indirectly. The subjective individual is not didactic, doctrinizing, or proselytizing and has not the slightest assurance for his or her faith. The object of faith is the infinite, the unknown, and thus steers clear of idolatry. Socrates, Climacus's analogue to faith, was not at all one who should be thought of as a fanatic.

There is another sense of "human madness" as seen from an enlightened or divine perspective.[32] The objective, speculative thinker who lacks inwardness or would build an existential system is mad in this sense. An existing spirit cannot form a system of reality. This does not imply, however, that such a system does not exist. "Reality itself is a system—for God" (CUP 107), but a finite human being could never conceive and formulate this system.

Passionate readers are not likely to forget that Climacus posed the problem of an eternal happiness on the title page of his *Philosophical Fragments.* If one will assume the possibility of an eternal happiness, which is admittedly objectively uncertain, then one will agree that this is the greatest good possible for an existing individual. In the final third (roughly) of Climacus's weighty text he presents a more detailed and sharper discussion of the problem itself, which involves the various degrees of expressing an existential pathos.

According to Niels Thulstrup's résumé of the *Postscript,* the pathos of truth consists

> in allowing the conception of an eternal happiness to transform the individual's entire existence; it is not merely a matter of words or understanding. This means, then, that religious pathos consists in existing and in doing so ethically, and not in singing psalms or writing song books.[33]

"If then an existing individual is to realize a pathetic relationship to an eternal happiness," writes Climacus, "his existence must express the relationship" (CUP 352). One must therefore will the absolute telos, which involves a heightened sense of active concentration. Climacus continues: "To will absolutely is to will the infinite, and to will an eternal happiness is to will absolutely, because this is an end which can be willed every moment" (CUP 353). What follows in the text might very well be termed Climacus's "(non-)philosophy of the act," in which he distinguishes between relative and absolute acts of the will. The latter can and need be repeated every moment. The duty of the ethically and religiously qualified individual is to will the absolute acts absolutely and the relative acts relatively. Any shirking of this obligation will result in a failure to maintain the true ethical attitude, because all relative volition is a means to some end, and the true ethical attitude is indifferent to results.[34] With existence as a period of continual striving, only choice and determination are relevant to ethical activity.

So "the decision lies in the subject" (CUP 540), and in this subjectivity there is truth. As the early Kierkegaard marked the beginning of subjectivity in the life-view of irony, a look at the textual appearances of the concept of irony and the conception of Socrates in the *Postscript* is of much significance when reading the Kierkegaardian corpus. What, then, does Climacus have to say about irony?

First, he criticizes Magister Kierkegaard's understanding of Socrates. It is important to note that this criticism is directed against Kierkegaard's (Is this the same person as the editor? Is this a serious question?) earlier interpretation that Socrates was completely negative in his relationship to the absolute and therefore did not become the fullness of subjectivity. But this does nothing to undermine the concept of irony itself, which is not what Climacus wants to do. Socrates is still considered an ironist, but this ironist is now portrayed as a subjective ethicist with religious leanings.

Climacus elaborates on irony in the *Postscript*. One relatively small part of his discussion includes the rather mysterious assertion that irony is the boundary zone between the aesthetic and the ethical spheres of existence, with humor cited as the boundary zone between the ethical and religious spheres (CUP 448). This is immediately problematic in that the manifestations of irony are so heterogeneous that, on the account one finds in Climacus, it is possible for an ironist to be an aesthete, an ethicist, or a person whose existence brings faith to view and who stands on the frontier of the religious realm.[35] In the case of the ethical and/or religious individual, irony must execute an infinite movement, which in *The Concept of Irony* was spelled out as considering the totality of existence—not the particularities—*sub specie ironiæ* (CI 271). With a more careful eye to the ethical, Climacus describes irony as

> the constant placing of the particularities of the finite together with the infinite ethical requirement, thus permitting the contradiction to come into being. Whoever can do this with facility, so that he does not permit himself to be caught off guard by any relativity where his skill is shy, must have executed the movement of infinitude in his soul, and in so far it is possible that he is an ethicist [CUP 448–49].

"It is possible that he is an ethicist," but this is not necessarily the case. An additional step must be made, and it is this step that the early Kierkegaard, consciously or unconsciously, did not present with regard to Socrates. This step involves maintaining an inner relationship to what is variously called "the absolute requirement," "the (infinite) ethical requirement," simply "the absolute," or "the infinite." It is therefore clear from the beginning of Climacus's treatise that irony—defined in *The Concept of Irony* as "infinite absolute negativity"—fits the form for maintaining the absolute in one's subjectivity.

> The subjective existing thinker who has the infinite in his soul has it always, and for this reason his form is always negative. When it is the case that he actually reflects existentially the structure of existence in his own existence, he will always be precisely as negative as he is positive; for his positiveness consists in the continuous realization of the inwardness through which he becomes conscious of the negative [CUP 78].

In other words, "the positive"—which Socrates may now be conceived as maintaining—is the continuous relating to the infinite, which is additionally referred to as the idea or the negative.[36] This more or less synonymous use of multiple terms and expressions shows that the nature of the infinite is extremely elusive. To cite a much needed example at this point, the possibility of death at any moment may be likened to the elusiveness of the infinite. To become conscious of this powerful thought and maintain a continual relationship to it will transform one's existence unspeakably—"into a vanishing nothing," says Climacus (CUP 76).

Climacus then raises the question directly: "What is irony?"

> Irony is a synthesis of ethical passion which infinitely accentuates inwardly the person of the individual in relation to the ethical requirement—and of culture, which infinitely abstracts externally from the personal ego, as one finitude among all the other finitudes and particularities. This abstraction causes the emphasis in the first attitude to pass unnoticed, and herein lies the art of the ironist, which also insures that the first movement shall be truly infinite [CUP 448–50].

The language of this passage may be initially puzzling to readers. The reference to irony as a "synthesis between ethical passion and culture [*Dannelse*]" has not yet found a clear interpretation in the secondary scholarship.[37] Rather than strictly defining irony, Climacus is here disclosing the necessary conditions that make irony possible. There must be the tension of individual inwardness in relation to a social culture.

A culture presents itself as being valid for all persons within it, but the subjective thinker knows better. It is the contrast between society and the individual that makes irony possible. Insofar as an individual lives and moves in a social culture and is conscious of his or her infinite inwardness, that individual travels under the incognito of irony. "Irony is an existential determination"; it is not merely an intellectual qualification involving a certain means of expression. "Whoever has essential irony has it all day long, not bound to any specific form, because it is the infinite within him" (CUP 450).

Another way to get a grip on the movement of infinitude made by the "ironic ethicist" is by contrasting it with what Climacus calls "the derelict Hegelian ethics." Hegelian ethicists reduce themselves to finitude by identifying the ethical with the state (or culture). This obliterates the inwardness of irony and the category of the "free individual," while it establishes in its place the category of race.

There is another brief passage on the spheres of existence that seems to present problems for my reading of Kierkegaard.

> Irony is a specific culture of the spirit, and therefore follows next after immediacy; then comes the ethicist, then the humorist, and finally the religious individual [CUP 450].

Based on my reading of *The Concept of Irony*, I have read irony as crossing all boundary situations and significant for each and every form of individual existence. The attempt to classify the structures of the various forms of existence into more or less rigid categories appears at times in the Kierkegaardian literature, but I do not think that it sits well with the overall implications of Kierkegaard's argument, one of which is that the spheres of existence continually overlap and interpenetrate each other. Kierkegaard's writings clearly exhibit this point.

Moreover, the repeated preoccupation with elaborating life's stages may be viewed as a Hegelian impulse sparked by Kierkegaard's close reading of *The Phenomenology of Mind*. The similarity with Hegel's project, however undesired, is present within Kierkegaard, who in his journal remarks that "everything has its particular stages with me." The possibility of reading Kierkegaard as constructing a phenomenology of stages is clearly evident in the secondary literature:

> In fact, though Kierkegaard never directly claimed any such thing, the development of the so-called stages or spheres of existence through his pseudonymous writings amounts to the construction of a new "phenomenology of spirit" alternative to Hegel's.[38]

The conclusion that one should draw is that Kierkegaard's intimacy with Hegel's writing has led him to express matters—on the surface—in a strictly hierarchical manner, while not being truly persuaded of the hard and fast gradations, as was Hegel. Hegel's influence lies deep and may be found beneath Kierkegaard's discourse that irony is mixed with culture and directly precedes the ethical stage. Although Hegel does not specifically identify irony as such, he writes about faith as inner individual and culture as outer individual, and he locates the self's completion of the stage of culture prior to becoming moral and, then, self-consciously ethical.

But the ironist, Climacus writes, is "not bound to any specific form," and Socrates, the ironist par excellence, is "an ethicist tending toward the borders of the religious" (CUP 450), who in Kierkegaard's mind ultimately becomes a Christian (PV 41; SV XVIII 105). Therefore, I conclude, first, that Climacus should never be interpreted as presenting a system of existence; and, second, that an ironist can be many things, but in the mastered sense that Kierkegaard develops, irony is fundamental to the personal life that fits the essential nature of existence.

Socrates's existence is considered as presenting an analogy to faith, and for Kierkegaard, both the ironist and the Christian always travel incognito. A further important similarity between Socrates and the Christian is that the truth is "an inward transformation, a realization of inwardness." Climacus calls this the "Socratic secret,"

> which must be preserved in Christianity unless the latter is to be an infinite backward step, and which in Christianity receives an intensification, by means of a more profound inwardness which makes it infinite, is that the movement of the spirit is inward, that the truth is the subject's transformation in himself [CUP 37–38].

Clearly, Climacus's text witnesses to Kierkegaard's recurring ruminations on the character of Socrates and his continually developing conception of the man. But it is equally apparent that the conception has not yet reached its zenith, for Socrates is now conceived as falling short of "the humorous stage."

Obviously, it is Kierkegaard, not the dead Socrates, who is experiencing difficulties, so it is apparently Kierkegaard who has not yet realized the transcendence of irony. His case for the position remains puzzling:

> Just as there is to be found in him [Socrates] an analogy to faith, so there must also be found an analogy to the hidden inwardness, only that he outwardly expressed this by means of negative action, by abstention, and in so far contributed toward helping people to become aware of him. The secret inwardness of religiosity in the incognito of humor evades attention by being like others, only that there is an echo of the humorist in the even response, and a tinge of it in the everyday mode of living, but it nevertheless requires a skilled observer to notice anything; the abstention practiced by Socrates, nobody could fail to perceive [CUP 450].

The point being, I gather, that if one's irony is not noticed, then it becomes humor. Is Kierkegaard's irony then infinitely deep?

But the ironist is conscious that one is always striving—in the process of becoming which corresponds to the infinite in existence—that the outward form is negative while the inward, in contradiction with the outward, maintains a deeper positivity. However, the inward—that is, the formless—can never be brought out in finitude, can never be communicated directly, because of the absolute distance between language and reality and between the world and one's subjectivity.

As already seen, Climacus distinguishes subjectivity from objectivity using an analogy of the "what" and the "how." The ironist is concerned solely with the "how," and it is possible that "merely by describing the 'how' of his inwardness (the ironist) can show indirectly that he is a Christian without mentioning God's name" (CUP 542).

The total impression readers gain from this Climacian text resembles the Socratic. What is characterized in the case of both Socrates and Climacus/Kierkegaard is that a negative (ironic) dialectic produces nothing whatsoever. The "result" is, in truth, a "non-result," and an ethicist who pays no attention to results can only be designated an ironic ethicist.

Consequently, the ironic ethicist (let us simply say "ironist") is impotent when it comes to communicating his ends. But it is precisely the ironic method's practice of impotence (this was seen in Socrates, and I think it holds for Christ and Kierkegaard as well) that serves to empower an individual. A conclusion from *The Concept of Irony* is also valid here: the negativity of irony frees the individual and makes existential growth possible. The same may be said of humor, which is only relatively different from irony, which itself is surely preserved in the humorist. One has only to consider Johannes Climacus.

To close this chapter on the non-philosophy of truth—or the truth of non-philosophy—is not easy. Can it be done without capriciousness? There is a handful of propositions that may be considered more or less equivalent:

Irony is subjectivity.[39]
Subjectivity is truth.
Truth is faith.
Faith is inwardness.
Inwardness is subjectivity.
Subjectivity is irony.
....
Irony is truth.

These statements return readers to the problem of reading Kierkegaard and to a specific literary problem concerning the situation of language and writing, for, somehow, taken at face value, they do not quite seem to work. Taken in a deeper, more personal sense, their effect is indeterminate and undeterminable. They call to mind two different but similar comments on the strategy of Kierkegaard's writing.

> (1) The Kierkegaardian gambit: to say by unsaying and unsay by saying. In writing. That is the deconstructive force of Kierkegaard's "indirect communication."
>
> The Kierkegaardian gambit: it can neither be accepted nor declined; but must either be accepted or declined.[40]

> (2) If you take (say) Christ's parable of the sower and the seed as an unvarnished tale, it is utterly trivial, pointless; heard and understood, it teaches the reception of the word of salvation. He that hath

> ears to hear, let him hear. Kierkegaard, bent on knowing the distance between what Christendom says and what it understands, tries to unstop its ears, to awaken the Christian by producing for him the irony, the comedy and the tragedy of his existence. Above all the irony, which is the specific for words and deeds which have the opposite of their intended effect, which mask what they seem to reveal, or produce what they were meant to avoid.[41]

The force of Kierkegaard's writing, his strategy, his irony, was not fashioned or intended for academia. In clarifying the meanings of the above propositions, one may well find an unceasing flow of things to say, although much of it, in all likelihood, cannot be properly said. A defense of a thesis of "indirect communication" will never succeed if done so directly or in a scholarly fashion. Done otherwise, the results are quite impossible to ascertain. One does best, perhaps, merely to point out the irony involved and to remember that no scientific or scholarly communication of the truth is admissible, accessible, or achievable.

Notes

1. "Philosophy and Non-Philosophy since Hegel," *Telos* 29 (1976): 75.

2. "The similarity between Christ and Socrates consists essentially in dissimilarity" (KW II 5–6).

3. The anonymous (Andreas Frederik Beck) review appeared in the German periodical *Neues Repertorium für die theologische Literatur und kirchliche Statistik*, 2, No. 1 (April 30, 1845), 44–45. Kierkegaard discusses it in a lengthy footnote to the appendix "A Glance at a Contemporary Effort in Danish Literature."

4. In accordance with the suggestions in chapter 4, I do not see any fundamental difficulty in occasionally referring to Kierkegaard certain views expressed figuratively by Johannes Climacus. Although, in general, I try to respect Kierkegaard's wish and prayer that "if it should occur to anyone to want to quote a particular passage from the books . . . that he will do me the kindness of citing the respective pseudonymous author's name, not mine" (KW XII 1 (627)), after having discoursed on the problem of language at the heart of Kierkegaard's writings which prevents both the identification of and search for an authorial point of view, and given that Kierkegaard is no longer with us and that I am not in pursuit of his historical being or, strictly speaking, his intellectual position, any overzealous, didactic concern to follow

Kierkegaard on this point might be considered the work of an associate professor or Kierkegaardologist.

5. Or, to cite Louis Mackey's more obvious example: "Reflections on Round Squares." See *Kierkegaard: A Kind of Poet* (Philadelphia: University of Pennsylvania Press, 1971), p. 150.

6. This further bit of evidence confutes Hartshorne's thesis.

7. For the seventh-century work from which Kierkegaard derives the pseudonym Johannes Climacus, see John Climacus, *The Ladder of Divine Ascent*, trans. Colm Luibheid and Norman Russell (New York: Paulist Press, 1982).

8. The interplay of irony and earnestness is so great that Robert C. Roberts describes it as the problematic "general tension between the deceit of the hypothesis and the serious intent of Climacus's project" as well as "the tension between Climacus's 'demonstration' of the truth of Christianity (in Chapter One) and the Moral, which maintains strictly the hypothetical character of *Fragments* with respect to the truth of Christianity." See *Faith, Reason, and History: Rethinking Kierkegaard's "Philosophical Fragments"* (Macon, Ga.: Mercer University Press, 1986), p. 22.

9. Ibid., p. 24.

10. In addition to Roberts's *Faith, Reason,* and *History* noted above, there are the following commentaries on the *Fragments*: Niels Thulstrup in PF 143–260; H. A. Nielsen, *Where the Passion Is: A Reading of Kierkegaard's "Philosophical Fragments"* (Tallahassee: Florida State University Press, 1983); and C. Stephen Evans, *Passionate Reason: Making Sense of Kierkegaard's "Philosophical Fragments"* (Bloomington: Indiana University Press, 1992).

11. Roberts, *Faith, Reason, and History*, p. 57.

12. Since I am unable to transcend my own understanding, I should prefer not to follow the custom of capitalizing the noun "god," for to do so usually gives the impression that one is really thinking and writing about "God" and that "God" itself may actually be disclosed in the discourse. According to Climacus, all such discourse is "capricious arbitrariness," which simply cannot transcend its own understanding. But I shall not do so consistently throughout this reading, for this might appear too shocking to some readers.

In the *Fragments* and the *Postscript*, however, Kierkegaard uses the unusual word *Guden*, a noun with a definite article. The Hongs translate this as "the god" and note that it "emphasizes the Socratic-Platonic context of the hypothesis" (KW VII 278). Therefore, I shall write of "god" in the present chapter.

Kierkegaard, incidentally, did not have to face what I imagine he would have considered a most vexing problem, because in the Danish of his day all nouns were capitalized. For example, it made no difference if one were discoursing on "the fly" (*Fluen*) or "the god" (*Guden*) for both required a capital letter. This lack of grammatical difference does not come across in the English translations.

13. *Faith, Reason, and History*, p. 64. Although Roberts criticizes this premise, he seems to get its serious import right— "the highest pitch of passionate thinking about how to live one's life results in a skepticism about the norms of self-understanding proposed by common sense."

14. Poul Lübcke, review of *Faith, Reason, and History*, by Robert C. Roberts, in *Kierkegaardiana*, 15 (1991), 169.

15. Moreover, Kierkegaard confides in his journal that "only when I write do I feel well" (DSK 52; P VII[1] A 222).

16. And that his initials are identical to Jesus Christ's is purely coincidental.

17. "Rasmus Nielsen (1809–1884) succeeded Poul Møller as professor in philosophy at Copenhagen's University in 1841. He was originally a proponent of Hegel's philosophy, but later became—under the influence of Kierkegaard—spokesman for an absolute distinction between faith and knowledge. The hearty relationship to Kierkegaard was not mutual, however, for in his papers Kierkegaard describes Nielsen as 'characterless' and like a 'weathercock'" (Poul Lübcke, ed., *Filosofilexikonet* [Dictionary of Philosophy], trans. Jan Hartmann [Stockholm: Forum, 1988], p. 390).

18. "Socratic Midwifery" has rightly been regarded as the method and purpose of Kierkegaard's whole authorship. See, for example, Taylor's *Kierkegaard's Pseudonymous Authorship*, pp. 52ff. It is important to realize, however, that if Kierkegaard is in possession of the positive as he came to see Socrates as being, he would still refuse all scholarly attempts to approach the positive or absolute, which, strictly speaking, must always reside outside the text. While I must be careful to avoid the same objection, I read Taylor's early study as providing a generally too positive account of the pseudonymous literature.

19. See *Phaedrus* 244a. Cited by Merold Westphal in *Kierkegaard's Critique of Reason and Society*, p. 86.

20. Stephen Evans rightly points out in *Kierkegaard's "Fragments" and "Postscript"* that "the contradictions he (Climacus) focuses on are not logical but existential. He is discussing the incongruity, tension, or contrast between one state of affairs and another" (p. 188).

Westphal offers a similar perspective in *Kierkegaard's Critique of Reason and Society*: "We dare not assume that Kierkegaard, speaking in a Hegelian context, must mean by 'contradiction' what we mean by it in the context of the propositional calculus, since he may well have learned from Hegel how to use the term in a variety of nonformal senses to refer to otherness, conflict, tension, and so forth (p. 101)."

21. See Gregor Malantschuk, *Kierkegaard's Way to the Truth*, trans. Mary Michelsen (Montreal: Inter Editions, 1987), pp. 20ff. This study is what I would consider a much too positive account of Kierkegaard's philosophy, particularly his theory of the stages, because it leaves little open to the reader's imagination. It is as if in discussing this basic premise, which may also be signified by the word "temporality" in the Heideggerian sense, one has hit upon Kierkegaard's fundamental ontology. Such a didactic account must certainly be viewed with suspicion.

22. One finds this idea repeated in a variety of places. For example, Anti-Climacus writes in the beginning of *The Sickness Unto Death*: "A human being is spirit. But what is spirit? Spirit is the self. But what is the self? The self is a relation that relates itself to itself or is the relation's relating itself to itself in the relation; the self is not the relation but is the relation's relating itself to itself. A human being is a synthesis of the finite and the infinite, of the temporal and the eternal, of freedom and necessity, in short, a synthesis" (KW XIX 13).

This passage clearly directs one to another problem in reading Kierkegaard and writing "after" him, for how does one come to understand and, when writing, avoid what has rightly been called the "most ironizing Hegelianese"?

23. It can be argued, however, that the frequent presentation of Hegel's dialectic as the development from a thesis to an antithesis to a synthesis of contradictory moments is mistaken. This dialectical method is more heartily embraced by the young Schelling than by Hegel, who "already in 1807 rejected the triadic scheme thesis-antithesis-synthesis as 'superficial' and 'lifeless' (and it is consequently a myth that arose during the 1830s that Hegel's dialectic was supposed to be built of this triad)" (*Filosofilexikonet*, ed. Lübcke, p. 113).

24. To say "objective knowledge" would be redundant.

25. Karl Jaspers also notes the problem of attempting to condense Kierkegaard in his comment: "Beim Referieren Kierkegaards merkte ich, dass er nicht referierbar ist" (By reporting on Kierkegaard I noticed that he is not reportable) (quoted by Walter Kaufmann in *Existentialism from Dostoevsky to Sartre* [New York: New American Library, 1975], p. 24).

26. While the general characterization of scientists and scholars as disinterested persons is accurate, nothing prevents them from raising the question of existential truth in an inward manner.

27. See my article, "Welcome to the Jungle: The Problem of Language in Kierkegaard and Wittgenstein," *Topicos*, 2 (1992), 97–110.

28. At this point Climacus's anti-Hegelianism is perspicuous as the objective, speculative philosopher's claims to truth do not necessarily

involve any action, passion, or risk. Put plainly: purely objective thinkers forget what it means to exist as human beings. They are mad—in a human sense—and if their thought is their ultimate concern they will ultimately be led to commit suicide. See CUP 273. See also Gordon D. Marino, "S. Kierkegaard: The Objective Thinker Is a Suicide," *Philosophy Today* (Fall 1985), 203–12.

29. Malantschuk, *Kierkegaard's Way to the Truth*, p. 44.

30. In his journal Kierkegaard writes: "Faith therefore hopes for this life, but, be it noted, by virtue of the absurd, not by virtue of human understanding. . . . Faith is therefore what the Greeks called divine madness" (JP 1 5).

31. *Kierkegaard, Godly Deceiver*, p. 42.

32. Although Climacus does not deal with it directly, there is, of course, a type of madness that is today classified as clinical. Friedrich Nietzsche and Louis Althusser, both of whom were officially over the edge for exactly ten years, are two fine, philosophical examples of clinical madness.

33. Niels Thulstrup, *Commentary on Kierkegaard's "Concluding Unscientific Postscript,"* trans. Robert J. Widenman (Princeton, N.J.: Princeton University Press, 1984), p. 348.

34. Climacus explains this point using an example concerning Napoleon. See CUP 356–57.

35. Here one finds a clear indication of how the spheres or stages and "boundary zones" interpenetrate each other such that to speak of them as hard and fast categories of existence is to miss the significance of the negativity of existence. The sum of individuals presents a quite mixed bunch, many of whom may most frequently exhibit aspects of divergent spheres or zones. I can hardly imagine that Kierkegaard intended for his writing on the stages to be taken as a new "phenomenology of spirit" which, as a written, propositional account abstracts from existing itself.

It is really high time that the vast majority of talk and writing about the "theory of the stages" be seen as a blatant misunderstanding. If Kierkegaard resembles Socrates in any regard it is this: he was also trying "to prevent getting on his hands a moved and believing listener, who would proceed to appropriate positively the proposition that existence is negative" (CUP 77). If existence is negative, so too are its stages: *ergo*.

36. Here my explication will in all likelihood present readers with a certain uneasiness. This witnesses to the real tension involved in commenting on Climacus's text. Imagine the difficulty—no, impossibility—of teaching it.

37. Evans interprets irony, and humor with it, not as universal existential possibilities, but as obtainable only by the relatively few members of a cultural elite. See *Kierkegaard's "Fragments" and "Post-*

script," pp. 186–92. I find his account to be a fabrication which misreads the above paragraph and ignores the practical, personal aspects of irony developed in *The Concept of Irony*, together with this work's significant fifteenth thesis.

38. Stephen Crites, *In the Twilight of Christendom: Hegel* vs. *Kierkegaard on Faith and History* (Chambersburg, Pa.: American Academy of Religion, 1971), p. 6.

39. This is certainly the most debatable of the propositions, but one which I feel Climacus implicitly supports. In *The Concept of Irony* Socrates' standpoint was classified as irony, in contrast to subjectivity which maintains a deeper positivity. (This was not without its problems, however. See p. 45 above.) Now, in the *Postscript*, this is precisely the point that Climacus criticizes in Magister Kierkegaard, and he thereby presents Socrates's standpoint as both subjectivity and irony. Nowhere does he deny the irony. Socrates's irony is therefore more than an abstract determination of subjectivity. It is subjectivity, incognito, of course.

40. Bigelow, *Kierkegaard and the Problem of Writing* (Tallahassee: Florida State University Press, 1987), p. 3.

41. Stanley Cavell, "Existentialism and Analytical Philosophy," *Daedalus*, 93 (1964), 968.

7

Training in Christian Maieutics

> Christianly understood, the truth consists not in knowing the truth, but in being the truth.
>
> S. Kierkegaard, TC 201; SV XVI 193

THE PSEUDONYM THAT SHARES the most things with Johannes Climacus is Anti-Climacus. As the names themselves indicate, these two personae belong to the same family. It is therefore fitting that this "look at the pseudonymous writings," which has centered on the Climacian texts, includes a glance at the work of Anti-Climacus.

Despite the obvious relatedness of Johannes and Anti-Climacus, the first impression the prefix "anti-" presents to readers is that this pseudonym stands in opposition to Johannes Climacus. This is partially accurate, in the sense that the positioning of Anti-Climacus against Johannes highlights the difference between the latter's not being a Christian (CUP 545) and the former's being a Christian in an extraordinary sense (P X^2 A 517).[1] However, it is inaccurate to read Anti-Climacus as being hostile toward or attacking Johannes Climacus, such as someone who is anti-abortion would act toward a pro-choice supporter. The strongest evidence here is found in the contents of the texts. I shall return to the conundrum of interpretation caused by the Climacus/Anti-Climacus pseudonyms following my examination of Anti-Climacus's text.

In the previous chapter we saw that both Climacus and Anti-Climacus share a deep appreciation of that individual, Socrates. That this is not an incidental impression but a fundamental orientation is one ostensible thesis of this reading. There are, of course, other similarities to be found in *Sygdommen til Døden*[2] (The Sickness Unto Death [1849]), Anti-Climacus's first publication, but they will not be pursued here.

Rather, the continuity of looking at the non-philosophical, and equally non-theological, approach to the truth is maintained in Anti-Climacus's second writing, *Indøvelse i Christendom* (Training in Christianity[3]). This text, which was written in 1848 but published in 1850, constitutes the second major turning point in Kierkegaard's productivity. Historically, the position of *Training in Christianity*, may be viewed as follows:

> It marks the beginning of a relentless and single-minded campaign against "Christendom," in which SK no longer takes time to discourse in detail upon ethics or Christian love or the psychology of the individual but moves steadily into an increasingly open posture of conflict with the established Church and the Golden Age notion of Christian culture.[4]

It would be wrong, however, to read the complete absence of "existential-theoretical" concerns into this writing, and the one that will be of no small interest in this chapter is the unavoidability of indirect communication in all matters Christian that is clearly developed in Part Two. Still, this writing does signify the beginning of the end (especially the theme of Part Three), which is the no-holds-barred attack on Christendom during the last year of Kierkegaard's brief life. This attack, waged in newspaper articles in *Fædrelandet* (The fatherland), Denmark's leading serious newspaper, and Kierkegaard's own publication *Øieblikket* (The Moment), "contained nothing that had not at least been adumbrated in this book" (TC xxii).

On a philosophical level, however, this text is very much in tune with *Philosophical Fragments* and *Concluding Unscientific Postscript*. Indeed, according to the Danish editors of Kierkegaard's collected works, "*Training in Christianity* is a more existential reproduction of what had already been philosophically discussed in *Philosophical Fragments*" (SV XVI 243). These points will, of course, have to be exhibited in further detail, but it is interesting to note at the outset that this work serves as a connecting link between the *Fragments* of 1844 and the "Attack" of 1855. Consequently, it is arguable that the philosophical background to Kierkegaard's criticism of Denmark's "Christian" culture was worked out pseudonymously.

In general, one approaches this text with an impulse to ask, "What is it to train in Christianity? Whose training in Christianity?" But also, thanks to the pseudonym, "Whose *Training in Christianity*?" While the first two questions must remain open for the time being, a discussion of the last one may prevent some initial confusion. The simple fact that this text is pseudonymous and presents an ideal persona in the person of Anti-Climacus does not seem to have been fully accepted by Kierkegaard's commentators. Many are those who have followed Walter Lowrie's "argument," in the first English translation, that *Training in Christianity* is a non-pseudonymous work(!) that presents one with "the essential Kierkegaard." Actually, the "argument" is non-existent (Lowrie would perhaps excuse himself as not being a professor), unless one considers that Kierkegaard, by sending a copy of the book to Bishop Mynster, was disavowing his pseudonym. For this is what one finds in Lowrie's introduction:

> It was ascribed to the pseudonym Anti-Climacus, but it is so far from being pseudonymous that he sent a copy, as he was accustomed to do with all his works, to the Bishop . . . [TC xxii].

Presumably, the idea is that if Kierkegaard is known to be the author, then the intended effect of the pseudonym is lost. A false presumption, of course.

But I shall not argue the obvious. *Training in Christianity* has Anti-Climacus as pseudonym and S. Kierkegaard as editor. This is in keeping with the strategy of the Climacian works, which were read above as exemplifying the writer/reader's nature as a third person—someone who has to mediate between existence (immediacy) and language (ideality). Thus, a reduplication of earlier analyses underlies the strategy of this text. That Kierkegaard originally thought to publish this work under his own name[5]—like the *Philosophical Fragments*—may indicate his intimacy with this text, but it does not absolve it of indirectness, nor does it eradicate the name of Anti-Climacus, "a Christian in a superlative degree—to a degree, S. K. thought, almost repulsive, almost demoniacal" (TC xxiii).

Training in Christianity, then, belongs to Kierkegaard in the legal sense, belongs to Anti-Climacus in the ideal sense, and, like his other works, belongs to the readers in the truest sense. Kierkegaard clearly understands himself in the role of the reader, particularly the reader for whom this book was written. In the "Editor's Foreword," which appears before each of the three parts to *Training in Christianity*, the editor writes:

> In this little book, which originated in the year 1848, the requirement for being a Christian is strained by the pseudonym to ideality's highest degree.
>
> The requirement must be heard, and I understand what is said as said to me alone—that I might learn to take refuge in "grace," but to take refuge in such a way as to make use of "grace" [TC 7; SV XVI 13].

Once again, the simple point of pseudonymity is to express the maieutic—and, as we shall see, Christian—practice, which, in Kierkegaardian terms, endeavors to permit readers to relate themselves to the truth freely, without violence or authoritative persuasion. The pseudonym has the effect of immediately freeing readers from the claims of the text, so that they may then enter into these claims through their own choosing.

Anti-Climacus explains the maieutic practice as the erection of a "dialectical duplexity, but with the opposite intent of turning the other person away from oneself, of turning him in upon himself, of making him free, not of drawing him to oneself" (TC 141; SV XVI 137). This effect would surely be hindered were the stringent demands of the text uttered by one Magister Kierkegaard in absolute, straightforward earnestness. And given Magister Kierkegaard's ironic beginnings, the possibility of straightforward earnestness could never shake off its character as a possibility, to which certainty simply does not apply.

As Kierkegaard's dialectic of communication (maieutics) is inseparable from his dialectic of freedom (subjectivity), so is the readers' freedom inseparable from their responsibility. It is a misunderstanding to read Kierkegaard's use of the maieutic method as an attempt either to offer readers the truth with the right hand or to show them the way to the truth with the left. This practice would be a fundamental obstruction of their personal freedom. The point of Kierkegaard's employment of ironic maieutics is not to force readers to notice the truth—although that they do is entirely possible—but, more modestly, to make them aware of their personal responsibility for their conduct toward the truth. Thus, whether persons are within or without the truth cannot be decided by the midwife without authority. The ramifications of this view[6] are quite significant. The heavy-handed Kierkegaardologist explains dogmatically how the life of the aesthete is wrong, and does likewise for the ethicist and for the individual under "religiousness A." Kierkegaard, however, does not want to decide the issue. He would rather point to the need for personal responsibility and honesty in each of these lives, and hope that individuals could come to decide the issue for themselves.[7]

A further consequence of pseudonymity, which has been seen as a sign of indirect communication, is that it frees Kierkegaard from thinking that he has obtained the result and is no longer training in Christianity but rather proclaiming this practice to others. In possession of a result, it would then be possible for Kierkegaard to become an object of faith. This possibility, however, is canceled through the maieutic method.

> If one person uses dialectical redoubling in relation to another, he must conversely use it maieutically, in order to avoid becoming an object of faith to another person or any approximation to it [TC 142; SV XVI 138].

This is, indeed, a strong reason for supposing that maieutics were never fundamentally abandoned by Kierkegaard throughout his work as a writer.

Accordingly, it seems that to speak of this and Kierkegaard's other later works as giving an "exact expression to his thought and faith" is to miss the point of his becoming a Christian. In other words, it is to make of Kierkegaard a positive thesis rather than a synthesis involved in existing. Furthermore, that Kierkegaard strove to avoid any such place of rest and repose while living appears to be the point behind his not wanting merely to take refuge in grace but wanting to do so in such a way as to make use of grace.

Nevertheless, there are significant differences between this text and those of the other pseudonyms—differences that may point to the progressive mastery of Kierkegaard's writing, a mastery of irony, a mastery of the self. The content is strongly Christological, and a prolonged meditation on biblical passages such as this does not take place in any other pseudonymous writing. In this regard, then, this text represents a transition from the pseudonymous to the veronymous writings.

Another change in this text is that the general tone becomes sharper, and the life-view contained within is expressed more concisely and plainly. This occurs for the obvious reason that the philosophical foundation of the life-view striven after by Kierkegaard had by this time been worked out in the earlier academic and pseudonymous works, writings that "were his own schooling in Christianity" (TC xx) and the writings to which one must ultimately return to plumb the depths of the compact presentation of *Training in Christianity*.

As the voice is also clearer, it is evident that were this text not pseudonymous or maieutically communicated, Kierkegaard would be left without any safe defense against what in this case would be very severe didacticism. We have already seen how he forcefully deplored all doctrinizing didactics with regard to existential truth, and it would have been unthinking of him now to forget the contradictory nature of the truth and express it in a direct fashion. So he does not seek to "express" the truth, although this position is not incompatible with attacking false conceptions of truth. Even in the veronymous writings, Kierkegaard seeks in different ways to avoid the charge of didacticism.[8]

Yet how can readers be sure that Kierkegaard would not be willing to say directly that this book presents the truth of Christianity? Does it not come frightfully close to the attempt to do so? Strictly speaking—and one must be very strict in this regard—the answer the text discloses is that when the nature of truth is Christianly qualified it cannot be directly communicated. Consider, for example, that Part Two is a reflection on the verse "Blessed is the one who is not offended by me" and that the second heading reads "A Biblical Exposition and Christian Definition of Concepts" (*En Bibelsk Fremstilling og Christelig Begrebsbestemmelse*). Could such a reading directly expose the truth? Anti-Climacus writes:

> Christ is the truth in such a sense that to be the truth is the only true explanation of what truth is. . . . [T]he truth, in the sense in which Christ was the truth, is not a sum of sentences, not a definition of concepts [*Begrebsbestemmelse*], etc., but a life. The being of truth is not the direct [*ligefremme*[9]] reduplication of being in terms of thought, which yields only being as thought. . . . No, the being of truth is the reduplication in you, in me, in him, that your, that my, that his life, approximately in the striving thereafter, expresses the truth, so that your, that my, that his life, approximately in the striving thereafter, is the being of truth, as the truth was in Christ, a *life*, for he was the truth [TC 201; SV XVI 192–93].

This passage makes it Christologically crystal clear that Kierkegaard could never in good faith claim that his writings were carried out to give a direct or positive presentation of the truth. The irony and paradoxicality of the truth would not allow him to say such a thing.

But something does get said through these significant words. Truth shines through in its absence, its negativity, in that it is nowhere to be found in these words or in the thoughts they bring to mind in a human being. The being of truth does not reside in the statement "Christ is the truth" nor in any other statement or set of propositions. According to Anti-Climacus, truth has its being in the life of Christ, not in the accounts of his life and not in the texts of the New Testament. Truth is decidedly extratextual. The irony of this text, then, is that for all the moving and disquieting things Anti-Climacus has to say concerning the truth, he does not mean that what he says is the truth. The practice of Christianity must of necessity take place outside the covers of *Training in Christianity*.

The idea that truth is not a "what" (a knowledge of something) but a "how" (a way of life and the responsibility thereof) is carried over from the non-philosophy of Johannes Climacus to Anti-Climacus. The difference is that the latter has no qualms about explicitly identifying the truth with Christ. There is a manifest agreement, however, in the significant attack on the Socratic-Platonic doctrine of recollection. Anti-Climacus writes:

> Is "truth" the sort of thing that one might conceivably appropriate without more ado by means of another person? Without more ado, that is, without being willing to be developed and tried, to fight and to suffer, just as he did who acquired the truth for himself? Is not that as impossible as to sleep or dream oneself into the truth? Is it not just as impossible to appropriate it thus without more ado however wide awake one may be? Or is one really wide awake, is not this a vain conceit, when one does not understand or will not understand that with respect to the truth there is no short cut which dispenses with the necessity of acquiring it, and that with respect to acquiring it from generation to generation, there is no essential short cut, so that every generation and everyone in the generation must essentially begin again from the start [TC 198–99; SV XVI 190–91]?

Here is also a lead-in reference to one of Anti-Climacus's central developments, "the dialectic of contemporaneity," which was appropriated from Johannes Climacus's *Philosophical Fragments*. A point that is not often exhibited, however, is that, although the importance of the ironic-maieutic method that Kierkegaard appropriated from Socrates could hardly be overemphasized, there is in Kierkegaard's account the recognition of a definite limit to midwifery when the question is one of the truth of existence. Hence the need "to master" irony. Kierkegaard repeatedly claims that there can be no teacher of existence. With reference to Socrates, who maintained an ironic ignorance and taught by saying he was not teaching, it is arguable that one might even imagine that he respected this limit, in pointed contrast to his gifted student and the Hegelian philosophizers of Kierkegaard's day. Indeed, evidence for this inclination may be found in the so-called "aporetic" dialogues, which end inconclusively without Socrates actually leading his dialogist to the truth, and thus result in the provocation that "the learner" stands outside the truth and needs to search himself more carefully.[10]

To repeat, then, the point of Kierkegaard's Socratic maieutics is to show readers their responsibility with regard to the truth. In this way readers are deceived, teased, and perplexed into seeking a relationship with the truth. But the "deception" itself (the text) cannot yield the truth or establish the relationship. At best, it can free readers (learners) from the illusion that they are not individually responsible for their lives. Kierkegaard's polemical attacks on the philosophizers, the press, the church, and the crowd were all directed toward the goal of reinstating the individual responsibility that had been lost, or "leveled," in the modern age.

Anti-Climacus's Christological focus empowers him to explain the matter of truth more unequivocally when discussing Christ's relation to Pilate. As already seen, the knowledge of the truth does not capture the being of truth. More precisely determined, the knowledge of the truth is untruth when one regards truth ontologically.

> For knowing the truth is something which follows as a matter of course from being the truth, and not conversely; and precisely for this reason it becomes untruth when knowing the truth is treated as one and the same thing as being the truth. . . . Indeed, one cannot know the truth; for if one knows the truth one must know that the truth is to be the truth, and so one knows in one's

> knowledge of the truth that this thing of knowing the truth is an untruth [TC 201; SV XVI 193].

As in the earlier Climacian writings, the focus here is on truth and not truths. Kierkegaard is conscious of the difference, and has Anti-Climacus give several examples to illuminate this (TC 203–204; SV XVI 194–95). Christendom, the Church, however, has not respected the qualitative difference between the truth as the "way" and truths as "results." Truth as the way is—if it is at all—a being, a life. There are no short cuts to obtaining or receiving the truth. Alternatively, truths in the sense of results may be acquired more quickly and without as much effort once the way has been discovered. It is not necessary to repeat long years of scientific experimentation once a result is obtained. The way may then be transferred to knowledge and passed on by learned professors in academic lectures. But, for the truth that is being, a life, lecturing or instruction is a monstrous error. For Anti-Climacus, "to impart Christianity by lecturing is very nearly the greatest possible error" (TC 202; SV XVI 194). The error of Christendom is that it comports itself as if the truth of Christianity were a result and not a way. It teaches; it preaches; it tries to give direct expression to those dimensions of truth that elude direct communication. Consequently, what is needed in order to reintroduce Christianity into Christendom is a renewed focus on the irony, the paradoxicality, the uncertainty, and the possibility of offense, all of which were the inseparable elements of Christ's life.

Readers should not forget that *Practice in Christianity* is an indirect communication which "seriously" holds that, humanly viewed, Christianity appears as "the higher madness" (TC 55; SV XVI 60) or "senseless lunacy" (TC 57; SV XVI 61), which follows "the logic of insanity"[11] (TC 58; SV XVI 62). To ignore this would make the author sound religiously doctrinizing in his provocative statements that "Christianity is the absolute" and "Christ is the absolute."[12] Even more so is his interpretation that being a Christian means being contemporaneous with Christ:

> If you cannot prevail upon yourself to become a Christian in the situation of contemporaneity with him, or if he in the situation of contemporaneity cannot move you and draw you to him: then you will never become a Christian. . . .
>
> If you cannot endure contemporaneity, cannot endure the sight

> of reality, if you are unable to go out in the street and perceive that it is God in this horrible procession, and that this is your case were you to fall down and worship him: then you are not *essentially* a Christian. What you have to do is unconditionally to admit this to yourself that above all you may preserve humility and fear and trembling with relation to what it means in truth to be a Christian. For this is the way you must go in order to learn and practice to take refuge in grace such that you do not take it in vain. And for God's sake, do not go to anyone to be "reassured" [TC 68–69; SV XVI 71–72].[13]

Kierkegaard must have been aware that his earnestness in the higher madness is off(ense)-putting when it is viewed as coming from one who knows better and is convinced of the accuracy of what he says. But since this writing is an indirect communication, in that it is internally self-negating—as signified by the pseudonym, although deeper reasons are to come—readers should see that they are responsible for their reaction to the text. In other words, the possibility of offense or belief lies in the act of reading; it lies with the existing readers. In this regard, Kierkegaard succeeds in reduplicating the possibility of offense that awaits individuals who react in one way or another to the contradictory truth of Christianity.

The non-doctrine of "the offense" (*forargelsen*) plays a momentous role in Kierkegaard's complex life-view. It was first developed in the *Philosophical Fragments* in an appendix entitled "Offense at the Paradox" (KW VII 49–54). Here Johannes Climacus shows, with the help of ordinary language usage, that all offense is an act, not an event, and a suffering. The offense is brought into existence through the paradox, which Climacus defines as the God-human (*Gud-Mennesket*) but no further, for he wished to steer clear of all Christological discourse (although he certainly did not expect to be regarded as the originator of the "new" philosophical thoughts he discussed).

In contrast, Anti-Climacus devotes much of Part One and all of Part Two in *Practice in Christianity* to searching out the implications of the offense. These ultimately entail that, with regard to Christianity, "all direct communication is impossible" (TC 123; SV XVI 121). Offense is still essentially related to the paradoxical God-human—that is, "the unity of God and an individual human being" (TC 84; SV XVI 86)—but it is now disclosed as a determination that is particularly characteristic of Christianity. Indeed, without the possibility of the offense, there is no Christianity. To remove this possibility is to remove Christ.

The pronounced importance of the possibility of offense for faith (some examples of which follow here) is repeated throughout the text. In a footnote, Anti-Climacus writes: "personality's relationship to Christianity is not: either to doubt or to believe; but either to be offended or to believe" (TC 83; SV XVI 85). Moreover, "the one who believes must, in order to come to believe, have passed the possibility of offense" (TC 102; SV XVI 101). And, conclusively, "the possibility of offense is precisely the repellent force by which faith can come into existence" (TC 122; SV XVI 120).

If to become a Christian means passing through the possibility of the offense that is posited by the paradox, then it would follow that "there is no *direct* transition to becoming a Christian" (TC 98; SV XVI 97). And if one can become a Christian only indirectly, it makes sense—within the context of insanity in which Anti-Climacus is admittedly operating—that this can be achieved only by maintaining the incognito of inwardness, a practice that could be further, if not better, designated as irony.

Although Anti-Climacus does not specifically mention irony, if his text has the status of a "sign of contradiction," which it most surely does, then this self-negating communication is ironic in the deepest sense. References to maieutics and the mention of the Socratic position in the discussion of the incognito may serve as further evidence to make this interpretation stick. Moreover, the language Anti-Climacus employs in his overall discussion of the impossibility of direct communication points to descriptive features that fit the concept of total irony—not merely the figure of speech—as it was initially, but not exhaustively, set forth by Magister Kierkegaard. As we shall see, there are some conspicuous examples: the sign of contradiction, the incognito, self-abnegation, and the superiority that allows for self-transcendence.

An additional comment on the connection between Christianity and irony: an early fragment from Kierkegaard's journal gives the impression that Christ was conceived and born in irony: "Irony, the ignorance Socrates began with, the world created from nothing, the pure virgin who gave birth to Christ—" (P 1 A 190). The point seems to be that contradictory phenomena such as these have irony as their beginning, a point that was carried over with relation to the truth of personal life in Kierkegaard's dissertation, and a point we have no reason to suppose was later abandoned by Kierkegaard.

I turn now to consider what I regard as one of the most interesting chapters of *Practice in Christianity*. Its subject matter involves what Anti-Climacus calls "the essential thought-determinations of the offense." The seven sections that follow elaborate on the specific nature of Christian communication, which is most accurately seen from the standpoint of rhetoric, a way of using language, and not from the standpoint of expressing knowledge, as would be the case in dogmatics.[14] The first section presents readers with a fine example of what might be labeled "Christological semiotics." It is entitled "The God-human is a 'sign' " (TC 124–27; SV XVI 122–25).[15]

A sign is first broadly defined as "the negation of immediacy, or a second state of being." This does not mean, however, that a first immediacy is lacking, for, to the person who does not know what a sign signifies, the first immediacy is all one sees. Someone who does not understand sign language sees only waving hands and fingers, and has not the slightest notion of what is signified. Consequently, in order to understand a sign as a sign, there must be a reflective act that determines what a sign signifies.

The "word," of course, is a sign. But what kind of a sign is it? As if in answer to this question, Anti-Climacus leaps from explaining the definition of a sign to a discourse on a "sign of contradiction." Two examples of a sign of contradiction are given: one, of the word as text; the other, of the word as Christ, the God-human. With regard to the former, a communication is a sign of contradiction when it is "the unity of jest and seriousness" or "defense and attack,"[16] such that neither term absolutely predominates (as would be the case in direct communication) and that the resultant impression of the communication is not galimatias.

"A sign of contradiction is a sign which contains in its very constitution a contradiction." The contradiction is the unity of two opposing terms that are not resolved in the sign. A text that is the unity of jest and seriousness does not directly communicate either jest or seriousness. These are communicated indirectly, and Anti-Climacus explains that "the seriousness of such a communication lies in another place, or in a second instance; it lies in making the receiver independently active—which, dialectically understood, is the highest seriousness in the case of communication." And where lies the jest? Anti-Climacus does not answer this question, but it must lie in the impression that a book gives in the first instance, where all appearances would indicate that a writer has something to communicate directly. If this jest is not present, then the highest seriousness of the maieutic method cannot be present, and it is a considerable leap to assume that Kierkegaard abandons this method—his incognito, the irony that endeavors to activate readers in their reading—at any time in his writing.

Furthermore, readers find out later that to maintain seriousness requires being "infinitely introverted, such that the introvert has nothing to do with anybody else" (TC 220; SV XVI 210). This follows the claim that "the very first condition for becoming a Christian is to be absolutely introverted" (TC 219; SV XVI 210). Anti-Climacus, later Kierkegaard, explains:

> Being thus introverted, the learner then understands, or learns to understand, what the task of becoming and being a Christian is—every moment he is extraverted is wasted, and if there are many such moments, all is lost. . . . [T]he thing that is Christianly decisive [is] that what he says applies to him in endless introversion [TC 219; SV XVI 210].

While this polemic was directed primarily against Bishop Mynster, it could apply equally to Kierkegaard himself, and could then throw into question the task of openly attacking Christendom, and also the supposedly direct self-revelation in *The Point of View*, for these were apparently focused on outward, rather than inward, concerns. One might even raise the question of whether the "attack" and the "direct report to history" make of Kierkegaard a "sign of contradiction." As a preview of a coming attraction, the argument that they do remains for my concluding holistic interpretation of Kierkegaard's writings.

The second example of a sign of contradiction presented by Anti-Climacus is the God-human. In the scripture, he finds that Christ is called a sign of contradiction (Luke 2:34—the Greek *antilego* means "to contradict or speak against") and takes this to represent the greatest possible qualitative contradiction between being God and being an individual human. In contrast, the speculative unity of God and humankind in general cancels the sign of contradiction, which "is to be another thing that stands in opposition to what one immediately is." Immediately, Christ is a simple man, and to say that he is God directly contradicts this.

Were Anti-Climacus to reduce Christianity to a single assertion, it would be Christ's implicit claim that "I am God." To all appearances, this sentence is both direct and a knowledge communication. Is this the case, or was Jesus a master of irony? Anti-Climacus may be read as affirming the latter position, since he interprets this statement as indirect; it is not "to be regarded as absolutely direct communication; for then the contradiction would *eo ipso* be removed." A summary explanation is presented in a note to the second section.

> One can easily perceive that direct communication is an impossibility, if only one will be so kind as to take the communicator into account, and if one is not so distrait as to forget Christ when thinking about Christianity. . . . If there is to be direct communication which remains direct communication, one must step out of one's incognito, for otherwise that which in the first instance is direct communication (the direct assertion) becomes in the second instance (the communicator's incognito) non-direct communication [TC 132; SV XVI 129].

And does it not follow that if direct communication is impossible for the unrecognizable God-human, who never once forsook his incognito, then this impossibility must make itself felt all the more in the communication of the follower of the sign of contradiction? It is arguable that, on this point, Anti-Climacus leans in the direction of this actually being the case, although there is a slight hesitation felt in putting Christ and his followers in a similar situation, that is to say, one where direct communication is an impossibility. My argument is that Anti-Climacus does, and must, embrace this conclusion—in effect, the secondary impossibility of employing direct communication—if the sign of contradiction is to be maintained.

Hence, when Anti-Climacus repeatedly declares "that direct communication is an impossibility for the God-human," the corollary—that direct communication is impossible for the followers of the God-human—must follow if the contradiction, the paradox, and the offense are to be maintained. (But we should note that this secondary impossibility is entirely dependent on the first and refers not to the nature of the human communicator but to the subject of his or her communication, the God-human.) That Anti-Climacus accepts the corollary is implicit in his stark criticism of the modern confusion that has turned Christianity into direct communication and thereby left out Christ—the teacher, the communicator, the God-human, the paradox. In other words, he advocates very clearly and forcefully that direct communication from pastors and professors does not work.

Moreover, if the follower is essentially involved in the teaching, aware that he or she exists in the communication, then there is a reduplication. And whenever there is reduplication, "the communication is far from being the direct paragraph- or professor-communication." But is it then indirect communication? Not necessarily—and here is the hitch: an additional qualification is needed.

> But the fact that there is a communicator who himself exists in what he communicates does not suffice to characterize such communication as indirect communication. If, however, the communicator himself is dialectically qualified, his own being a determination of reflection [*Reflexions-Bestemmelse*], then all direct communication is impossible [TC 133–34; SV XVI 130].

For Anti-Climacus, it is unquestionable that the God-human is thus qualified. But what about an individual human being? This he does not decide, perhaps because the necessity to maintain the vast qualitative gap between humans and God dominates his thought. Or is it perhaps a sign of concealed irony?

How does Kierkegaard understand human communicators or human beings in general? The question is not considered in *Practice in Christianity*, but in Kierkegaard's early philosophical meditations[17] we have seen that human consciousness is a determination of reflection: "consciousness presupposes reflection" (KW VII 169; P IV B 1 147–8). And of great interest in the present context is that Kierkegaard defines consciousness as contradiction (KW VII 168; P IV B 1 146). In general, we saw that the early phenomenological and entirely un-Christological considerations of "the contradiction" led Kierkegaard to reject any linguistic communication of truth (reality/immediacy). "I cannot express reality in language," he writes, "because I use ideality to characterize it, which is contradiction, an untruth" (KW VII 255; P IV B 14:6). Kierkegaard's writing thus seems to duplicate the dialectical duplexity of both human beings and the God-human.

For when the context is Christianly qualified, the author's position is surprisingly similar. Here the sign of contradiction motivates the thesis that "all direct communication is impossible." Based on Kierkegaard's phenomenology of consciousness, which he never found cause to repudiate, it is reasonable to conclude that human beings can also be regarded as dialectically qualified, particularly when they are aware of their inherent nature as a determination of reflection. Consequently, they (we) become impotent in the act of direct intercourse.

To be dialectically qualified corresponds to existing in the deeper sense, the sense in which, according to Anti-Climacus, most people do not exist. The reason that follows is this: Most people "have never made themselves existentially familiar with the thought of willing to be incognito, that is, they have never attempted and executed this thought" (TC 128; SV XVI 126). Christ's incognito was the most profound, but it is evident from the text that humans also can choose to be incognito. In the consideration of simple human relations, Anti-Climacus imagines an example of a person who is able successfully to maintain an incognito:

> He *wills* to be incognito; he wants presumably to be recognized, but not *directly*. Still there is nothing that happens to him such that he is not recognized directly for what he is, because it is, of course, his own free decision. But precisely here lies the secret: most people have no notion about the superiority over oneself. And the superiority over oneself in willing to be incognito such that one appears much lowlier than one is, that they do not suspect at all [TC 128–29; SV XVI 126].

The way one masters oneself or transcends oneself in superiority is through self-denial. Here Socrates serves as the example—"that in order to will the good in truth one must avoid the appearance of doing it" (TC 129; SV XVI 126)—for in the service of the good he stresses the need to maintain an incognito, an unrecognizability, and this is done through self-denial. Anti-Climacus will later explain how "to be a Christian is to deny oneself" (TC 217; SV XVI 207), which leads to suffering and, quite possibly, but not necessarily, martyrdom.

Incognito is unrecognizability, and this is the form that the servant of truth takes. According to Anti-Climacus, the God-human assumed this form, which, if it is true, makes him the most profound servant who has ever lived.

But Anti-Climacus also suggests that Socrates assumed this form, which is now easily recognized as irony. To be more specific, we have here a descriptive elaboration of the "mastered irony" with which Magister Kierkegaard abruptly concluded his dissertation, now carried out in terms of the most profound irony of Christ. Christian self-denial, the incognito, and indirect communication may thus be understood as the works of mastered irony, the function of which is of the utmost importance for "the personal life to acquire health [*Sundhed*] and truth [*Sandhed*]" (CI 340; SV I 330).

The deepest irony of *Practice in Christianity* is that the maieutic method of indirect communication is shown to be essential to all Christian communication—with the "whys" and "wherefores" originating in the paradox—and yet Anti-Climacus declines to say this. Instead he writes: "With respect to the maieutic method [*det Maieutiske*], I do not decide how far, Christianly understood, it can be approved" (TC 143; SV XVI 138). In this way, Kierkegaard comes across as being clearly aware of the logical difficulty involved in affirming the indirect method directly. Therefore, the maieutic method is presented maieutically. Anti-Climacus does not decide the matter. The choice lies with the readers, who are impelled by the possibility of offense with constant reference to the God-human.

For these reasons, then, we may read *Practice in Christianity* as an exercise in mastered irony, Christianly qualified. Such deep, practical irony could never be communicated directly, and thus the ubiquitous practice of indirect communication is set fast. If the complex determination of mastered irony is an accurate description for the living sign of contradiction—namely, Christ (certainly it is more accurate than the one found in Christendom)—and if a follower of Christ is one who maintains a life that resembles his as much as is humanly possible (TC 108; SV XVI 107), then would it not be possible (albeit anachronistic) to imagine Socrates, that original ironic master, a Christian? Such an imagination has Kierkegaard.

It now remains to clear up the explicit difference between the pseudonyms Johannes Climacus and Anti-Climacus, as well as to address a foreseeable objection to the significance granted the relation between irony and Christianity. Are readers (potential Christians) forced to choose—as they would be if the two names were truly contradictory—between the standpoint of the one who maintains an incognito of humor/irony and the one who is strenuously exercising in Christianity? Or are these two standpoints compatible, if not essentially related to each other? To motivate the answer to these questions, I shall consider a possible objection to my thesis.

Perhaps certain circumspect readers are shaking their heads at the conjunction of irony and Christianity, which I have argued for and tried to demonstrate from Kierkegaard's texts. As the close connection between humor and Christianity seems to be called into question in Johannes Climacus's *Concluding Unscientific Postscript*, adding irony into the equation makes matters all the more problematic. That Climacus conceives irony and humor as essentially similar is given in the text, but the possibility of conceiving irony (and humor) and Christianity together is thrown into doubt. Particularly with the following passage:

> When humor uses the Christian terminology it is a false reflection of the Christian truth, since humor is not essentially different from irony, but essentially different from Christianity, and essentially not otherwise different from Christianity than irony is [CUP 242; SV IX 227].

The implication that irony is essentially different from Christianity would seem to prohibit the interpretation of irony as an important element in the life of the Christian. Hence, this is a troublesome passage that presents problems in reading Kierkegaard. It also presents internal problems for Johannes Climacus, who is attempting to reflect the problem of becoming a Christian in a clear and decisive manner. For Climacus is a self-proclaimed humorist, and "when humor uses the Christian terminology (sin, the forgiveness of sins, atonement, God in time, etc.) it is not Christianity, but a pagan speculation which has acquired a *knowledge* of the Christian ideas" (CUP 243; SV IX 228). Climacus must realize that in his attempt to define what it is to become a Christian as a non-Christian, he directly contradicts himself, because, following his own argument, the content of his assertion must be reduplicated in his life. "For to be a Christian is something so deeply reflected that it does not admit of the aesthetic dialectic, which teleologically allows one human being to be for others something he is not for himself" (CUP 542–43; SV X 275). In his claims that he is not a Christian and the whole matter is a mere thought experiment, it is clear that Climacus has put knowledge above being,[18] which—as Anti-Climacus would say—is an expressly false presentation of Christianity. Were this the end of the matter, we could conclude that there is a sharp, essential difference between Climacus and Anti-Climacus.

However, it is not. Climacus is aware that his very words turn against him, and he is forced to recant the entire *Postscript* in the appendix entitled "For an Understanding with the Reader." Here we read:

> [S]o what I write contains also a piece of information to the effect that everything is so to be understood that it is understood to be revoked, and the book has not only a conclusion but a revocation [CUP 547; SV X 280].

It is in this act of revocation (of knowledge) that the possibility of Climacus's becoming a Christian lies. While he appears to be left standing at the edge of the abyss, waiting to be carried over to the decisively Christian realm, he has actually enacted the move from knowledge (thinking about Christianity, determining the difficulty of becoming a Christian) to being (acting on Christianity in order to become a Christian) in his revocation. Through this consideration any determinate opposition to Anti-Climacus is abolished.

Let us not stop here but also consider matters the other way around. When we get to the decisively Christian Anti-Climacus, is he essentially different from his predecessor? Is he without an incognito? Obviously not, for Anti-Climacus is an incognito for one who speaks of the necessity of being incognito whenever one endeavors to present the truth of Christianity. Moreover, as we have seen above, Anti-Climacus faces the same impossibility of directly defining what it is to become a Christian. Therefore, I conclude that Johannes Climacus and Anti-Climacus are truly brothers in the same family of thought (against thought) and that Kierkegaard does not force readers to choose between them but allows them to complement each other in a most illuminating way.

How, then, shall readers resolve the tension between irony[19] and Christianity? Are they essentially distinct or essentially conjoined in Kierkegaard's writings? Given the evidence of a holistic reading of the texts, my argument is that the latter holds true. But here readers must understand that I am speaking of irony in the broad—persuasively expressed but not ostensibly defined—Kierkegaardian sense, which I should call "existential irony." This is not romantic irony. Thus, I should not claim that irony-in-general is linked with Christianity. Kierkegaard's irony is lived; theoretically expressed, it is a paradigm for self-transcendence. It is not always called by name, but it may be recognized in the ideas (and deeds) of contradiction, incognito, inwardness, silence, subjectivity, and, ultimately, offense (for the ironist appears haughty and superior[20]).

According to Johannes de Silentio, irony is practically "everything that is based on the premise that subjectivity is higher than actuality" (KW VI 111). This is admittedly very general, but, in addition, de Silentio mentions that the New Testament praises irony, "provided that it is used to conceal the better part," and he provides one biblical example in the text and one in a passage deleted from the final copy of *Frygt og Bæven* (Fear and Trembling) of 1843. The former example suggests Jesus as a teacher of irony:[21] "When you fast, anoint your head and wash your face, that your fasting may not be seen by men" (KW VI 111). The latter reads as follows:

> One of the gospels tells the parable of two sons,[22] one of whom always promised to do his father's will but did not do it, and the other always said "No" but did it. The latter is also a form of irony, and yet the gospel commends this son [KW VI 253].

In this we recognize the Socratic maxim quoted by Anti-Climacus: put briefly, "to do good without appearing to do so." These examples may be used to show that irony is not foreign to Christ, Christianity, or becoming a Christian.

It is in the meanings that Kierkegaard continually lends to the word that "existential irony" becomes a fundamental aspect of Christian faith—not the least of which is his ultimate conception of Socrates as a Christian. Kierkegaard's conception of Socrates and irony are, for all practical purposes, one, as they undergo similar modifications and elaborations throughout Kierkegaard's writings. "Existential irony" is then broader than the conception reached in *The Concept of Irony.*[23] It is a life-view (*Livsanskuelse*)—the operative word being "life," for it is an entire existence, a form of life. Contrary to Climacus's presentation in the *Postscript*—which, to be fair, is ambiguous[24]—it is more than a boundary zone or phase through which one passes. And contrary to certain Kierkegaardologists, it is not a concept that is important only to the early Kierkegaard but not to the more mature writer. Here Kierkegaard's journal supports this interpretation. In as late as 1854—the year before his death—Kierkegaard writes that his "whole existence is the deepest irony." He continues in the same entry to speak of Socrates, a pagan who comes closer to being a Christian than do the "Christians" in Christendom (cf. DSK 127; P X^5 A 133).

> What did Socrates' irony actually consist of? Could it be certain terms and terms of speech or such? No, these are mere trifles; maybe virtuosity in speaking ironically? Such things do not constitute a Socrates. No, his entire life was irony and consisted of this: while the whole contemporary population . . . [was] absolutely sure that they were human beings and knew what it meant to be a human being, Socrates probed in depth (ironically) and busied himself with the problem: *what does it mean to be a human being* [DSK 128; P XI^2 A 189]?

In this entry Kierkegaard expressly affirms his similarity with Socrates in maintaining an existence of irony while tackling a more elaborate problem with the most intense irony. The problem Kierkegaard faces is that not only do people "imagine themselves to be human beings (here of course Socrates halts) but they also imagine themselves to be that historically concrete thing which being a Christian represents." As an existential ironist, Kierkegaard would strive to become a Christian outside Christendom, or, conversely, he would strive to become a non-Christian within Christendom.

I shall have reason to discourse on this relation in what follows, but it is now established that within Kierkegaard's writings there is a very significant relation between irony and Christianity.

Notes

1. It might be mentioned here that, as I read it, the argument of *Practice in Christianity* confutes the notion of ranks or levels to being a Christian.

2. According to one commentator this is Kierkegaard's "most perfect work" (Kirmmse, *Kierkegaard in Golden Age Denmark*, p. 359).

3. The recent Hongs' translation is *Practice in Christianity* (KW XX). It is peculiar that the Danish word *Christendom* (modern spelling *Kristendom*) is "Christianity" in English, while *Christenhed* (*Kristenhed*) is "Christendom."

4. Kirmmse, *Kierkegaard in Golden Age Denmark*, p. 379.

5. Although, for my purposes, I shall be interpreting *Practice in Christianity* as it originally appeared in 1850, that is, under a pseudonym, it should be noted that a second edition was published four and one-half years later under Kierkegaard's own name. He also retracted the "Editor's Foreword" and "The Moral" in order to be as severe as possible in his attack on the indefensible established church. For, as he says in the text, "severity is the only thing that can help a person" (TC 223; SV XVI 213). Does this mean that the text is thereby rendered absolutely direct? Not by any means. For, as we shall see, the "sign of contradiction" still lies at its heart, sustaining its status as indirect communication.

6. For this view I am indebted to George Pattison's *Kierkegaard: The Aesthetic and the Religious: From the Magic Theatre to the Crucifixion of the Image* (London: Macmillian, 1992), p. 79. Pattison explains how this view derives from Kierkegaard's "Lectures on Communication" (P VIII^2 B 79, 812–89; JP I 648–57).

7. In general, Kierkegaard's open attack during the last year of his life may seem to complicate matters, in so far as he appears to abandon the maieutic practice in order to directly impel readers out of their deluded state. Still, this should not be interpreted as an argument against the maieutic method, which remains suitable to existential truth; Kierkegaard continued to be more negative than positive, although more attention was drawn to himself. Rather, it should be seen as an acknowledgement that his readers were not yet able to appropriate the truth that is subjectivity—given that the unprecedented illusion of Christendom was so powerful.

8. Perhaps the most obvious example is found in the "edifying discourses" where Magister Kierkegaard repeats in the preface "that he is not a teacher." Johannes Climacus notes this point in his "Glance at a Contemporary Effort in Danish Literature" (CUP 244).

9. For an unknown but suspicious reason, Lowrie does not translate this word.

10. This view of Socrates is fully argued for by Gregory Vlastos in "Socrates' Disavowal of Knowledge," *The Philosophical Quarterly*, 35 (January 1985), 1–31. However, Vlastos finds reason to beg to differ with Kierkegaard (p. 30), but it is not at all clear that he has been as careful in interpreting Kierkegaard as he has been in interpreting Socrates.

11. In the original this last phrase is *Afsindighedens Sammenhæng*, literally, "the context of insanity."

12. Throughout this writing and elsewhere Kierkegaard clearly equates Christianity with Christ. Without Christ there is no Christianity, "for Christ is a person, and he is the teacher who is more important than his teaching" (TC 123; SV XVI 121).

13. I have quoted this passage at some length to enable readers to derive a more distinct impression from the text. Admittedly, Lowrie's translation using old-fashioned English pronouns and verb inflections contributes to making the dogmatics of Anti-Climacus unbecoming, no matter how much one sympathizes with the message. One further note on the original: Kierkegaard's pronominal references to Christ are lowercase, whereas the references to the reader—to "you" and "your"—are uppercase.

14. For this insight I am indebted again to George Pattison's *Kierkegaard: The Aesthetic and the Religious*, p. 87.

15. All the unnoted quotes that follow are from this section.

16. When this writing was published, Kierkegaard saw it as a sign of contradiction in this latter sense with regard to Christendom.

17. See my reading of *Johannes Climacus* in chapter 3 above.

18. Not a few Kierkegaardologists have followed, and are still following, Climacus in this regard.

19. As Climacus maintained the essential similarity between irony and humor, this tension could include humor as well. I explain below, however, that irony may be broadly conceived as the Kierkegaardian paradigm for authentic existence. To be specific, I think Kierkegaard prompts an overall impression of what could be called "existential irony," which has both humor and mastered irony as elements.

Explaining humor and Christianity involves a closely related problem, but it is also evident that humor is a fundamental aspect of Christianity. As in the case with irony, a reflection from Kierkegaard's journal proves relevant here: "the humorous is present throughout Christianity" (JP II 1682). Such a perspective is gathered through reading Kierkegaard holistically. That "humor itself is a fundamental aspect of Christian faith" is argued by C. Stephen Evans in his article "Kierkegaard's View of Humor: Must Christians Always Be Solemn?" *Faith and Philosophy*, 4 (April 1987), 176–86.

20. "It is so that the very power of being superior ends in loss of power. Socrates possessed the power of superiority, that was why he was executed" (DSK 123; P IX A 453).

21. From Jesus's Sermon on the Mount (Matt. 6:17–18). Further examples of ironic teachings may be found in this same chapter.

22. Matt. 21:28–30.

23. Jens Himmelstrup addresses Kierkegaard's changing concept of irony in his *Terminological Dictionary* to Kierkegaard's collected works:

"When Kierkegaard's real 'authorship' presents a rather different view of the concept of irony, it is due to the following heterogeneous relation:

"In Kierkegaard's dissertation ethical seriousness was only possible within a totality. Therefore irony, which removed the subject from the totality, was without seriousness. After the category of 'that individual' was constituted more and more, actual seriousness is only first possible in that individual. And on the other hand: when Kierkegaard, as he now does, expressly says that irony does not exclude seriousness, such a pronouncement must obviously also be seen in the light of Kierkegaard's own changed conception of the ethical foundation of what ethical seriousness is.

"But at the same time there also occurs, however the causal relation is, a change in the conception of Socrates. There is room for a much warmer, deeper, and fuller conception of Socrates. And as now Kierkegaard, for both historical reasons and because he continually understands irony as also an actual spiritual standpoint, must protect Socrates as an ironist, there also occurs a widening of his concept of irony" (SV XX 106–107).

24. For example, how can irony be both a boundary zone (prior to the ethical stage) and the incognito of the ethical individual? And compare this discussion with the one at the end of the treatise, where Climacus uses irony more generally to express a keen attentiveness to the "how" of communication (CUP 543; SV X 275).

PART THREE

The Veronymous Writings

8

The "Indirectness" of the Signed Writings*

> It is with the subjective thinker as it is with a writer and his style; for he only has a style who never has anything finished, but "moves the waters of language" every time he begins, so that the most common expression comes into being for him with the freshness of a new birth.
>
> Johannes Climacus, CUP 79; SV IX 74

> The most interesting reading is the one where the reader himself is productive to a certain degree.
>
> Judge Wilhelm, SV III 21

> People would rather have direct communication as assurance and insurance; it is so comfortable, and most comfortable, that it thus amounts to nothing.
>
> S. Kierkegaard, CD 115; SV XIII 109

When readers turn to Kierkegaard's veronymous writings, are they supposed to suspend the possibility of irony? Shall they forget the unforgettable—that these discourses were written, that they were not dictated by God? Or shall they not speak of them as literature, fearing the truth that "there is no literature without a suspended relation to meaning and reference?"[1] This chapter will show that these writings are not intended to be so direct or straightforward that they are closed to individual interpretation.

---

*An earlier version of this chapter was first published as "The Indirectness of Kierkegaard's Signed Writings," in the *International Journal of Philosophical Studies*, 1 (March 1995), 73–90.

Quite the contrary, they are explicitly textual discourses, in which the goal of the indirect, maieutic method remains valid, as they accordingly petition the personal appropriation of each single reader. This chapter will attempt to show that all of Kierkegaard's writings are indirect in the primary sense of not wishing to speak to the reader directly, as from one person to another, from an "I" to a "you," but to have each reader communicate in private with her- or himself, from an "I" to a "me."

For the many who wittingly or unwittingly privilege the pseudonymous writings, it must be asserted at the outset that these veronymous writings are not so authoritative, didactic, or pious that one should be disinclined to read them carefully, not to mention reading them aloud.

Specifically, my aim here is to show that Kierkegaard's signed writings may be read as ironic instances of indirect communication. My argument is twofold. First, I shall endeavor to show that the commonplace distinctions between the aesthetic and the religious writings and the direct and the indirect writings, no matter how helpful to academics, ultimately fail Kierkegaard's readers. In their place I shall propose a weaker but more accurate distinction between the pseudonymous and the veronymous writings. Second, a careful reading of the various prefaces signed by S. Kierkegaard supports the view that the maieutic method is not abandoned in these works. In general, I want to suggest that edification is possible only through indirect communication.

Failed Dichotomies and a Renewed Distinction

Kierkegaard's body of literature is so complex and multifarious that one is persuaded to create a new word in order to provide an accurate overall description of it. To this end I have coined the word "veronymous,"[2] in the hope that readers will find this genuinely useful in describing Kierkegaard's writings, and not an awkward eccentricity. Let me explain why.

That there exists a certain bipolarity in Kierkegaard's writings is well known, but the terms that are usually used to describe it can be misleading, if not inaccurate. Readers who approach Kierkegaard without the presuppositions of mutually exclusive binary oppositions are in a better position to judge the nature of a given text and its overall impression than are those who do not, for the commonplace oppositions between (1) the "aesthetic" and the "religious" writings and (2) the "indirect" and the "direct" writings ultimately fail Kierkegaard's readers in two crucial respects. First, they have the effect of prescribing the way in which a given text is to be read. Second, they often work to describe in advance what is to be found in the reading (a seduction, Kierkegaard's own opinions, etc.). Consequently, matters may be simplified considerably, and unnecessary presuppositions avoided, with the plain, factual distinction between the pseudonymous and the veronymous writings.[3]

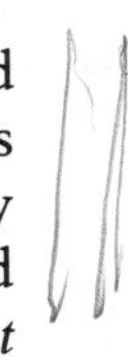

The problem with the distinction between the "aesthetic" and the "religious" writings is that each one of Kierkegaard's texts contains aesthetic and religious elements such that it can earnestly be approached both aesthetically and religiously. Kierkegaard recognizes as much when, a year after he composes *The Point of View*, he writes in his journal under the heading "On My Authorship Totally":

> In a certain sense it is like a choice; one must choose either to make the aesthetic the central thought [*Totaltanke*] and so explain everything in that respect, or the religious. Precisely herein lies something revitalizing [P X^2 A 150].

Regardless of Kierkegaard's own individual choice, a textual both/and must be present in order for there to be a reader's either/or. (Kierkegaard obviously recognized this point when he wrote *Either/Or*, and to claim that he forgot it when he wrote *The Point of View* would need explaining.)

Based on Kierkegaard's own classification of his writings in *The Point of View* (SV XVIII 85), it is commonly held that the aesthetic writings are those written pseudonymously and the religious ones are those authored by S. Kierkegaard. (What about the earliest veronymous writings, most notably *The Concept of Irony*, which Kierkegaard fails to mention?) Understandably, Kierkegaard's English translators have followed their author in this regard and promulgated what has become the received interpretation (there are aesthetic writings and there are religious writings), which has been so prevalent that it would be too time-consuming to cite all the writers who have followed suit. Not until deconstructive and rhetorical readings of Kierkegaard appeared in the 1980s have the implications of this distinction come under question. While a clear-cut distinction between the aesthetic and the religious writings no doubt makes it easier for associate professors (*docenter*) to teach Kierkegaard—a dubious task at best—it obscures a very basic impression borne out in the reading, namely, that the workings of "aesthetics" and "religiosity" are inextricably intertwined and coexist in every Kierkegaardian text. Indeed, Kierkegaard considered himself a religious author from the start, and the pseudonymous productivity as his "training in Christianity," such that to consider the pseudonymous works as absolutely aesthetic (as, most recently, Hartshorne attempts to do, without success[4]) would be a serious interpretive mistake. To consider the veronymous works as absolutely religious is equally erroneous.

What, then, are we to make of the meanings of "the aesthetic" and "the religious" in the claim that each posture is embraced by the Kierkegaardian text? In short, they may be broadly conceived as having to do with "perceiving" (*aisthetikos*) and "believing." Accordingly, Kierkegaard is writing to perceive in the aesthetic works, and he writes to believe in the religious ones. Thus, in order to observe the phenomena better, he strives to put himself at a considerable distance—the distance of double reflection—from the pseudonymous writings, while he affirms his "active belief," a working toward his personal faith, in the veronymous ones. In turn, each reader is then implicitly asked to follow the movements of reflective perception and active belief.

With precisely these meanings,[5] however, the sharp distinction within Kierkegaard's overall activity as a writer between the aesthetic productivity and the religious productivity becomes blurred, for there exists a movement toward faith in the pseudonymous writings and an endeavor to perceive a most beautiful sight, the love of God, in the veronymous writings. Furthermore, as we shall see, the distance established through the maieutic method, the ironic detachment of our author, is just as evident in the veronymous writings as it is in the pseudonymous ones, which means that each reader is individually responsible for bearing the meaning of any given text. The idea implied by Kierkegaard's choice of his first pseudonym, Victor Eremita, remains valid throughout the authorship: readers "must win through to an understanding of the text in solitude, without the support either of authorial guarantees or of the received opinion of fellow readers."[6]

Another point is that both "sets" of writings are characterized by the reflective sensitivity of an aesthete. Although one could maintain that dialectical concept analysis is somewhat less prevalent in the veronymous writings (it is not found in Kierkegaard's prayers, for example), it is certainly not absent. Each kind of writing is equally limited by its textuality. A religious writing cannot express the immediacy of faith (the immediacy after reflection)—or it does it as well as an aesthetic writing expresses the immediacy of, say, "the sensuous genius" (*sandselig Genialitet*)[7]—for it is always carried out in language, in reflection. Therefore, it is arguable that, in significant respects, both aesthetics and religiosity are found within each of Kierkegaard's writings,[8] an argument that serves merely to strengthen what is impressed in a primitive reading of the texts.

One could also attribute a less abstract meaning to the aesthetic/religious distinction. If by an aesthetic writing one means a text strictly devoted to romantic or speculative themes, and by a religious writing one devoted to biblical or theological themes, then the distinction still does not work, for these distinctive themes have the facility of appearing where they will, irrespective of their particular authors. I shall consider some examples.

Either/Or ends with an "Ultimatum," which is explicitly religious, and its religiosity is not different from the life-view developed in the first *Two Edifying Discourses* (1843). Consequently, the very first of Kierkegaard's edifying discourses is "The Edification Implied in the Thought that as Against God We Are Always in the Wrong," which appears in the Chinese puzzle-box of texts edited by Victor Eremita. Here we may also note that the significance of this pseudonymous editor also applies to Kierkegaard himself, for we learn later that he is a hermit who apparently thinks himself victorious in living in a "religious" monastery (cf. SV XVIII 90).

Fear and Trembling strikes a decisively religious note and has the character of Abraham, the father of faith, as its central focus. *Repetition* also focuses on a biblical character, Job. Obviously, religious themes lie behind the aesthetic lyricism of these writings.

Furthermore, if one were strict in the distinction between the aesthetic and the religious writings based on the usage of pseudonyms, then Vigilius Haufniensis's *The Concept of Angst*[9] and Anti-Climacus's two publications would have to be considered as merely aesthetic writings. Surely this would be a gross misrepresentation of "dogmatic reflections on original sin" and other specifically Christian analyses, which is why not a few commentators have wanted to claim that these writings—particularly those by Anti-Climacus—should be regarded as non-pseudonymous, by which they mean absolutely religious. More examples could be given, but one starts to get the point that, ultimately, the either/or of the aesthetic/religious distinction does not work when applied to Kierkegaard's writings.

Clearly it is not difficult to see that the religious is represented in the aesthetic. This is, of course, what Kierkegaard argued in *The Point of View*, while realizing full well the need for textual demonstration:

> I do not believe in assurances with respect to literary productions. . . . If, in my capacity as a third party, as a reader, I cannot establish on the basis of the writings themselves that things are as I claim them to be . . . then it would never occur to me to attempt to win a battle which I would have to regard as lost [SV XVIII 87–88].

In that the religious is represented in the aesthetic, Kierkegaard's argument is cogent, but it only goes halfway in showing that the distinction between the aesthetic and the religious is not intended to be taken as absolute.

No matter how forcefully the "posthumous Kierkegaard" privileges the religious over the aesthetic, it is still an exaggeration to claim that "Kierkegaard himself has in a most energetic way criminalized the aesthetic and devalued it to a marginal note in the authorship's great text."[10] While I shall show in the conclusion how the privileging of the religious in *The Point of View* need only be interpreted as a part of the authorship's great text, my present interest lies in seeing how the aesthetic is represented in the religious.

A close grammatological look at the original Danish texts provides indisputable evidence of the presence of the aesthetic in the religious—and quite literally at that. The single word that Kierkegaard designates as the outstanding characteristic of Christ is *Forbillede*, which may be rendered into English as "model," "pattern," or even "prototype."[11] In Part Two of *Judge for Yourself!*, for example, Kierkegaard discourses on "Christ as the Model or No One Can Serve Two Masters." Another striking discussion of "Christ as the model" is found in Part Three of *Practice in Christianity*, a work that, quite significantly in the present context, was the only one of Kierkegaard's writings to be published both pseudonymously (1850) and veronymously (1855). In considering Christ as the perfect "model," Kierkegaard endeavors to make clear the point that a follower of Christ does not admire him—"there verily was not the least thing to admire" (TC 234; SV XVI 223)—but instead strives to imitate him: "Christ is the model, and to this corresponds 'imitation' " (TC 237; SV XVI 226). Specifically, one would seemingly be called to imitate Christ's "existential irony"—his "will to be unconditionally: Nothing" (SV XVII 196), his absolute self-annihilation—for this is surely reminiscent of the ironist's "infinite absolute negativity."

Kierkegaard's veronymous writings are thus focused on perceiving, on better beholding the "model" (*Forbillede*) of Christ, and it is significant that Kierkegaard can also speak without compunction of the *Billede* (image or picture) of Christ as motivating the imitative response. Hence, the well-known passage in *Practice in Christianity* where a child is shown a picture of Christ on the cross for the first time and then told the story of Christ's life (TC 174f.; SV XVI 168f.). The visual image of the crucifixion and the narration of the humiliation of Christ—two principal forms of the aesthetic—have a profound effect on the child and continue to move him throughout his life, until he ultimately wishes to imitate the image he retains from his childhood. When older and mature he wishes

> only one thing, to suffer in some measure as He suffered in this world, which the philosophers always have called the best of worlds, but which nevertheless crucified love and cried *Viva*! to Barabbas . . . [TC 178; SV XVI 171].

In such a way the aesthetic is present in the religious, and this is by no means communicated directly to readers, for only through the author's narration of a story told to a child (a triple reflection) are readers led to behold Christ through the eyes of a child. Therefore, only through aesthetic, indirect means does Kierkegaard work to communicate the religious truth of Christianity. The case for the role of the aesthetic in Kierkegaard's theological thinking is summarized nicely by the Danish scholar Joakim Garff:

> That the aesthetic is repeated in writings which Kierkegaard himself classifies as specifically religious directs attention to the point that it is precisely iconography's *mimesis*, i.e., its metaphorical or aesthetic representation of Christ, which transforms itself in the young person's imitation, his *imitatio Christi*. By representing this picture the iconography gets the young person to want to repeat it, for he is, as Anti-Climacus notes, "solely occupied with wanting to resemble this picture. And it exercises its power over him; his whole inwardness is transformed little by little . . ." (SV XVI 183). That the picture's exercise of power is the re-presentation's mimesis, which transforms itself in an imitatio, exposes with other words how the aesthetic [picture: *billede*] is active in the religious [model: *forbillede*]. An aesthetic surface has been given transforming significance for the "inwardness."
>
> Thus, it is not for nothing that it is only the little difference of a prefix between the picture [*billede*] and the model [*forbillede*]. That Kierkegaard nowhere comments on this difference himself, perhaps conveys in itself "the most beautiful evidence" of how aesthetic he imagined the religious.[12]

For all these reasons, the reader can clearly perceive the failed nature of the absolute dichotomy between the aesthetic and the religious.

What, then, are the problems with the second generally accepted distinction, that between direct and indirect communication?[13] What is misleading here? I shall once again consider the subject of the relationship between direct and indirect discourse, but from a slightly different angle.

What is the difference between direct and indirect communication? Are they as distinct as is generally assumed? In an interesting recent study entitled *Kierkegaard: The Aesthetic and the Religious: From the Magic Theatre to the Crucifixion of the Image*, George Pattison explains how the relationship between direct and indirect communication is much more intimate than is usually perceived. As far as Kierkegaardology is concerned, this is a rather novel view. Consider a passage from the chapter entitled "The Dialectics of Communication":

> The Kierkegaardian apostle, then, despite the vocabulary of "authority" which encompasses him, does not occupy a safe house, immune from the complex and problematic dialectics of communication. This situation is, on the contrary, extremely complex

> and dialectical and his message is disturbingly direct-indirect. Its directness (its claim to divine authority) means that we cannot comfortably dismiss it as a literary game, a thought-experiment (and, in this respect, it is quite distinct from the altogether indirect communication offered by the pseudonyms). On the other hand, its indirectness (its "failure" to substantiate its knowledge element) means that we cannot evade our responsibility for interpreting it the way we interpret it. The authority of the apostle does not therefore overrule the freedom of the recipient of the message. The communication of the paradox expects and requires the full activity of the freedom and interpretative responsibility of the recipient (as is also the case with the indirect communication contained in the pseudonymous authorship).[14]

Here Pattison leads one in the right direction, for it is initially important to be made aware of the indirect nature of the veronymous discourses, so that one may later grasp its deep significance. But Pattison does not go far enough, for he seemingly wishes to maintain an element of directness that is altogether lacking in the writings signed by Kierkegaard.

Perhaps the greatest confusion resides in the awkward, oxymoronic designation "the Kierkegaardian apostle." Given the state of the modern world, a world that Kierkegaard would call "leveled" (which means approximately what we mean today when we speak of our "postmodern" world), the religious apostle cannot directly express him- or herself as such; and cannot be known as an apostle, for the claim to divine authority cannot be legitimized. Kierkegaard does not hesitate when speaking of Paul as a Christian apostle, yet nowhere does he seem prepared to accept any modern-day apostles, although he does not thereby deem it absolutely impossible that such a person could appear.[15] Clearly, Kierkegaard himself is no Kierkegaardian apostle, for there is no direct claim to divine authority within his project.

Quite the contrary, he repeatedly denies any possible misreading by strictly maintaining that he is "without authority." This designation serves as a clear characteristic of a given work's indirectness, for by claiming his lack of author-ity Kierkegaard absents himself from his veronymous texts, such that he "is no more directly present in the text of the religious discourses than in the case of the pseudonymous works (or, to put it another way, there are comparable structures of absence)."[16] Even when the "vocabulary of authority" cannot be altogether avoided in the veronymous writings, Kierkegaard makes sure that it gets expressed under the incognito of irony—the jest of earnestness.

To begin again, but more simplistically, what do we usually mean by the terms "direct" and "indirect" communication? In the first instance, the meanings of direct and indirect discourse are determined by grammar. These are quite easy to understand. Grammatically, indirect discourse involves statements about what another person has said. Kierkegaard's use of pseudonyms signals indirect discourse in this sense, which means that the statements within a pseudonymous text are said by another person. As indirect discourse, Kierkegaard himself must say, "He says so and so," even though a pseudonym can still speak in the first person. But whether Kierkegaard agrees or disagrees with these statements cannot be decided by the simple fact that they are indirect. When Kierkegaard relates that "in the pseudonymous books there is not a single word by me" (KW XII 1 [626]), he is stating not that he disagrees but simply that they are meant to be understood as being by other personae.

On the other hand, in a direct discourse, Kierkegaard chooses to assert, "I say this." While this may reduce some of the personal distance between the writer and his work, the use of his own name does not, in and of itself, entail that irony is absent or that the words Kierkegaard uses are direct representations of the meanings he is after. The grammatical structure does not prevent direct discourse from being "indirect" in a deeper sense, which could more appropriately be called "ironic" in a broad sense, since this fits well with Kierkegaard's overall Socratic strategy. In this sense, there is a suspended relation between meaning and reference, essence and phenomenon; and, as Magister Kierkegaard would have it, such a ubiquitous suspension allows for the mastery of irony within the writer's own actuality.

Therefore, with application to Kierkegaard's writings, the meanings of direct and indirect communication may be summarized as follows:

	Grammatical Meaning	*Deep Meaning*
Pseudonymous Writings	Indirect	Indirect/Ironic
Veronymous Writings	Direct	Indirect/Ironic

In general terms, one may question whether irony and indirect communication are equivalent, but in the case of Kierkegaard it is useful to conceive of an equivalent relation, for his indirect method of communication (deep meaning) can be understood as being determined by his conception of irony and, what is practically equivalent, his conception of Socrates. This style of communication by one whose "existence was the deepest irony" (DSK 128; P X^5 A 133) could, then, arguably be called ironic communication, for if Kierkegaard is trying to will the good, he certainly does it without his readers' having any conscious knowledge of it. The pervasiveness of irony runs throughout all of Kierkegaard's writings, and we shall see below how it is expressed in selected edifying texts.

For the reasons explained above, by replacing the aesthetic/religious and direct/indirect distinctions with the admittedly weaker, but more accurate, pseudonymous/veronymous one, the reader should not be misled into regarding the veronymous writings as lacking in indirectness or irony.

Edifying Prefaces: Hopeful Superfluity by S. K.

> State-of-mind and understanding are characterized equiprimordially by *discourse*.
>
> Martin Heidegger, *Being and Time*[17]

I shall now consider the general nature of the first veronymous writings to appear after the early academic ones. These are the *Opbyggelige Taler* (Edifying Discourses), published in six books, in groupings of two to four discourses, during 1843 and 1844. The first edition of the collected eighteen discourses was published in 1845.

First, what is a discourse? Unlike its modifier, the translation of the Danish word *Tale* as "discourse" has been agreed upon by both the old and the new English translators. More common translations of *Tale* include "speech," "oration," "address," "conversation," and "talk."[18] *Tale* is also a verb meaning to speak or talk, and it may thus be compared to *logos*. But this should hardly prompt any hesitation as to the appropriateness of "discourse," a word that etymologically is particularly suggestive. The prefix dis- points to a separation, such as, for example, between the speaker and the speech; and a written dis-course may be said "to run away" from itself, which is a rather clear suggestion of a "suspended relation between reference and meaning." As it were, both the Danish and its English equivalent are more commonly understood as significations of oral communication. Quite reasonably then, Kierkegaard explains in one of the seemingly "insignificant"[19] prefaces the significance of reading aloud. Specifically, his words seek

> that favorably disposed person who reads aloud to himself what I write in stillness, who with his voice breaks the spell on the letters, with his voice summons forth what the mute letters have on their lips, as it were, but are unable to express without great effort, stammering and stuttering, who in his moods rescues the captive thoughts that long for release [KW V 53].

In a journal entry describing the reasons for his rather unique method of punctuation—which translators have never hoped to reproduce in translation—Kierkegaard indicates that he is particularly interested in "the architectonic-dialectical phenomenon that the eye sees the structure of the sentences which at the same time, when one reads them aloud, becomes their rhythm" (DSK 48; P VIII[1] 33). Such a keen awareness of the manner of writing and an ear for the reading of the reader lead Kierkegaard to visualize the reader reading aloud all that he writes.

What does the emphasis on reading aloud say about the interpretation of Kierkegaard's writings? In general, it is evidence of the view that language and a certain use of language are determinative of a certain way of thought. Thought is dependent on language, not vice versa. Kierkegaard is interested in rhythm and mood, aspects of language that are intensified through the vocalization of the written word, which then become factors of thought. As explained earlier, for Kierkegaard, existence (immediacy, being) cannot be directly expressed by language; it cannot be captured by thought. (Recall Johannes Climacus's words: "The only thing-in-itself which cannot be thought is existence, and this does not come within the province of thought to think" [CUP 292].) Words are universal but moods are not. Thus, is it not possible that the successful creation of a mood can, indirectly of course, come closer to expressing the ineffable as it relates to each individual in particular? If so, then could we not view the call to be read aloud as an important feature of the method of indirect communication, in which the reader is given the opportunity to create a complex of meaning by breathing life into the words of the text? Indeed, such an explanation is plausible, for our author does not explain, expound, describe, or demonstrate the mood, and yet through a very careful style of writing he hopes to make it possible for readers to communicate to themselves what could not be said in the text. Consequently, writing to be read aloud is another facet of indirect communication, which, in turn, may be viewed as an integral part of Kierkegaardian edification.

Readers may then wonder what Kierkegaard would have thought about translating his writings into dozens of foreign languages. While he does not specifically consider the possibility, his emphasis on writing to be read aloud points to the impossibility of translating the total expressiveness of a Kierkegaardian text. The peculiarity of his punctuation and the vocal vibrations of the guttural Danish language simply cannot be captured in translation. It seems that, at best, the rhythm of the Kierkegaardian text is altered by translation; at worst, it is lost altogether. If we then consider how this rhythm contributes to the thought of a piece, we can only question the validity of the understanding that is acquired through a translation. Still, even though one can learn to read the original text, it would not be without great effort, years and years of practice, that in reading aloud one could hope to come close to reproducing the rhythmic pronunciation of a native Danish speaker. (Perhaps reading aloud with a mouthful of porridge would be of some help![20])

Kierkegaard does not give up in later years the idea of writing to be read aloud; instead, he reaffirms its significance. The preface to *Dømmer Selv!*[21] (Judge for Yourself!), dated August 1, 1851, reads:

> My dear reader! Read, if possible, aloud! If you do this, let me thank you; if you not only do it yourself, but induce others to it, then let me thank each one particularly, and you again and again! By reading aloud you will receive the strongest impression that you have only to do with yourself, not with me, who am "without authority," nor with others, which would be a diversion [KW XXI 3; SV XVII 51].

Here the significance of reading aloud is given a more explicit interpretation. Not only do readers who read aloud re-create the rhythm and mood of a text, but also, in so doing, they focus their on their individual responsibility for what transpires in the reading. Through the act of reading aloud one "brings the cold thoughts into flame again, transforms the discourse into a conversation" (KW V 231), albeit a conversation with oneself.[22]

In such a way, each reader can be addressed in particular, for Kierkegaard knows that he cannot hope to edify readers in general. "Above all, generality is not for edifying, because one is never edified in general, any more than a house is erected in general" (KW V 276). Therefore, readers are enjoined—although without authority—to have nothing to do with the author (S. K.), which, again, makes the idea of direct communication appear quite inappropriate here. Kierkegaard's text is a meager offering, where the reader is the "temple box," which "sanctifies the gift, gives it meaning, and transforms it into much" (KW V 107). Consequently, if this is the primary import of reading aloud—to change a faded old mite into a shiny new penny—then perhaps using a translation when the original is inaccessible is not so bad after all, for all reading (unto edification) is itself an act of transferral, of translation.

Each of the six prefaces contained in *Eighteen Upbuilding Discourses* begins identically with a parenthetical comment on the book's title. Each little book

> is called "discourses," not sermons, because its author does not have the authority to *preach*, "upbuilding discourses," not discourses for upbuilding, because the speaker by no means claims to be a *teacher* [KW V 5, 53, 107, 179, 231, 295].

The affinity with certain pseudonymous authors—particularly Johannes Climacus—strikes one straightaway in Kierkegaard's disavowal of any pedagogical authority. From the word Go, the *Edifying Discourses* are thus cast in an indirect light, as the ironic writer subtracts any presumed author-ity. From the start of his veronymous productivity, Kierkegaard is emphatically "without authority," such that, even in relation to these discourses, he is to be regarded as "a reader of the books, not as the author" (KW V xv; SV XVIII 69).

The reasoning behind the distinction between a discourse and a sermon needs to be fleshed out, however, because, as it stands, it gives the false impression that, practically speaking, a sermon is something higher than a discourse. While it is true that Kierkegaard points to the sermon as something higher, he does this to express in an uncharacteristically non-polemical way the virtual impossibility of the sermon as a form of communicating Christianity. Kierkegaard should not be read as saying that, in general, pastors do something higher than he does with his upbuilding discourses. No, he implies that this is a misunderstanding, for he is not comparing himself to pastors whose sermons "constitute a form of communication in complete discord with Christianity" (DSK 180; P X³ A 59). Surely he could compete on their level as a sermonizer, a preacher, but he must admit to falling well short of the ideal of the sermon, and he thus concedes to writing mere edifying discourses (KW V 489; P X⁶ B 145). As a direct communication of the contradictory truth of Christianity, the sermon is so high indeed that it is an impossibility for an individual human being. This is what Kierkegaard wants to suggest, and precisely this is missed or ignored by the many Kierkegaardologists who speak of the sermon as something higher. In his day, as far as is discernible, Kierkegaard did not think that anyone had the authority to preach or teach regarding matters existential or Christian.[23] Thus, the effect of his work in the field of edification is the abolition of the sermon as an acceptable form of Christian communication. No apostles, no sermons; in matters of communication the master to be imitated is Socrates, and the method to be called upon is irony.

In a similar fashion, the distinction between "edifying discourses" and "discourses for edification" rests upon the one between the writer as learner and the writer as teacher, respectively. Kierkegaard never grew tired of disclaiming the role of teacher in either his pseudonymous or veronymous writings.[24]

In this way, one rightly perceives an important methodological agreement between the pseudonymous writings and the edifying discourses. Not surprisingly, then, the first preface continues in a very Climacian vain: "This little book . . . wishes to be only what it is, a superfluity, and desires only to remain in hiding" (KW V 5). The concealment of our author even when he signs his own name is a further indication of his "existential irony."[25]

I have reflected above on the term "discourse" (*Tale*), but what do readers initially make of the designation "edifying" (*opbyggelige*)? The Hongs have preferred the term "upbuilding" to "edifying," for reasons given in a lengthy note to *Eighteen Upbuilding Discourses*. Here they suggest that the word "edify" will sound off-putting to readers of English, but, in their view, what is worse is that it "lends itself readily to an ironical tone" or "occasionally has an ironical touch" (KW V 503). From the point of view of the present inquiry, this is particularly striking, since I am arguing for the interrelatedness and interdependence of irony and edification, such that the dichotomy between the ironic writings and the edifying ones must also ultimately fail.

Because my interpretation sees the interpenetration of the methods of irony and edification in Kierkegaard's overall productivity, I shall prefer the use of "edify" over "upbuild," and thank the Hongs for pointing out the potential irony that lurks behind this word. I do not actually object to the use of "upbuilding," although I should not think that this word and the Danish *opbyggelig* are completely free from annoying connotations. For, concerning the latter, is it not likely that a certain negative view would have been found among the cultured Danish public, when one remembers the repulsion Hegel felt toward the term and how influential his writings were in Denmark? Regardless, what is more significant with respect to Kierkegaard's writings is that once it is understood that the possibility of the offense is essential to Kierkegaard's Christianity, it seems ludicrous to wish to avoid being put off.

One further point: if a prominent contemporary American philosopher[26] can use "edifying" to designate a salutary kind of philosophy—knowing full well that if "edifying" is off-putting to the general reading public (an exaggeration) it would certainly be considered much worse by academic philosophers—then I should hardly think that this word needs to be avoided at all costs. What we have here is actually a good example of the Kierkegaardian view that the individual reader is ultimately responsible for both the mood and the meaning of a given text, for in and of themselves the terms "edifying," "upbuilding," and *opbyggelig* are neither disconcerting nor distasteful.[27]

Another important, repeated feature of the prefaces to the *Edifying Discourses* is Kierkegaard's reference to "that single individual [*hiin Enkelte*] whom I with joy and gratitude call my reader" (KW V 5, 53, 107, 179, 231, 295). Within the field of

Kierkegaardology, the "category" of that single individual has taken on enormous proportions, but what is surprisingly missing is a thorough critical account of the earliest mention of this epithet. So it is said that Kierkegaard originally had his ex-fiancée Regine *in mente*, but what really incites one's wonder is how the sheer contingency of this situation would come to leave its mark on most of the future writings. Moreover, one rarely hears of Kierkegaard's serious misgivings, for after reflecting on his first mention of "that single individual, my reader" he actually objected to its implications and chose to have the reference removed. A journal entry records what happened.

> Quite curious, I must say. I had decided to change the small preface to the "Two Sermons," because I somehow felt that it concealed a certain spiritual eroticism, and because it is so extraordinarily hard for me to give myself so calmly that the polemic contrast is not pointedly present. So I rush to the printing shop. What happens? The compositor intercedes for this preface. Though I laughed a little at him I thought to myself: "So let him be 'the single individual,' my reader." In my joy about this idea I first decided to have only two copies printed and present one of them to the compositor. There was really something fine in seeing his emotion. A compositor who, one would think, gets even more bored with a manuscript than the author himself [DSK 49; P IV A 83]!

What Kierkegaard recognizes here is that writing for "that single individual whom I with joy and gratitude call my reader" implies only one reader. Perhaps he did have only one reader in mind when he made the first reference in *Two Edifying Discourses* (1843)—which certainly does conceal a spiritual eroticism—but on the verge of publication became aware of the wrong-thinking involved in such a reference, and sought to have it changed. Unfortunately, the compositor, probably trying to save himself the extra work of changing the text, convinced Kierkegaard to allow the type to stay as set. As it remains, then, the singular references to "the reader" prompt a suspicion on the part of many of today's readers, for these references would seem to entail a defined essence, such as when we write: "The square is a closed plane figure."

Does Kierkegaard's "that single individual" (*hiin Enkelte*) present an abstraction that exists only as an idea and invokes an essentialist posture? While it does seem very likely that Kierkegaard idealized his reader from time to time—even after, to his credit, wishing to change the reference—the intimate way in which he continuously refers to "the reader" throughout the authorship seems calculated primarily to bring his readers into a close relationship with the text, such that an abstraction seems to be precisely what he wishes to avoid.

As I see it, there are two preeminent interpretations of the reader who is "that single individual." First, Kierkegaard wishes to stress the freedom and responsibility of each reader, such that by focusing on the unknown individual reader Kierkegaard is privileging the subjective reading over the objective book. In the preface to *Tre Taler ved taenkte Leiligheder* (Three Discourses on Imagined Occasions), published the day before *Stadier paa Livets Vei* (Stages on Life's Way) in 1845, Kierkegaard implies that the person whom he calls his reader is one who would understand what is involved in the edifying words of Johannes Climacus, "truth is subjectivity," for a correlate of this statement is given here as "the meaning lies in the appropriation" (SV VI 245). To elaborate: the meaning of a book lies in the appropriation of the reader. "Therefore *the book's* happy *submission*," writes Kierkegaard. However, he also adds that the dialectic of appropriation is such that appropriation is even greater, given the *reader's* victorious *submission*.

The second level of meaning to "that single individual" is that Kierkegaard is addressing himself. This comes forward in the preface to the posthumously published *Judge for Yourself!*:

> I address myself to the single individual [*den Enkelte*], every individual, or to everyone as an individual; if it pleases God all would read, but everyone as an individual.
>
> If every individual does as I have done when I wrote, locks his door and reads for himself, fully convinced of the truth that I have not even in the slightest degree thought about writing to tread too closely to him or speaking to others about him, since I have only thought about myself; if he thus reads as an individual, then it does not in the slightest degree occur to him to think of others rather than himself; then I certainly do not need to fear that he would be mad at me for this communication [KW XXI 191; SV XVII 127].

Obviously, for Kierkegaard to remain consistent with his own suggestion, he need only think of himself, not authors or others, when he reads the "contemporary efforts in Danish literature."

Further evidence that Kierkegaard understood himself as designated by this noncategorical epithet is given in his choosing the term *den Enkelte* as his epitaph.[28] This is a deeper indication that Kierkegaard understood himself primarily as a reader of his works, such that his own subjective reading would take precedent over any literal interpretation of his own writings.

The consideration of one additional preface will also demonstrate, like those previously discussed, that the veronymous text is far from being direct in the sense of a straightforward communication of knowledge. This preface belongs to *Kjerlighedens Gjerninger* (Works of Love [1847]). Additionally, a deliberation on this work's subtitle and Kierkegaard's reflections thereupon will provide concrete evidence that the act of irony has been committed in this important text.

In short, Kierkegaard's *Works of Love* cannot communicate love; they cannot even describe it. Before even getting to the body of the text, Kierkegaard admits that one cannot describe "works of love," for they are *essentially* indescribable. The Danish word translated as "describe" is *beskrive*, which has the root *skrive* (write) preceded by the prefix *be*, which makes the verb transitive. Literally, then, *beskrive* means "to write about some object," but the object Kierkegaard has before him exists essentially as that about which one cannot write, that which cannot be put into words, that which defies language. Works of love—to say nothing of love itself—defy language because they are inexhaustible (*uudtømmeligt*) and cannot be grasped by the written word. In other words, works of love cannot be directly communicated.

The subtitle reads "Several Christian Deliberations in the Form of Discourses" (*Nogle christelige Overveielser i Talers Form*). Although the form itself (part of the "how") would seem to suggest a close affinity to the edifying discourses, Kierkegaard writes a piece called "The Difference between Edifying Discourse and a Deliberation" in his journal of the same year. While the distinction may look good on paper, there can be disagreement as to whether it comes across unequivocally in the reading. Many an edifying discourse sounds like a deliberation, and may even be called a deliberation internally—for example, the edifying discourses "The Expectancy of Eternal Salvation" and "He Must Increase; I Must Decrease" (See KW V 254–5, 279). Thus, one should hesitate to accept this distinction as hard and fast, for there is clearly a deliberative quality to be found in the edifying discourses.

Then Kierkegaard proceeds to indicate that "a deliberation ought to be a 'gadfly,' " and "irony is necessary here" (JP I 641; P VIII[1] A 293), which presents readers with explicit textual evidence that Kierkegaard recognizes irony as an important ingredient of the veronymous writings. Specifically, it is necessary within all "Christian deliberations," which could also be edifying discourses, for they are intended to precede and motivate action. That irony is necessary within Christian writings is anything but surprising when one recalls the Anti-Climacian point that if a work is to be considered Christian, or as progressing toward a Christian life-view, then it must be mindful of the person of Christ, and the sign of contradiction must lie at its heart.

In conclusion, a close reading of the prefaces signed by S. K. accentuates the inapplicability of the term "direct communication" to describe these works. It also points to the irony of edification—that irony is a part of edification and that one can only hope to edify from the vast distance of ironic detachment.

Notes

1. Jacques Derrida, *Acts of Literature*, ed. Derek Attridge (New York: Routledge, 1992).

2. As noted above, this will be useful in distinguishing between the writings Kierkegaard signed with his own name and those he did not, without giving the impression that the former are works of "direct communication."

3. Even if this distinction were used as the ultimate means of classification, there would still be problematic cases. Three of these have already been noted: (1) Kierkegaard conceived of publishing *Philosophical Fragments* veronymously, (2) he considered publishing *The Point of View* pseudonymously, and (3) uniquely, *Practice in Christianity* was published both pseudonymously and veronymously.

4. See chapter 5 above, "Are the Pseudonymous Views Completely Bogus? On Hartshorne's *Kierkegaard: Godly Deceiver.*"

5. There are obviously other meanings and shades of meanings for these words, but I think that "perceiving" and "believing" come close to capturing what Kierkegaard signifies when he speaks of his "aesthetic" productivity and "religious" productivity (see SV XVIII 85). What else

might he mean by "aesthetic" in this context? Surely he makes use of a narrower, Baumgartenian sense of the word (which would apply to essays such as "The Immediate Stages of the Erotic or the Musical Erotic" in volume 1 of *Either/Or* and *The Crisis and a Crisis in the Life of an Actress*), which is well defined in the *Dictionary of the Danish Language* (Ordbog over det Danske Sprog) as "pertaining to a person's philosophy of life, as this is determined by the fact that the person exclusively or to a great extent values life's various relationships on the basis of their possibility of evoking a strong feeling of pleasure, enjoyment, and the like" (quoted by Hartshorne in *Kierkegaard: Godly Deceiver*, p. 5). But this sense of the aesthetic—valuing phenomena from the point of view of beauty or enjoyment—would hardly seem to describe accurately the contents of volume 2 of *Either/Or*, parts of *Stages on Life's Way, Fear and Trembling, The Concept of Angst*, and *The Sickness Unto Death*. It is more likely the case that when referring to his "aesthetic" productivity, Kierkegaard, a scholar of ancient Greek literature, has in mind the original and more general meaning of *aisthetikos*, "perceiving," from *aisthanesthai*, "to perceive," in which he would seek to express the propaedeutic nature of the pseudonymous works, which enabled him to "perceive" the problem of his authorship as it manifested itself in the process of his writing, for as he was well aware, it was not preconceived.

6. Pattison, *Kierkegaard: The Aesthetic and the Religious*, pp. 71–72.

7. See "The Immediate Stages of the Erotic," in *Either/Or*.

8. The central thesis of Pattison's *Kierkegaard: The Aesthetic and the Religious* is an affirmation of this view, namely, that "the tension between the aesthetic and the religious runs throughout virtually every line of the authorship" (p. 155).

9. This is the only work that can clearly be seen to have inspired the philosophies of the ontologist Martin Heidegger and the existentialist Jean-Paul Sartre. The former would make the distinction between Kierkegaard's "theoretical" writings and his "edifying" ones. In *Being and Time* (trans. John Macquarrie and Edward Robinson [New York: Harper & Row, 1962]), he writes: "There is more to be learned philosophically from his 'edifying' writings than from his theoretical ones—with the exception of his treatise on the concept of anxiety" (p. 494).

10. Joakim Garff, "Det aesthetiske hos Kierkegaard: dets flertydighed og dets rolle i hans teologiske tænkning" (The Aesthetic in Kierkegaard: Its Ambiguity and Its Role in His Theological Thinking), *Dansk Teologisk Tidskrift*, 55 (1992), 37.

11. Although the distinction may be slight, I think that English readers would feel that "model" gets closer to the heart of the matter, and will use this term throughout. "Pattern," however, has been preferred by Kierkegaard's English translators.

12. "Det aesthetiske hos Kierkegaard," 54.

13. It is unfortunate that the translators of the definitive English translation promulgate this distinction. For example, in the "Historical Introduction" to *Eighteen Upbuilding Discourses*, they write that "the signed discourses are from first to last direct" (KW V xi) and go so far as to include the pseudonymous works, *Practice in Christianity* and *The Sickness Unto Death*, in the category of direct communication.

14. P. 86.

15. A case in point is Adolph Adler (1812–1869), a Danish priest who in 1842 claimed to receive a personal revelation from Jesus Christ. The case provoked considerable debate, and Kierkegaard wrote a book on the subject, which is largely concerned with the issues of revelation and authority. He never published this writing, which has appeared in English under the title *On Authority and Revelation* and separately in Danish as *Nutidens Religieuse Forvirring* (The Religious Confusion of the Modern Age).

16. George Pattison, "'Who' Is the Discourse? A Study in Kierkegaard's Religious Literature," *Kierkegaardiana*, 16 (1993), 42. Here Pattison seems to come one step closer to abandoning any claim of "directness" in Kierkegaard's veronymous writings when he writes: "This paper might contribute to supporting the suggestion that his [Kierkegaard's] best works and most fruitful insights transcend this duality in such a way that even the direct is indirect, that is, that even the 'direct communication' of the religious writings turns out to be somewhat 'indirect' after all" (p. 43).

17. P. 172.

18. These are the translations found in the most common Danish-English dictionary. See Jens Axelsen, *Dansk-engelsk Ordbog*, 9th ed. (Copenhagen: Gyldendal, 1984), p. 538.

19. At least in the view of Nicolaus Notabene, who, writing at the same time as the author of the *Edifying Discourses*, writes in his "book" *Forord* (Prefaces): "In relation to a book a preface is an insignificance" (PR 17).

20. A typical Swedish response to hearing a Dane speak is "*svälj gröten*" ("swallow your porridge").

21. This text was written during 1851–52 and published by Peter Christian Kierkegaard in 1876.

22. In order to make Kierkegaard's point clear we must distinguish between silent reading, reading aloud to oneself, and speaking to another person. The ordinary opinion is that reading to oneself is silent reading, whereas reading aloud is, at least hypothetically, a way of speaking to other persons. Thus Kierkegaard's emphasis on reading aloud has usually been interpreted as giving words their proper existential power within a

public, rather than private, setting. Kierkegaard's remark about transforming "the discourse into a conversation" might seem to suggest this as well. My reading, however, views this ordinary interpretation as mistaken. It is quite clear from the last two quoted passages that the reading aloud that Kierkegaard envisions is meant to be done in private. Particularly in the last passage, where Kierkegaard writes: "By reading aloud you will receive the strongest impression that you have only to do with yourself, not with me, nor with others, which would be a diversion."

Consequently, we have to draw a distinction between reading aloud to oneself and reading aloud to others, for there is surely an important difference. Consider the difference in reading a difficult text aloud to oneself in order to grasp its meaning and appropriate that meaning for oneself, and then the following day reading the same text aloud—perhaps without thinking so much about it while doing so—to another person. Reading aloud to oneself is a more intensive way of learning and appropriating the written word. And because of the tripartite nature of consciousness, one can truly be said to converse with oneself.

23. Properly understood, Kierkegaard's anti-authoritarianism only applies to existential truth, for on this subject we are all truly learners, as no one can possess the "power to give orders and make others obey," i.e., authority, regarding questions of existence. When one speaks with authority on the authentic religious life, readers do not face a free choice, posited by themselves, but only a choice between obeying or disobeying the speaker. This is not the higher freedom Kierkegaard esteems, for he wants readers to face individually life's choices without influence or coercion. Hence, the method he practices is irony.

24. Here, again, the similarity between Kierkegaard's supposedly diverse sets of writings takes the upper hand. Consider: if the pseudonymous works are claimed to be false representations of Kierkegaard's viewpoint, then what would it have mattered for him to claim being a teacher when he meant the opposite? Or, if he pseudonymously claims that he is not a teacher, then is he to be understood as being one? If so, then this would conflict with the claim of the veronymous writings that he is not to be understood as a teacher. The point is that the wall erected by Kierkegaardologists between Kierkegaard's "indirect" and "direct" writings is made of paper.

25. An existential irony departs from the classical conception in that it does not wish to be revealed to the wise and discerning reader, but rather to remain forever in opaqueness. Consider a "secret note on the secret" found among Kierkegaard's papers: "After my death no one shall find in my papers (this is my consolation) a single piece of information on what has actually made up my life, nor find the writing in my most inward being that explains everything . . ." (P IV A 85).

For this reason Kierkegaard knew that not only his writings, but his entire life, "the whole machinery's scheming secrecy would be studied and studied" (P VIII[1] A 424). In an article entitled "The Machinery's Scheming Secrecy," a Danish couple—a parson and a psychiatrist—have attempted to solve Kierkegaard's mystery by arguing that Kierkegaard, like Doestoevsky, suffered from epilepsy. Although such a hypothesis is uninteresting from the perspective of reading Kierkegaard's writings, it did prompt me to recall a passage out of Doestoevsky's *The Idiot* (trans. Constance Garnett [New York: Bantam Books, 1958]), which shares an illuminating similarity to Kierkegaard's note: "It's life that matters, nothing but life—the process of discovering, the everlasting and perpetual process, not the discovery itself, at all. But what's the use of talking! I suspect that all I'm saying now is so like the usual commonplaces that I shall certainly be taken for a lower-form schoolboy sending in his essay on 'sunrise,' or they'll say perhaps that I had something to say, but that I did not know how to "explain' it. But I'll add though that there is something at the bottom of every new human thought, every thought of genius, or even every earnest thought that springs up in any brain, which can never be communicated to others, even if one were to write volumes about it and were explaining one's idea for thirty-five years; there's something left which cannot be induced to emerge from your brain, and remains with you for ever; and with it you will die, without communicating to anyone perhaps, the most important of your ideas" (pp. 382–83).

Thus, what is interesting is the existential irony—that is, in the Kierkegaardian sense, the lack of desire and inability to express one's essence—alluded to by each author. To view this in strictly objective (e.g., medical) terms, however, does a grave injustice to the texts involved.

26. See Richard Rorty, *Philosophy and the Mirror of Nature* (Princeton: Princeton University Press, 1979). Rorty's explanation of "edification" is quite different from Kierkegaard's, although not therefore necessarily incompatible. He writes: "Since 'education' sounds a bit too flat, and *Bildung* a bit too foreign, I shall use 'edification' to stand for this project of finding new, better, more interesting, more fruitful ways of speaking. The attempt to edify may consist in the . . . 'poetic' activity of thinking up such new aims, new words, or new disciplines, followed by, so to speak, the inverse of hermeneutics: the attempt to reinterpret our familiar surroundings in the unfamiliar terms of our new inventions. In either case, the activity is (despite the etymological relation between the two words) edifying without being constructive—at least if 'constructive' means the sort of cooperation in the accomplishment of research programs which takes place in normal discourse. For edifying discourse is

supposed to be abnormal, to take us out of our old selves by the power of strangeness, to aid us in becoming new beings" (p. 360).

By contrast, Kierkegaard pays particularly close attention to the etymology of "edify," although he too would hardly consider it "constructive" in the scholarly sense defined by Rorty. It would no doubt be interesting to pursue the comparison between Kierkegaard and Rorty on edification, for both would agree that edifying discourse helps us to become "new beings." Although it cannot be done here, I would particularly like to raise the question of whether it is contingency or solidarity that associates their "edifying philosophies."

27. The etymology of *opbyggelig* is discussed by Kierkegaard in *Works of Love*, and will be considered in the following chapter.

28. However, this polemical epitaph does not mark his gravestone. He had also chosen these verses from a Danish hymn:

> In yet a little while
> I shall have won;
> Then the whole fight
> Will all at once be done.
> Then I may rest
> In bowers of roses
> And perpetually
> Speak with my Jesus [KW XXV 27].

9

The Love of Edification and the Edification of Love

> But let us never forget that in the midst of life's earnestness there really is and ought to be a time to jest, and that this thought, too, is an edifying observation.
>
> S. Kierkegaard, KW V 253

> Woe to the person who wants to edify without knowing the terror; indeed, he does not know what he himself wants!
>
> S. Kierkegaard, KW V 344

> Wherever the edifying is, there is love; and wherever love is, there is the edifying.
>
> S. Kierkegaard, WL 173; SV XII 208

For Orientation

We have seen how Kierkegaardian irony provides the original perspective for reading the body of literature called "Kierkegaard." Within this literature we have seen also that a more precisely determined existential irony is fundamental to any worthy human existence (recall the fifteenth thesis to *The Concept of Irony*). Concurrent with the ever-deepening non-concept of irony harmoniously runs another dominant aspect of Kierkegaard's life-view: his non-concept of edification. Without a reflection on the method of edification, a comprehensive interpretive reading of the Kierkegaardian corpus would be as incomplete as it would without a reflection on the method of irony. Consequently, the main concern of this chapter is twofold: first, to ensure that no such omission occurs; second, to understand how the method of edification takes the form of existential irony.

In the preceding chapter we saw that however hard Kierkegaard tries to distinguish between seemingly different types of writings, the dichotomies that are generated ultimately fail his readers when they are presented as the final word of interpretation. In a similar manner, the commonplace distinction between the "edifying" writings and the "ironic" ones does not work when applied to Kierkegaard's writings holistically read. In general, what is rather the case is that edification and irony together form a deeply interrelated perspective for reading Kierkegaard. While I have pointed to textual evidence of irony in the veronymous writings (and we shall see more below), it would, by contrast, present no difficulty to return to the pseudonymous works to show how they may be read as edifying. But this may be left to the readers, for they will have little doubt that this is possible or accurate—Is it not how Kierkegaard read these works?—as the movement in the pseudonymous writings endeavors to build one up as a new creation, namely, a worthy, honest human being. And, in Kierkegaard's life-view, honesty before God is undoubtedly the most crucial and necessary aspect of the Christian existence.

To pursue this view a little further, clearly the final sentence of *Either/Or* is of epigraphic effect for the rest of Kierkegaard's writings: "For only the truth that edifies is true for you" (EO II 356; SV III 324). The validity of this suggestion from an unknown parson holds for Kierkegaard throughout all the pseudonymous and veronymous texts. It highlights the centrality of edification in the act of reading Kierkegaard, for the subjective truth is constituted such that it must lead to edification if there is to be truth for the individual reader. Whether it does, however, depends more on the readers than it does on the texts. This idea is expressed figuratively in a famous passage by Georg Christoph Lichtenberg (1742–1799), that Kierkegaard used as the motto for "In Vino Veritas" in *Stages on Life's Way*: "Solche Werke sind Spiegel: wenn ein Affe hineinguckt, kan kein Apostel heraus sehen" (Such works are mirrors: when a monkey looks in, no apostle can look out) (SV VII 14).

Granted this, and given that Kierkegaard's various writings are explorations in subjective truth, it follows that there should be an edifying component to each writing. Hence the inappropriateness of distinguishing between the "ironic" writings and the "edifying" ones. Still, if there is a distinction to be made—and it should go without saying that, like all the other distinctions, this one could not endure the tension of being pushed to the realm of ultimate significance—it might be as follows. Generally speaking, much of the edifying in the pseudonymous writings is immanent, which is to say that it lies within individuals to will themselves to be built up as new persons—whereas the edifying in the veronymous writings is transcendent.

However, with the positing of the absolute paradox in the *Philosophical Fragments*, the transcendental is clearly also at hand within the pseudonymous literature, even if it is not explicitly developed. Johannes Climacus would be the last to claim that the absolute paradox is a product of an immanent thought experiment, which is, indeed, part of the irony, for it is presented as such. But he knows that his ironic project does not deduce the concept of the God in time. No, such a thought lies far from the minds of human beings; it is a product of revelation, of God's disclosure. If there is any decisive difference between the pseudonymous writings and the veronymous ones, it would be that the former culminate their existential analyses in an openness for the possibility of presupposing the need of a revelatory disclosure of the absolute. While, in contrast, the latter proceed in a way that assumes this presupposition has already been made.

As indicated, the general impression of the veronymous writings is that the work of edification is transcendent; it lies outside an individual. This is expressed in one way through the emphasis on the need for the love of God, which is, for Kierkegaard, the basis of all true edification and completely beyond our own human capabilities. To become a new creation in this context depends solely on the love of God.

Nevertheless, here again it is helpful to speak of a point of contact between the two terms rather than so sharply distinguishing them that one overlooks the transition. The immanent and the transcendent must come together in at least one sense. An individual must choose to be open to this love. The "openness" itself is understood by Kierkegaard as the love within, which might also be described as the condition, analogous to that of which Climacus spoke. Unsurprisingly, then, the paradoxical is also propounded here, for in order to be edified by love, one must first have love.

To be sure, the pseudonymous literature is an edifying propaedeutic to the veronymous texts, which are edifying through discoursing on the disclosure of the divine love of Jesus Christ, who is, *nota bene*, not always nominally present. But whether pseudonymous or veronymous, no Kierkegaardian text is directly edifying. The same principle of the ironic-maieutic method holds for the method of edification—namely, readers are responsible for freely acting on a text. It cannot work the other way around. Like the sons (and daughters) of Korah, readers need to "incline their ears to the parable, and propound their dark sayings on the harp" (Psalm 49:4).

The line of interpretation being pursued comes into seeming conflict with the non-philosophy of Johannes Climacus, for whom the edifying as a category appears as distinct from the pseudonymous writings. Kierkegaard also takes pains to distinguish the edifying discourses from the later Christian discourses. The initial distinction, however, is already present in Climacus's *Concluding Unscientific Postscript*.

> For the Christian truth as inwardness is edifying, but from this it does not follow that every edifying truth is Christian; the edifying is a wider category [CUP 229].

Clearly, Climacus is right in suggesting that we would not want to call all edifying thoughts Christian.[1] But from his argument it does not necessarily follow that the *Edifying Discourses* of Magister Kierkegaard are not decisively Christian. Because Kierkegaard places such great emphasis on the paradox and sin, this is, however, the argument he wishes to develop. Climacus lays the groundwork for the argument even before the *Christian Discourses* were conceived. To describe a contemporary effort in Danish literature, he writes:

> Magister Kierkegaard doubtless knew what he was doing when he called the edifying discourses Edifying Discourses, and abstained from the use of a Christian-dogmatic terminology, from mentioning the name of Christ,[2] and so forth; all of which is in our day commonly indulged in without hesitation, although the categories, the thoughts, the dialectical element in the exposition, are entirely those of immanence [CUP 243].

Readers can be sure that Climacus considers the *Edifying Discourses* to be within the realm of immanence, for, shortly before this quote, he had remarked how "the last four discourses took on a carefully modulated humoristic tone," which is "doubtless the sum of what can be reached within the sphere of the immanent" (CUP 241).

As is well known, immanence is the defining characteristic of what Climacus calls "religiousness A," whereas transcendence marks "religiousness B," which has its beginning in the paradoxical figure of Jesus Christ. Thus, at this point in the authorship, so the argument would run, Kierkegaard sees himself as peaking in the upper limit of religiousness A, the so-called border of humor (and perhaps with an uncertain view of the future, for he had of course intended to "conclude" his authorship with Climacus's *Unscientific Postscript*).

For all practical purposes, it is more helpful, however, to emphasize the continuity of the overall religiousness developing in Kierkegaard's writings than it is to stick to distinctions that are not borne out by the letter of the text. While the distinctions may prove useful in evaluating other texts by different authors, in the specific case of Kierkegaard, his religiousness is undeniably both edifying and Christian, immanent and transcendent, focusing on "Jesus" and "Christ."

For readers, then, it seems futile to follow Kierkegaard in his attempt to separate the edifying from the decisively Christian writings. In the first place, they all share a common literary style. Second, a look at the diverse titles and subtitles that grace the veronymous writings[3] witnesses to the virtual impossibility of conceptually distinguishing between the different yet similar writings. There are *Edifying Discourses* and *Edifying Discourses in Diverse Spirits*; *Christian Discourses*, some—specifically Part Three, "The Thoughts that Wound from Behind"—for edification (*til Opbyggelse*, a designation Kierkegaard would not accept in the earlier discourses); "Some Christian Deliberations in the Form of Discourses" (*Works of Love*); "Godly Discourses" (*The Lilies of the Field and the Birds of the Air*; or simply unqualified "Discourses," such as "God's Unchangeableness." Additionally, there are the pseudonym Anti-Climacus's "Christian Expositions," one of which, *The Sickness Unto Death,* is "for edification." All this perplexing diversity within the veronymous writings suggests the need for simplification when we read Kierkegaard's discourses as a whole. Indeed, it may even be appropriate to draw the conclusion that, for Kierkegaard, the hope of edification has a specifically Christian character.[4] That this is the case in the pseudonymous works is clear, first from their obviously propaedeutic character and then from their orientation toward the theme posed by the question of what it means to become a Christian. Thus, Kierkegaard's overall strategy is to edify his readers ironically, such that, if they perceive the irony, they will become new creations who face the choice of becoming Christians.

The way of edification is of undoubtedly great moment in Kierkegaard's production. In the recent Danish secondary literature, Anders Kingo has persuasively argued for the widening of the category of "the edifying discourse," such that it may serve as "the principle for the reading of Kierkegaard's whole authorship."[5] This thesis is compatible with my reading, but, although Kingo has rightly argued for the specifically Christian character of the edifying discourse qua category, he has erroneously stated that "the authoritative word constitutes the edifying discourse."[6] It was clear in the previous chapter how a careful reading of Kierkegaard's "edifying prefaces" dispels any superficial impression of "authoritative words."

Nonetheless, Kingo's analysis is interesting and insightful. He describes the edifying discourse as "the pseudonymous discourse's navigation mark," and sets its place in the authorship as "the authorship's doubly reflected point of orientation."[7] Kingo writes:

> The edifying discourse is the constant in the authorship. Categorically there is no development from the "Ultimatum" to "God's Unchangeableness." From first to last, the discourses conduct the same discourse on the same thing, and it is as such, as the constant, that the edifying discourse is the pseudonymous writings' point of orientation: "that to which they should come" [SV XVIII 66]. In relation to the edifying discourse the pseudonyms assume a forerunner's mission: they are to break down and do away with the time of reflection's sensual illusions and the mediation in order to afterwards let the edifying discourse speak.[8]

In order to determine concretely the constancy of the method of edification, I shall proceed by detailing what this method signifies.

Readings on Edification's Way

A. *Either/Or*

How interesting that one always hears that *Either/Or* ends with the positing of a choice, either the aesthetic or the ethical. But when we read the "Ultimatum" we find that the choice does not lie here. Rather, it involves whether or not one will be edified, whether or not one will love. Let us begin by rereading the "Ultimatum."

Kierkegaard's first published edifying discourse is entitled "The Edification Implied in the Thought that as Against God We Are always in the Wrong." This sermon also contains a brief, but significant, dialectical analysis of edification, for, in reading this text, we gather some important defining characteristics of the phenomenon.

The first of these is that only thoughts pertaining to the infinite are edifying. According to the text, finite relationships are not edifying, "for only the infinite edifies" (EO II 350; SV III 320). Thus, "to wish to be in the right" and "to find it difficult to be in the wrong" are not edifying thoughts, for these represent finite perspectives. In contrast, to delight in willing to be in the wrong expresses an infinite relationship.

The second important determination of edification may be formulated thus: There is no edification without freedom. This explains why Kierkegaard pursued a subtle ironic method in the edifying discourses. In the language of the unknown Jutland parson, if one must recognize that one is of necessity always in the wrong, then the thought is not edifying. This is because in order for the thought to be edifying, one must freely choose to recognize it. No thought is edifying if one is coerced by logic or by authority that it must be so. These are the words of the parson:

> So it is an edifying thought that against God we are always in the wrong. If this were not the case, if this conviction did not have its source in your whole being, that is, did not spring from the love within you, then your reflection also would have taken a different turn; you would have recognized that God is always in the right, this you are compelled to recognize, and as a consequence of this you are compelled to recognize that you are always in the wrong . . . . So you recognize that God is always in the right, and, as a

> consequence of this, that you are always in the wrong; but this recognition does not edify you. There is no edification in recognizing that God is always in the right, and so, too, there is none in any thought which follows from this by necessity [EO II 352; SV III 321].

The element of individual freedom must be maintained in order for one to be edified. It is also quite interesting to note that already in the pseudonymous *Either/Or*, the source of the edifying is recognized as "the love within" (i.e., immanent). Moreover,

> The thought that one is always in the wrong is the wing whereby one soars above finitude, it is the longing wherewith one seeks God, it is the love wherein one finds God [EO II 354; SV III 323].

Edification, then, presupposes love. This insight will be made explicit several years later in the *Works of Love*.

The remaining two characteristics of "the edifying" that we find in this text are closely interrelated. Edification "allays doubt" and "animates to action." Just as in *Johannes Climacus, Or, De omnibus dubitandum est*, here also it is true that the doubter cannot act. Unlike the ruminations of modern philosophy, however, the edifying silences the rumblings of doubt. The text reads:

> He is in an infinite relationship to God when he recognizes that God is always in the right, in an infinitely free relationship to God when he recognizes that he himself is in the wrong. In this way, therefore, doubt is checked, for the movement of doubt consists precisely in the fact that at one instant he might be in the right, at another in the wrong, to a certain degree in the right, to a certain degree in the wrong, and this was supposed to characterize his relationship to God. But such a relationship to God is no relationship, and it was the nutriment of doubt [EO II 354; SV III 322–23].

While it is not the case that certainty edifies—even though it is true that certainty lies opposite doubt—it is the case, according to the parson, that edification produces what might be called an inward or subjective certainty. This is, however, not such as to make one complacent and lethargic. In reaction to the Hegelian view that the edifying "lulls one into a slumber," Kierkegaard here expresses the contrary view. The edifying thought that as against God we are always in the wrong should actually inspire one to act, because it stimulates a joy to act by empowering a person in spirit.

Kierkegaard will deepen this position later by affirming that whatever edifies obliges a person to act. In the *Christian Discourses* he writes:

> But beware of the edifying, there is nothing so gentle as the edifying, but there is nothing so imperious; the edifying is least of all loose talk, there is nothing so binding [CD 179; SV XIII 164].

On the note of constancy, the Jutland parson expresses a similar thought to "the edifying as binding" when in conclusion he refers to the edifying subject of his exposition as "that beautiful law, which for thousands of years has supported the race and every generation in the race, that beautiful law, more glorious than the law that supports the stars in their courses upon the vault of heaven" (EO II 356; SV III 324). As readers will find, the edification of this "beautiful law" remains the constant subject of the veronymous writings.

B. *Edifying Discourses*

As is well known, Kierkegaard paid considerably close attention to the order of publication of his works. He strove to impress the significance of this order, which in a comprehensive reading suggests that readers are led to perceive a constant faith on a similar theme rather than to view the religiosities of the "young" and the "old" Kierkegaard as fundamentally different. One can only wonder, then, why Climacus claims that the *Edifying Discourses* represent an immanent religiousness. We need not fault him too greatly, however, for he did not have the hindsight that we have, as Magister Kierkegaard's later writings remained hidden from him. And even if his keen dialectical distinctions have a certain applicability, it is still far more useful to emphasize the overall continuity in a holistic reading, in which the weight of the whole becomes greater than the sum of its parts. In this way we see the process of development—something often emphasized by Kierkegaard—as the Kierkegaardian life-view is continually built upon as it was itself built up.

A closer look at two particular edifying discourses will show that there is a definitive break with immanent religiousness insofar as a human being's utter incapability and powerlessness in reaching God is sketched. These discourses work out the overall position that "no one is good except God" (KW V 133) and that "God in heaven is capable of all things, and human beings of nothing at all" (KW V 310). Such views must presuppose an act of the divine, a revelation, to bridge the gap between human beings and God. While there are arguably countless points of interest in the *Edifying Discourses*, this point is of central importance in reading Kierkegaard and in understanding his life-view. Therefore, let us briefly consider the first example from the text.[9]

> So let us deliberate in more detail and do our part to understand and in our deliberation[10] be captured for freedom, as it were, by the beautiful apostolic words that explain both the what and the whence in: *that every good and every perfect gift is from above* [KW V 129].

These italicized words are from the epistle of James (1:17), which is a palpable constant in Kierkegaard's edifying life-view, for he was from first to last occupied with discoursing on "the Father of lights, with whom there is no variableness, neither shadow or turning." This biblical text serves as the title and the theme of the second of the initial *Two Edifying Discourses*, which appeared approximately three months after the publication of *Either/Or*, as well as the second (the discourse under consideration) and third of the *Four Edifying Discourses*, which were published at the end of 1843. It is, significantly also, the subject of Kierkegaard's last published discourse, "God's Unchangeableness," which appeared shortly before his death.

The words Kierkegaard uses to elucidate "every good gift and every perfect gift is from above" are taken from Jesus's Sermon on the Mount: "If you, who are evil, know how to give good gifts to your children, how much more will your heavenly Father give good things to those who ask Him?" (Matthew 7:11; Luke 11:13).

The first remark to be made is that Kierkegaard proceeds his examination of this metaphorical saying (*billedlig Tale*) indirectly, which is to say in the third person, as he describes how an individual may be affected by these words. This is a literary device in the service of edification, for it gives readers the freedom necessary to be edified by the difficult thought developed within the text. That it is a difficult thought is putting it mildly, for the verse under deliberation matter-of-factly states that human beings, God's highest creations, are evil. But listeners need not despair in this thought, for it works to illuminate the vast goodness of God. Human beings are seen as needy, imperfect creations who may try to give good gifts but can never know if the gifts they give are truly good. Perhaps many of us have received gifts from fathers who endeavored to do the good, only to find out upon receiving them that their gifts did us no good at all. Thus, to omit the phrase "who are evil" from the verse hardly inspires confidence in the awesome goodness of God. That the heavenly Father is analogous to earthly fathers could actually thwart the inspiration of hope in God. Therefore, there is no actual analogy that could illuminate the goodness of God.

Thus Jesus adds the phrase "you, who are evil." This is not to "pronounce a judgment of wrath" but, rather, to express metaphorically the unfathomable goodness of God, such "that God is the only good, that no one is good except God" (KW V 133). Even Jesus refuses to call himself good. What profound irony when he says, "Why callest thou me good? There is none good but one, that is, God" (Matthew 19:17). So it is that these words result in what the apostle says—every good gift and every perfect gift is from above.

> What earthly life does not have, what no man has, God alone has, and it is not a perfection on God's part that he alone has it, but a perfection on the part of the good that a human being, insofar as he participates in the good, does so through God. What, then, is the good? It is that which is from above. What is the perfect? It is that which is from above. Where does it come from? From above. What is the good? It is God. Who is the one who gives it? It is God. Why is the good a gift and this expression not a metaphor but the only real and true expression? Because the good is from God; if it were bestowed on the single individual by the person himself or by some other person, then it would not be the good, nor would it be a gift, but only seemingly so, because God is the only one who gives in such a way that he gives the condition along with the gift, the only one who in giving already has given [KW V 134].

A human being is completely dependent on God to partake in the good. The accent weighs heavily on the transcendent side in this discourse, for absolutely all credit for the good belongs to God, who "gives both to will and to bring to completion; he begins and completes the good work in a person" (KW V 134). So it is that Kierkegaard concludes that the need for God "itself is a good and perfect gift from God" (KW V 139).

The next discourse to which I shall turn my attention is entitled "To Need God Is a Human Being's Highest Perfection." Not more than one-third of the way into this text, Kierkegaard raises some very fundamental philosophical questions.

> But what is a human being? Is he just one more ornament in the series of creation; or has he no power, is he himself capable of nothing? And what is his power, then; what is the utmost he is able to will [KW V 307]?

Or what is the highest point a human being can reach? According to Kierkegaard, "the highest is this: that a person is fully convinced that he himself is capable of nothing, nothing at all" (KW V 307).

As it were, the "hidden inwardness" resulting from an individual's recognition of his or her nothingness appears as the culmination of Climacus's "religiousness A." This lends weight to Climacus's reading, and two pages later Magister Kierkegaard restates the highest in slightly different terms. After edifying readers with the thought that "one's annihilation is one's truth," Kierkegaard writes: "To comprehend this annihilation is the highest thing of which a human being is capable" (KW V 309). In the very next line, however, this understanding deemed the highest is referred to as a "God-given good," and Kierkegaard is shortly reflecting thus:

> This is the highest and most difficult thing of which a human being is capable—yet what am I saying—he is incapable even of this; at most he is capable of being willing to understand that this smoldering brand only consumes until the fire of God's love ignites the blaze in what the smoldering brand could not consume [KW V 309].

Thus, what Kierkegaard is saying is that even the knowledge of one's nothingness or annihilation must come from God. Hence another paradox arises, for human beings are not even capable of knowing that they are incapable. Here, too, we are directed away from knowledge that is beyond our reach, and we are left to focus on what does lie within our power, namely, willing, choosing, and acting.

Consequently, the religiosity that emerges from the text hardly resembles anything we would call immanent. And the God Kierkegaard sketches is about as transcendent as possible.

> Your very greatness makes you invisible, since in your wisdom you are much too far away from man's thoughts for him to be able to see you, and in your omnipresence you are too close to him for him to see you; in your goodness you conceal yourself from him, and your omnipotence makes it impossible for him to see you, since in that case he himself would become nothing [KW V 310]!

Furthermore, "where God is in truth, there he is always creating" (KW V 325). It is God who moves, who edifies, not human beings. But in order to be edified we must be willing, be open, to let God's powers form us into new human beings. In short, to be edified we must be open to love.

C. *Works of Love*

In its essence love (*Kjerlighed*[11]) is inexhaustible, indescribable, and unfathomable. To try to bring it under reflective determinations is therefore not one of Kierkegaard's goals. He is aware of the impossibility of putting into language what is, for him, the only absolute, and he would thus rather devote his "Christian reflections" to the "works of love," although these, too, are *essentially* inexhaustible, indescribable, and unfathomable. To this degree, there is a tension present in this text that is not unlike that first encountered in *The Concept of Irony*, for it is just as problematic to write about irony, or "infinite absolute negativity," as it is to write about love, or "infinite absolute positivity." A tension such as this one, however, is fitting for this work of indirect communication, in which the meaning of the text and the resolution of the tension lie in the hands of the reader.

I have already indicated that Kierkegaard himself speaks of the presence of irony in this powerful text. Appropriately, then, after the "Preface" comes a "Prayer," which ends on a rather ironic note.

> It is certainly true that there are some acts which the human language particularly and narrow-mindedly calls acts of charity [*Kjerlighedsgjerninger*]; but in heaven it is certainly true that no act can be pleasing unless it is a work of love [*Kjerlighedens Gjerning*]: sincere in its self-denial, a necessity for love, and, just because of this, without the claim of merit [WL 4; SV XII 10]!

That love would deny itself and endeavor to go without merit may be called the irony of love, for it takes the form of an incognito and is characterized by the maieutic method in loving another. Hence, it is not surprising that love would be unapproachable through reflection, for it remains hidden, an ineffable secret. Kierkegaard begins his deliberation in the discourse "The Hidden Life of Love and Its Recognition by Its Fruits."

Commenting on Luke 6:44, Kierkegaard explains that love must be known by its own fruit. The fruits of love, however, are not obvious to the eye. Nor are they necessarily pleasant to taste, as one might imagine. Indeed, Christian love has very little in common with earthly love; it appears, rather, as its opposite.

> Christian love is eternal. Therefore no one who understands himself would think of saying of Christian love that it blossoms. No poet who understands himself would think of celebrating it. For that which the poet celebrates must contain the sadness which is his own life's mystery: it must bloom—and, alas, it must perish. But the Christian love abides, and just for that reason it *is*: for what blooms perishes, and what perishes blooms, but what *is* cannot be sung, it must be believed and it must be lived [WL 7; SV XII 14].

This admonition extends to Kierkegaard himself, a self-proclaimed "kind of poet," for it is as misguided to try to capture Christian love in song as it is to try to capture it in reflection. Christian love is hidden, and, because of its secrecy, it cannot be known or directly communicated. "For words and expressions and the inventions of language can be a recognition [*et Kjende*] of love, but that is uncertain" (WL 10; SV XII 17). Ironically and by his own standards, Kierkegaard's *Works of Love* should not be considered a "work of love." This would be a deception, because "one must not love in words and forms of speech, nor should one recognize love in this way" (WL 10; SV XII 18). Words of love may be like leaves on the tree of love, but they are not its fruit.

Furthermore, Kierkegaard explains that the essential condition for love's bearing fruit is that the eternal God has "planted the human heart." This "planting" is, however, invisible. It cannot be known or expressed in language. Therefore, to repeat: "Love must be believed and it must be lived."

Yet, *how* it is to be lived, *how* it is to be shown—and for the existential ironist Kierkegaard the emphasis always falls on the "how"—remains more than slightly problematic. Reflecting on the mystery of love, Kierkegaard writes:

> Love's secret life is in the most inward, unfathomable, and it also has an unfathomable connection with the whole of existence. As the peaceful lake is grounded deep in the hidden spring which no eye can see, so a person's love is grounded even deeper in the love of God. If there were at bottom no wellspring, if God were not love, then there would be no quiet lake or human love. As the quiet lake is grounded darkly in the deep spring, so is human love mysteriously grounded in God's love. As the quiet lake invites you to look at it, but by its dark reflection prevents your looking down through it, so the mysterious origin of love in the love of God prevents you from seeing its source; if you think you see it, then you are deceived by a reflection, as if that which merely conceals the deeper source were the true source [WL 8; SV XII 15].

There is room here for mystical reflection on the hidden source of love, but Kierkegaard does not dwell long on the mystery. On the contrary, he would not recommend such mysticism to readers, and interprets the Gospel's emphasis on "the recognition of fruits" as reason enough to leave alone the hidden source of love. Kierkegaard would rather speak of the obligation (*Forpligtelse*) to love, which is in large measure the central theme of Part One, in which Kierkegaard scrutinizes the Christian command "Thou shalt love thy neighbor" in a most careful way.

The problem of recognizing love by its own fruits is that the essential condition (*den væsentlige Betingelse*) for all love makes it impossible to know or recognize love unconditionally. As was indicated above, this is why it must be believed. For Kierkegaard, the decisive thing is how an act is performed, "but there is nothing about which it can unconditionally be said that it unconditionally proves that love is not present" (WL 12; SV XII 19). Here it becomes clear that all acts are relative to the absolute, which cannot be objectively known but must be subjectively lived.

Nevertheless, love shall be known by its fruits. But now we realize that the import of this verse is not to promote looking for love and judging others but to bear fruit. It is "spoken admonishingly to the individual (to you, my hearer, and to me), in order to encourage him not to permit his love to become unfruitful, but to work so that it may be known by its fruits, whether others do recognize them or not" (WL 12; SV XIII 19). In this manner, it is very likely that Kierkegaard's interpretation of this verse may sting readers, causing them to look inward to make sure that their hearts are sown with seeds that bear good fruit.

But as it is the God of love who plants the essential condition for there to be human love, so, too, does this eternal lover plant the ground for the edifying. At this point in the authorship, the importance of edification has acquired decisive significance for Kierkegaard's life-view. But what is involved in edification? What does it mean to edify? Let us now turn to Kierkegaard's most direct analysis of edification. This is found in Part Two of *Works of Love*, in his commentary on I Corinthians 8:1: "but love edifies."

We read that "to edify" is a figurative or metaphorical (both words translate the Danish *overført*: literally "carried over") expression, but we must first consider "what this word signifies in direct speech [*ligefrem Tale*]" (WL 170; SV XIII 204).[12] Etymologically speaking, "to edify" means "to build up." Here the emphasis is on the adverb "up," for it is the case that "everyone who upbuilds builds, but not everyone who builds builds up." This "up," then, is significant, and while it indicates some upward direction, it is not dependent on height. For example, when we build an addition to a house, we do not say that the house has been built up, even if the height of a house has been increased. We say, rather, that the house has been built onto. If, however, a house is built from nothing, from the very beginning, we say that it has been built up. The point Kierkegaard draws is that in order to build up, one must build something from scratch, which means to start from the beginning by "digging deep" to lay the foundation. Therefore, we cannot understand "building up" without its contrary depth. For this reason we say "building castles in the sky"—building without a foundation—instead of "building up castles in the sky," which would be a thoughtless use of language (WL 171; SV XII 205).

After clarifying "to edify" in its direct sense, Kierkegaard moves to its indirect, metaphorical, and spiritual sense.

> All human speech . . . is essentially metaphorical. And this is quite proper as regards existence in general, since, although from the moment of his birth man is spirit, he does not become conscious of himself as spirit until later, and so sensuo-psychically he has already lived through a certain period of his life before the spiritual awakening. But this first period will not then be discarded . . . . The first period is simply taken over by the spirit, and thus employed, thus made the foundation, *it becomes the metaphorical* [*det Overførte*]. The spiritual man and the sensuo-psychical man therefore in a certain

> sense say the same thing. Yet there is an infinite difference . . . . The one has made the transition, or has allowed himself to be *carried over* [*føre over*] to that side, while the second remains on this side [WL 169; SV XII 203].

How, then, can the metaphorical word be known? Kierkegaard continues:

> The metaphorical word is not a brand-new word; on the contrary, it is the word that is already given. As the spirit is invisible, so too is its language a secret, and the secret lies precisely in the fact that it uses the same word as the child and the common person, but it uses it metaphorically, whereby the spirit denies that it is the sensuous or the sensuo-psychical, but does not deny it is a sensuous or sensuo-psychical manner. The difference is by no means a conspicuous difference. We rightly regard it, therefore, as a sign of false spirituality to make a parade of the conspicuous difference—which is the sign of the purely sensuous, whereas the essence of the spirit is the quiet, whispering secrecy of the metaphorical—to the one who has ears to hear with [WL 169; SV XII 203–204].

This is a rich passage. That Kierkegaard denies any conspicuous difference between the sensuous and the spiritual—the aesthetic and the religious—supports the present interpretation. As we have just read that anything can bear fruit if love is present, and that this cannot be known unconditionally, so can plain words convey the secret of language that edifies an individual. Kierkegaard could have been writing metaphorically from the start, and could still be doing so. To say that there is a conspicuous difference between the words he uses here and the words he uses there presents a false distinction. "As the spirit is invisible," the matter is undecidable. What do his words whisper to you?

The figurative use of "edifying" signifies to the one who has ears to hear that love is present. For "edifying" is "exclusively characteristic of love," and "there is nothing, simply nothing, which cannot be said or done so that it becomes edifying; but whatever it is, if it is edifying, then love is present" (WL 172; SV XII 206).

Love alone edifies. As the etymology of the word indicates, to edify is to build on some foundation, but how should we understand the foundation when the word is considered metaphorically? Spiritually understood, love is the foundation of love. "Love is the origin of everything," and love builds itself up. Thus it is the case, according to Kierkegaard, that, strictly speaking, humans cannot edify one another, for they cannot implant the ground that then builds itself up. We can act as love's midwives, however, by presupposing love in another, which then makes it possible for the other to be built up in love. Kierkegaard emphasizes that:

> *the lover presupposes that there is love in the other person's heart, and just through this presupposition he builds up the love in him—on that foundation, insofar as he lovingly presupposes that it exists at bottom* [WL 175; SV XII 210].

This is a lovely saying, and yet it is a difficult one to practice. To presuppose love in another, one's neighbor (i.e., any person next to you) is to view the actions and intentions of the person as honorable and praiseworthy—always without question or judgment—and, on top of this, to deny oneself, to recognize that one is nothing and that one should not be given credit for presupposing the presupposition, for this, too, depends on love itself. To begin with the presupposition is exceedingly difficult. "One's entire labor is discounted in advance, since the presupposition from first to last involves self-denial, or that the master builder be hidden and as nothing" (WL 176; SV XII 211). Based on love's incognito, its secrecy, and the true lover's self-denial, one may be said to "love forth love [*sic*] maieutically in the other."[13]

Lovers end where they begin, with the presupposition that love is present. Kierkegaard concludes his deliberation where it began:

> To edify is to presuppose love; to be loving is to presuppose love; only love edifies. For to edify is to build up something on a foundation, but spiritually love is the foundation of everything. No person can lay the foundation of love in another person's heart; nevertheless, love is the foundation, and one can only build on that foundation; hence one can only edify by presupposing love. Take love away, then there is nothing which edifies, and no one who is edified [WL 181; SV XII 217].

The self-denial of love is its irony, and a final example of the irony of *Works of Love* is found in the closing discourse, "The Work of Love in Praising Love." This is summarized nicely by Bruce Kirmmse:

> Alluding to himself as the author of *Works of Love* . . . SK writes that the person who praises Love, for example, *could* be vain and

> selfish, or *could* be performing a work of Love. So saying, SK himself disappears maieutically before the reader's eyes, and leaves one confronted with the problem of the book, which has nothing to do with whether or not *another person* (even the author of *Works of Love*) acts out of Love, but with whether one is oneself, at every moment, loving. SK's "real" intentions in writing *Works of Love* will never be fathomable, but as a demonstration of a self-disciplined act of maieutic disappearance it is unsurpassed.[14]

And what is "self-disciplined maieutic disappearance" if not "mastered irony"? Kierkegaard is still at a distance, and it remains quite possible that his text is a deception. There is no way to decide if his motives were pure and unselfish. In this sense this is an undecidable text. Upon Kierkegaard's own calculation, the decision to presuppose that love is present, or to presuppose that it is not, is left with the reader.[15]

D. *Christian Discourses*

The year following the publication of *Works of Love,* Kierkegaard published *Christelige Taler* (Christian Discourses, 1848). Like the earlier *Edifying Discourses in Diverse Spirits* and the later "Godly Discourses," these discourses contain a deep reflection on "the lilies of the field and the birds of the air" (Matthew 6:24–34), a point in which Kierkegaard successfully blurs the distinctions between the various writings and creates the impression of a more comprehensive whole.

Of deeper significance is that already in Part One, "The Heathens' Worries," the birds and the lilies are granted the esteemed place of assistant teachers of Christianity. This clearly introduces an aspect of immanence into these Christian discourses, for consider this statement: "if you live like the lilies and the birds, then you are a Christian" (CD 13; SV XIII 16). When one considers the behavior of birds in general, however, one will certainly realize that there are some aspects of their behavior, particularly the more predatory species, which ought not to be emulated. Kierkegaard is, of course, intent on perceiving them through the eyes of the Gospel, in which their greatest attribute is given in their complete lack of concern for the morrow. In other words, they live in the present, and Kierkegaard's Christian imperative could be stated thus: Be present!

Already in Kierkegaard's first edifying discourse, "The Expectancy of Faith," he speaks of the strong and sound life as the one in which the future is conquered and a person lives in the present (KW V 17). In *The Lilies of the Field and the Birds of the Air* (1849), he goes so far as to define joyfulness as "to be present to oneself; of truly *being today*" (CD 349).

In the *Christian Discourses*, Kierkegaard describes "The Worry of Self-Torment" as being preoccupied with "the next day." The bird does not have this worry; neither does the Christian, who has conquered his spirit "by *becoming* quit of the next day" (CD 74; SV XIII 72). In an interesting passage on "the most important thing in life," Kierkegaard compares the Christian with the actor:

> The most important thing in life is to be in the correct position, to assume the correct position. This the Christian assumes in relation to the next day; for to him it is non-existent. It is well known that in front of the actor, blinded as he is by the footlights, there is the deepest darkness, the blackest night. One might think that this would discompose him, render him uneasy. But no, ask him, and thou shalt hear him admit that this is precisely what gives him support, makes him calm, keeps him in the enchantment of deception. On the other hand, it would discompose him if he could see any single individual, catch a glimpse of an auditor. So it is with the next day [CD 76; SV XIII 74].

The self-tormentors live with continual anxiety over the next day, and thus lack faith. Christians, however, are believing and live in the present, a word which, Kierkegaard remarks, also means "mighty" in "that foreign language" (Latin). "The faithful one (the present one) is in the highest sense contemporary with himself" (CD 77; SV XIII 75), something that is by no means easily achieved, but with the help of the eternal one, as Kierkegaard describes it, it is the most educating and developing position in which an individual could be. This the birds teach us.

Kierkegaard's interpretation of the lilies and the birds contains a wealth of edifying discourse, most of which need not be explicated here. In general, it would be better to leave readers alone with the text, in which event they may choose to make some of the words their own. What is significant for the overall reading of Kierkegaard, however, is the importance that "jest" (*spøg*) plays in these *Christian Discourses*, a point that Kierkegaard makes in the opening introductory paragraph.

> It was on the summit of Sinai the Law was given, amidst the thunders of heaven; every beast that approached the holy mountain (alas, innocently and unawares) must be put to death—according to the Law. It is at the foot of the mountain; so mild is the Gospel, so close is the heavenly which descends, and yet all the more heavenly for that. It is at the foot of the mountain; yea, what is more, the birds and the lilies are in the company—it sounds almost as if it were turning the thing into a jest that they come along . . . playfully. For although the seriousness becomes all the more sacred just for the reason that the birds and the lilies are in the company, yet the jest continues, and it remains nevertheless a jest that the lilies and the birds are in the company, they are in the company, and what is more they are there to teach [CD 13; SV XIII 15–16].

Thus, from the outset, Kierkegaard proclaims the juxtaposition of jest and seriousness, as he had the juxtaposition of irony and earnestness earlier. The presence of jest in seriousness, and seriousness in jest, characterizes the ironist precisely, according to Magister Kierkegaard's doctoral dissertation: "The ironist hides his jest in earnestness, his earnestness in jest" (KW II 256).

What is more, in light of *The Concept of Irony,* readers may get the unmistaken impression that the jest of Kierkegaard's writings acts as the specter of irony, for "the ironic nothing is ultimately the dead silence in which irony walks again and *spøge*[16] (this last word taken altogether ambiguously)" (KW II 258). Consequently, in the peculiar case of Kierkegaard, readers must always suspect the very likely possibility that behind the jest there lies an ironist—or should we say a religious ironist—for, according to Johannes Climacus, "the highest earnestness of the religious life is distinguishable by jest" (SV VII 223).

One can then say that the irony of the Lord may be seen in his appointing the birds and the lilies as teachers of humankind. In *Judge for Yourself!* Kierkegaard again takes jest seriously.

> You lily of the field, you bird of the air! How much we owe to you! Some of our best and most blessed hours. When the Gospel appointed you as prototype and schoolmaster, the Law was abrogated and jest was assigned its place in the kingdom of heaven; thus we are no longer under the strict disciplinarian but under the Gospel: "Consider the lilies of the field; look at the birds of the air" [KW XXI 186]!

It is clear that jest is granted a privileged place in Kierkegaard's life-view—in which case he merely believes he is following the

Gospel—and, given its close relatedness to irony, one may conclude that the distinction between irony and edification fails in another way, for each method is equally playful (*spøgefuld*) and haunted (*spøgt*) by jest (*spøg*).

The jest involved in *Christian Discourses* may also be linked to indirect communication, for it is given in using the lilies and the birds to motivate the explication of the worries of the heathen. In other words, Kierkegaard is not saying that he has uncovered these unworthy worries and is judging the heathen; he is not so direct. Rather, it is through attending to the instruction of the lilies and the birds that these worries may be adduced. Thus, one should not read any condemnation of the heathen into Kierkegaard's discourse, for the lilies and the birds do not condemn and denounce. Neither does the Gospel. The lilies and the birds are the perfect teachers of Christianity, and one learns from them because they

> do not express any opinions, look neither to the right nor to the left, neither commend nor reprove, as teachers generally do, just as he, "the teacher," of whom it is said that "he cares for no man" (Mark 12:14), so they care for no man or they care for themselves . . . . Surely one can learn from them in the very first instance what it is to teach, what it is to teach Christianly, can learn from them the great art of teaching: to act as if it were nothing, to care for oneself, and yet to do this in such an arousing, arresting, ingratiating, and as far as expense is concerned cheap way, that it is thus so moving that it is impossible not to learn something from it [CD 14; SV XIII 16–17]!

Here is the jest: the serious task of teaching Christianity is to be done by those who have no concern for teaching, those without presumption, those who cannot have their students become indebted to them. Here is the seriousness: The lilies and the birds do teach, through their behavior, by being what they are. Consequently, if Kierkegaard has any thought of wishing to follow their example, he must be carefree and playful, wishing not to condemn; and, in struggling to edify, he does not forget the importance of a smile.

Part Two of *Christian Discourses* is entitled "Moods in Suffering's Strife" (*Stemninger i Lidelsers Strid*), although it might well have been entitled "The Joy of Christian Irony," for all seven chapters discourse on the contradictions of Christian theology (e.g., "the poorer you become, the richer you can make others"; "the weaker you become, the stronger God becomes in you"; "Misfortune is good fortune"). As my primary interest is in characterizing Kierkegaardian edification, I shall concern myself only with the concept of edification that is described here.

The first chapter is entitled "The Joy in—that One Suffers Only Once, but Triumphs Eternally." Kierkegaard begins this part of the *Christian Discourses* with a brief explanation of the edifying, the inclusion of which provides evidence that he also understands these later writings as edifying discourses. Here we read that, for Kierkegaard, the edifying is actually equivalent to the good-in-and-for-itself (CD 101; SV XIII 95). This being the case, any individuals who wish to be edified must, as a prerequisite, have understood themselves. Otherwise, such individuals risk taking their personal edification in vain.

And the edifying should not be taken in vain. In its first instance, 'the edifying' is defined as "the terrifying" (*det Forfærdende*).[17]

> Where there is nothing at all terrifying and no terror, there is nothing at all edifying and no edification. There is forgiveness of sin, that is edifying, the terrifying is that there is sin; and the degree of terror in the inwardness of the consciousness of guilt corresponds to the degree of edification. There is healing for all pain, victory in all conflict, salvation from all danger—that is edifying; the terrifying thing is that there is pain, conflict, danger; and the degree of the terrifying and of the terror corresponds to the edifying and to the edification [CD 102; SV XIII 96].

Hence, the edifying is very deep indeed. What is remarkable is that one need not be afraid of the terrifying. The more terror, horror, gloom, dismay one can absorb, the more triumphant one can be when transformed in edification. As the fear of the Lord is the beginning of wisdom (Proverbs 1:7), so is terror the beginning of edification; it is its presupposition. Christianity, too, is terrifying, for it views life as suffering. Thus, "in a worldly sense Christian consolation is more apt to drive (one) to despair." But this is how it should be, for it is precisely at the point of despair that edification begins, "the Christian edification, which is named after Him our Lord and Savior; for he too suffered only once—but his whole life was suffering" (CD 103; SV XIII 97).

Not surprisingly, then, thoughts that are explicitly designed for edification "wound from behind" (Part Three). This further adds to the characterization of the edifying as terrifying, for it comes from behind unexpectedly and aggressively in order to "stab one in the back."[18] Moreover, this title suggests an indirect approach in that the author chooses not to appeal to readers face to face. Here again we find evidence that the whole Kierkegaardian corpus invokes an indirect method, for in his journal Kierkegaard writes: "All my frightful authorship is one grand thought, that is: to wound from behind" (P VIII 1 A 548).

Another journal entry[19] shows that Kierkegaard specifically had irony and satire in mind when he sketched out the contents of these "Christian Lectures" (*Christelige Foredrag*). It is indeed ironic to discourse on the question "Behold, we have forsaken all and followed thee; what shall we have therefore?" (Matthew 19:27), when Kierkegaard expected to wound any prospective readers from within Christendom who had not forsaken anything at all.

In what became the third section of this part, "All things must work together for our good—if we love God," the journal entry notes irony in parentheses following this title. Within this section, Kierkegaard rewrites the biblical verse from Romans 8:28 in order to place the emphasis on whether or not one loves God and not on whether or not it is true that all things work to the good, which is the emphasis members of Christendom had always assumed. Kierkegaard's reading hinges on the word "if."[20]

> Thus the discourse really revolves around the word "if." It is a little word, but it has immense significance; it is a little word, about which nevertheless a world revolves, the world of personality . . . . Yes it is a little word this *if.* If God is love, then it follows as a matter of course that all things must work together for good to them that love God; but from the fact that God is love it by no means follows that you believe that God is love, or that you love him. On the other hand, if "you" believe, then it follows as a matter of course that you must believe that all things work together for good to "you," for this is implied in what you believe of God. In the one case it is the person who puts himself inside God and proves something about him, proves that he is love and what follows from this; in the other case the person humbly understands that the question is whether *he* believes that God is love, for if he believes this, then all the rest follows as a matter of course without

> proof: from proof nothing follows *for me*, from faith everything follows *for me* [CD 199–200; SV XIII 182–83].

In focusing on the little word "if," it is clear that Kierkegaard wants to follow Johannes Climacus in shifting the emphasis from the "what" to the "how," from the objective to the subjective, from proof to faith. It is the little word "if" that stabs from behind "and remains like an arrow in your heart; it will remain there until the last" (CD 201; SV XIII 184). For in the deepest depths of subjectivity there is always the possibility that one may doubt oneself; to doubt God—no, faith takes care of that, but it does not relieve the individual of the pain of the "if."[21]

> This word cannot give you the certainty that you love God, only God can give you that . . . . But this word can help you to seek this certainty. When despair would close around you, this word still provides a prospect of salvation; when you are about to collapse in weariness and to give up, then the word still holds the possibility of help open, if you love God [CD 206; SV XIII 188].

Kierkegaard then tells a parable about an intellectual author, which resembles the "parable of the wig" recounted by Climacus twice in his *Unscientific Postscript*. The gifted thinker has written a book on the subject that "all things must work together for the good," and then, after suffering a slight misfortune, he comes to doubt the truth of his thesis. He goes to see a pastor about his doubt, and the pastor counsels him thus: "There is a book about the love of God by so and so, read it, study it, if that does not help you, no man can help you" (CD 207; SV XIII 189). To this the thinker responds that he is the author of the book suggested by the pastor.

So it is that the accent falls on the objective, rather than the subjective, questions: Do you believe that God is love? Do you need God? This subjective questioning—and not some gifted intellectual proving that God is love—is what is decisive for an individual.

Kierkegaard concludes his thought by proclaiming the subjectivity of the listener of the discourse. "It all lies in the hearer. . . . For what effect this true discourse will produce depends solely upon who the hearer is."

> There may perhaps have been one in whom this discourse inspires such a dread as he never before has known; but this is not the fault

> of the discourse, it lies in the hearer. There was perhaps one who in entire agreement said yes and amen to it, listened to it with the most blissful tranquillity; but this is not to the merit of the discourse, it lies in the hearer. It is not the discourse which has terrified the one, and it is not the discourse which has tranquillized the other; it is the one and the other who in this discourse have understood themselves [CD 209; SV XIII 191].

And then there is the ironic writer, who is clearly free of the discourse and yet must choose a stance. The "if" applies to him as well. Kierkegaard does not reveal himself, and thereby succeeds in mastering the irony. His point of view remains undetermined and uninteresting to readers—except, of course, for one.

Notes

1. Consider, for example, Rorty's "edifying philosophy," which could certainly not be called "Christian."

2. Taken literally, the statement that Kierkegaard does not use the name of Christ in the *Edifying Discourses* is not true. Granted, he does for the most part refer to Jesus rather than Christ, but in the discourse "The Thorn in the Flesh," Christ's name does appear, albeit indirectly, as Kierkegaard relates Paul's views (KW V 341).

3. Here and in what follows reference to the veronymous writings does not include the early polemical writings discussed in Part One.

4. This view is corroborated in the chapter "Love Edifies" in *Works of Love*, which will be examined below.

5. *Den opbyggelige tale* (The Edifying Discourse) (Copenhagen: Gad, 1987).

6. Ibid., p. 138.

7. Ibid., pp. 139–40.

8. Ibid., p. 138.

9. This is not to suggest that there are not others which could be investigated at some length. Indeed, Anders Kingo has also argued that "the (edifying) discourse is a break with immanent religiousness" and has provided examples to support his argument. See Anders Kingo, "Den opbyggelige tale: Om Søren Kierkegaards *Atten opbyggelige Taler* og deras status i forfatterskabet" (The Edifying Discourse: On Søren Kierkegaard's *Eighteen Edifying Discourses* and Their Status in the Authorship), *Dansk Teologisk Tidskrift*, 45 (1985), 133–38.

10. Consider the point discussed above (pp. 191–92) that Kierkegaard later wishes to distinguish between the edifying discourse and a delibera-

tion, citing the latter as a call to action. Here the use of "deliberation . . . for freedom" signifies that this edifying discourse also hopes to capture one's will to act.

11. By *Kjerlighed* Kierkegaard means divine, Christian love, in contrast to *Elskov*, which he uses to designate human love. In Kierkegaard's writing, these Danish terms parallel the biblical distinction between *agape* and *eros* respectively. Today, however, *Kærlighed* is, like the English "love," used widely when speaking of love in general.

One does well to note from the outset that for Kierkegaard love is not a feeling or anything of the kind. Love is the works or acts of love. It is no doubt significant that Kierkegaard's religious writings both begin and end with a reflection on the letter of James. As is well known, this is the letter that Martin Luther disparagingly called the "Epistle of Straw," for it expresses a view that apparently flies in the face of grace, i.e., faith without works is dead. Kierkegaard clearly takes this view very seriously, however, and in his journal he writes: "Christ's love was not an inner feeling, a full heart and what not, it was the work of love which was his life" (J 317). For Christ, love is the only absolute, and for Kierkegaard, love is the only goal of edification.

12. *Ligefrem* means "direct." It is the same word Kierkegaard uses in the subtitle of *The Point of View*, "A Direct Communication, Report to History." But the English translators obscure the use of this word, which is pregnant with meaning in Kierkegaard's authorship, and translate *ligefrem Tale* as "ordinary use." As Kierkegaard is here contrasting direct speech with metaphorical speech, which could also be called "indirect speech," and as he maintains from the beginning that "all human speech, even the divine speech of the Holy Scriptures about spiritual matters, is essentially metaphorical," we have strongly supportive evidence that this text is an example of indirect discourse.

13. Kirmmse, *Kierkegaard in Golden Age Denmark*, p. 316.

14. Ibid., p. 318.

15. Two very divergent readings which might benefit from this discussion are Gene Fendt's *Works of Love?: Reflections on 'Works of Love'* (Potomac, Maryland: Scripta Humanistica, 1990) and Steven M. Emmanuel's review of this work in *International Journal for Philosophy and Religion*, 33 (1993), 125–27.

16. This word means both "to jest" and "to haunt."

17. Walter Lowrie's translation is "the dismaying," which, given the context that all of life is suffering, is too weak.

18. This is how Kirmmse translates "*Tanker som saare bagfra*": "Thoughts which Stab in the Back" (*Kierkegaard in Golden Age Denmark*, p. 347).

19. See CD 166. Lowrie does not include the reference to the original source.

20. In Danish the word is *naar*, which means both "when" and "if." I think Lowrie is right in sticking to "if."

21. This "if" also explains why Kierkegaard does not speak of being a Christian but of becoming one.

Conclusion: Rereading Kierkegaard as a Postmodern Philosopher

> In a certain sense it is like a choice; one must choose either to make the aesthetic the central thought (*Total-tanke*) and so explain everything in that respect, or the religious. Precisely herein lies something revitalizing.
>
> S. Kierkegaard, P X^2 A 150

> No, in truth I must say: I cannot understand the whole, just because I can understand the whole down to its smallest insignificance.
>
> S. Kierkegaard, PV 72; SV XIII 601[1]

> Deconstruction and reconstruction go together.
>
> Jacques Derrida[2]

IF THE CONCEPT OF IRONY is central to an understanding of Kierkegaard's life-view, and if the pursuit of irony constitutes a general anticipation of postmodern thought and literary practice, then Christopher Norris has rightly questioned, "Why has Kierkegaard so seldom been read or written about by deconstructionist literary critics who must surely realize that his work prefigures their own in many crucial respects?"[3] The answer to Norris's question may be found in the predominance of a supposedly definitive Kierkegaardian "point of view," a point of view that has been read as ending all other possible points of view, since it was Kierkegaard himself who had pronounced upon the matter. The text in question is the sharpest thorn in the side of the deconstructionists, because it does possess a seemingly conclusive nature, and if it also lies outside the Kierkegaardian canon proper—even more so than *The Concept of Irony*, which Kierkegaard did not mind publishing—it is appropriate that it be treated in the conclusion of the present study. What is the point of view to be taken on Kierkegaard? His own? If so, what was it? Another reader's own? Then what is to be made of that?

On the Point of View for Kierkegaard's Authorship

The problematic, "post-structural," and posthumous "conclusion" of Kierkegaard's body of literature is a slim volume entitled *Synspunktet for min Forfatter-Virksomhed* (The Point of View for My Activity as an Author). Although Kierkegaard seeks to come to a definitive conclusion with this text, he himself conceived an alternate conclusion several years later. I shall begin by considering the alternative first.

What might have become Kierkegaard's last work epitomizes the authorship in its totality:

My Program:
Either/Or
by
Søren Kierkegaard [JP VI 6944; P XI³ B 54]

Kierkegaard sketches another either/or, and this one written in 1854, several years after the second edition of *Either/Or* was released in 1848. The fragmentary journal entry following this one reads:

> It is laughter which must be used—therefore the line in the last diapsalm in *Either/Or*.
>
> But the laughter must first of all be divinely consecrated and devoutly dedicated. This was done on the greatest possible scale, Socrates [JP VI 6945; P XI³ B 55].

During the final full year of his life, Kierkegaard read the last diapsalm written by the aesthete and made it his own. It is quite a joyful thought. In a dreamlike state the narrator stands before the assembly of gods and is granted one wish. He says: "Most honorable contemporaries, I choose this one thing, that I may always have the laugh on my side" (EO I 42; SV II 44). The narrator of the diapsalm got his wish, and so, too, does Kierkegaard. His productivity is full of laughter, and behind the laughter lies a smile (cf. the preface to *Christian Discourses*), and behind the smile lies irony and jest.

Then there is the significant presence of Socrates, whose name must not be taken lightly, for it is the signpost for Kierkegaard's ever-developing life-view. When we remember that the Gospel assigns jest a place in the kingdom of heaven (KW XXI 186), it is easy to read Socrates's act of "divinely consecrating" laughter as a deed of (Christian) love. Who was a Christian? Kierkegaard poses the question to himself and offers an ironic answer: consider the case of Socrates, the spiritual founder of all those who give themselves over to philosophical questioning. When one then reads "Either/or by S. Kierkegaard," a choice faces the reader to the very end. But the realization of that choice, whether it has been engendered by the original or the alternative text, must finally eventuate into an implicit "both/and." No choice is ever limited to only one of two alternatives. The aesthetic and the ethical person give way to the religious personality, which unites them both. Why can't this second "Either/Or" indicate a similar solution?

Put another way: Kierkegaard's way, the totality of writings must be ambi-guous (the etymology of which shows that the word "both" comes from the prefix *ambi*-). Why, then, is the fundamental nature of the choice so often obliterated by reading *The Point of View* as if it unties the dialectical knot and frees readers from their responsibility for creating the meaning of the authorship by providing them with the "answer"? This would be quite ironic, of course, for to be freed of one's responsibility is to cease being free. Certainly, the blame for spinning such a weak, hole-ridden web rests with Kierkegaard. But is he as serious as the text? Moreover, how does he himself read the text once it is written? We know he considers himself more a reader than a writer, and that in relation to matters existential he views any positive determination as an encroachment when it is communicated as a result, excluding the negative that actually defines it.

Where do "individuals" find themselves most primordially, in the text or in their worlds? Was not Kierkegaard actually both the author and one of a series of readers, not merely one or the other? In the second of "Two Notes Concerning My Activity as an

Author," published posthumously with *The Point of View*, Kierkegaard cannot even come to regard himself as "the individual" (*den Enkelte*).

> [T]he individual . . . is something I do not pretend to be, although I have striven, without yet apprehending, and continue to strive, yet as one who does not forget that by the highest standards "the individual" is beyond a human being's powers [PV 128; SV XIII 647].

If Kierkegaard could not assert that he was "an individual" in the highest sense, then how could he rest assured that he was a Christian who had, at every turn, sought to develop the problem of becoming a Christian as only a solely religious author could? Or was he the first Christian reader of his own Christian texts? As readers, could we not suppose that perhaps Kierkegaard read his own *Point of View* with laughter, as he responded to his own existential bind?[4]

History clearly shows that this writing did not end matters for him. So we should not be surprised to see it as a false ending and also, when it is considered to be the key that unlocks Kierkegaard's secret well, as a false beginning. The task of this conclusion thus becomes the reevaluation of *The Point of View*'s significance for a holistic interpretation of Kierkegaard's writings. Such an interpretation will not be without consequence for the question of reading Kierkegaard as a postmodern philosopher.

Kierkegaard wrote *The Point of View* in the eventful year of 1848,[5] but for reasons that are perhaps too often ignored he did not deem the publication of this work as salutary to either himself or his readers. He chose, therefore, to shelve it. Apparently the text was far too personal to publish. According to a journal entry written after *The Point of View* in 1849:

> As yet I have not said a direct word about myself: the postscript to *Concluding Postscript* contains nothing of the sort. . . . The information given in *Concluding Postscript* about the character of the pseudonymous authors is by a third party. The conclusion of *Works of Love* ("The Work of Love in Praising Love") contains nothing direct about me; on the contrary, it says that "the most selfish person may be the one who undertakes to praise love." The review of *Two Ages* has one little hint about me, but that again is not direct communication . . . [JP VI 6523; P X^2 A 163].

The implication of this passage is that all Kierkegaard's writings have been indirect, for it is clear that he reads the veronymously authored texts (e.g., *Works of Love*, *Two Ages*) as yielding only an indirect communication. How, then, shall we read his "Direct Communication, Report to History?" Is this truly a piece of direct communication, or could Kierkegaard later disallow it in the same way that he here disallows the "directness" of the *Concluding Unscientific Postscript*'s postscript? He had signed that with his own name, while still playing the part of a third party, a reader of that same text.

The problem is intensified once we read that it is precisely this same role as a third party that Kierkegaard assumes while explaining his authorship in *The Point of View*. Readers have every right to doubt the directness of a writing in which Kierkegaard claims to reveal directly what he is as an author, and then is audacious enough to state that it is nevertheless quite in order for him to "possess a more exact and purely personal interpretation" of the personal content of his authorship (PV 98; SV XIII 621). The thought is not even paradoxical: Writers write for readers.

Although many readers may uncritically assume that Kierkegaard actually intended for *The Point of View* to be published posthumously, this is far from certain. The simple fact that he himself would not release it, coupled with his idea to publish it pseudonymously under the name of Johannes de Silentio (P X^1 A 78), is enough to cast Kierkegaard's own reading of this text in a very dubious light. Søren's brother, the pastor Peter Christian Kierkegaard, is responsible for seeing that the manuscript was published, and "almost symbolically" the original manuscript has since disappeared. Peter's estimation of his brother's "direct communication" is this: "One might almost be tempted to think that even what was signed 'S. K.' might not for certain be his final words, but only a point of view."[6] Indeed, for, as we shall see, the point of view of *The Point of View* does not constitute a final point of view, but rather engenders a further point of view, and that shall only generate still another.

What Kierkegaard did publish during his lifetime was the short paper (approximately ten pages of text) *Om min Forfatter-Virksomhed* (On My Activity as an Author [1851]), written in 1849. Kierkegaard describes his authorship as moving

> from "the poet"—from the aesthetic, from "philosophy"—from the speculative to the indication of the most inward determination in the Christian [*det Christelige*]. . . . This movement was accomplished or described *uno tenore*, in one breath, if I dare say, so the authorship, totally considered, is religious from first to last, something everyone who can see must see, if he wants to see it [PV 142–43; SV XIII 528–29].

In *The Point of View,* the central argument is that the author is a religious author. This is problematic in the sense pointed out by Joakim Garff, that

> if one assumes that Kierkegaard is a "religious author," this does not automatically establish that his "activity-as-an-author" was religious, because that depends less upon "the author" than upon "the activity," that is, upon the text.[7]

In *On My Activity as an Author,* however, the religiousness is specifically attributed to the authorship. As already suggested, the argument for the presence of religiousness from the very beginning—as far back as *From the Papers of One Still Living,* if you like—is confirmed in the reading. It is, however, possible to accept this argument and yet still doubt that its acceptance entails a disavowal of the aesthetic or that Kierkegaard remained a poet.

In a journal note written the same year, the first reason Kierkegaard gives for not publishing anything written about his own person in a direct way (e.g., *The Point of View)* is that he is "nevertheless essentially a poet" (P X^1 A 250). Moreover, is it not utterly ironic that in the conclusion to *The Point of View* Kierkegaard writes: "I have nothing further to say, but in conclusion I will let another speak, my poet" (PV 100; SV XIII 621)? Kierkegaard's poet clearly remains to the end, which signifies that the movement has not been away "from the poet" and that the presence of the aesthetic is maintained even to the unnatural conclusion of Kierkegaard's writings. On a deeper level, the appearance of the poet at the end of this work suggests an existential irony, which sets Kierkegaard free in relation to this work. Not surprisingly, then, our thoughts return to Magister Kierkegaard's *Concept of Irony*, where the whole project began.

On My Activity as an Author ends with a trace of existential irony. Printed in large type, Kierkegaard admits: "So it is that I understand the whole now" (PV 150; SV XIII 534). Thus he allows himself the freedom to reread this writing, and the whole, differently in the future. Once again, any authorial point of view is denied in favor of a reader's creative, subjective point of view.

> "Without authority" to *call attention* to the religious, the Christian, is the category for the whole of my activity as an author totally considered. That I was "without authority" I have from the first moment emphasized and repeated as a stereotype; I consider myself preferably as a reader of the books, not as the author.
>
> "Before God," religiously, when I talk with myself I call the whole activity as an author my own upbringing and development, not, however, meaning that I am now perfect or completely finished so as to need no more upbringing and development [PV 151; SV XIII 535].

The same is true of the "Explanation" appended to the *Concluding Unscientific Postscript*, where Kierkegaard regards himself as a reader of the books, not as their author. There he is referring to the pseudonymous writings. Here, however, it is clear from the context that he is talking about the entire authorship, veronymous writings included.[8] How interesting that Kierkegaard writes but does not want to consider himself the writer of the books. For Kierkegaard it seems that there is something more important (more worthy?) in being a reader.[9]

Unlike most of Kierkegaard's writings, *The Point of View* initially appears to be an easy read. This is, of course, a deception, for a deep dialectical tension lies coiled at the heart of this work. The introduction straightforwardly expresses the book's contents as a witness to what Kierkegaard is in truth as an author—namely, "a religious author," whose whole activity "relates to Christianity, to the problem of becoming a Christian" (PV 5–6; SV XIII 551). What Kierkegaard writes is "for orientation and attestation; it is not a defense or an apology." Although he is not on trial, Kierkegaard conceives his writing as analogous to Socrates's last speech, in which Socrates did not attempt to "defend" himself and clear his name, but chose, rather, to provoke and to sting his listeners in a way that would make him appear all the more contemptuous.

Kierkegaard's testimony is deeply personal. It is a matter of course, however, that he cannot present the purely subjective inwardness in which he possesses the explanation of his activity as an author (PV 9; SV XIII 554). Language cannot capture this "immediacy," which means that, to a certain extent, we are presented with an indirect (reflective) approximation of his point of view, not a direct disclosure. For when "the communication lies in reflexion, it is indirect communication. And when the communicator is determined in reflexion, he is negative" (PV 43; SV XIII 581).[10]

Even in this work, Kierkegaard does not say, "I am a Christian, or a Christian author." (Would this last determination be a contradiction in terms? The Scripture records that Christ wrote, but only, according to Kierkegaard, "to erase and forget" [see KW V 67].) The closest he comes is this claim: "The problem itself is one of reflection: namely, to become a Christian when one is a Christian of a sort" (PV 43; SV XIII 581). As a result, because the problem is one of reflection, Kierkegaard must be negative, "infinitely negative"; and, to recall his thesis from *The Concept of Irony*, the source of all authentic human existence lies in infinite absolute negativity, that is, irony.

Appropriately, then, as in his other texts, Kierkegaard does not regard himself, nor does he wish to be regarded, as an "author" (*Forfatter*: *for*, before; *fatte*, conceive, comprehend, understand—hence, literally, a "preconceiver"). He writes:

> The only thing that I could not submit to, and could not do without losing myself and the dialectical in my position (which is just what I could not submit to) is to defend myself qua author [PV 7; SV XIII 552].

Consequently, the aim of this little book is to affirm what Kierkegaard is in truth as author (*hvad jeg som Forfatter i Sandhed er*), while not affirming it in his capacity as an author, which would be an untruth (*en Usandhed*). In this way, this text becomes problematic, and Kierkegaard can be read as ironically undermining his authorial point of view by once again withdrawing himself as author.[11]

Just as there is in the pseudonymous writings, there is here a distinction to be made between the author and Kierkegaard. "An author is often merely an x, an impersonal something, even when he is given in name" (PV 45; SV XIII 582). Moreover, in light of the fact that the original manuscript was lost, for all we know, Kierkegaard's own name might not even have appeared on the title page of the text. Thus, as in the lives of all true poets, a profound mystery remains in the Kierkegaardian corpus *at spøge* (to jest and to haunt).

As indicated in the passage quoted above, Kierkegaard would just as much lose the dialectical structure of his position as he would lose himself. This is significant, for commonplace readings of *The Point of View* have so often entailed a breach with that structure by abrogating the aesthetic and embracing the religious. In other words, many have endeavored to remove the ambiguity that Kierkegaard himself wanted to maintain.

Part One begins by establishing "the ambiguity or duplicity of the whole authorship,"[12] something of which the author had been well aware from the publication of *Either/Or* and *Two Edifying Discourses* in 1842. Over the remarkably short span of seven years, Kierkegaard released a vast body of literature, but it is clear from this text that Kierkegaard intends to end it now, for he indirectly cites *The Crisis and a Crisis in the Life of an Actress* (1848) as completing "the whole dialectical structure of the authorship."

The dialectical structure is so tight that an equal amount of time appears to have been devoted to the aesthetic productivity and the religious productivity, with the writing of the turning point (i.e., *Concluding Unscientific Postscript*) falling squarely in the middle. But what would become of the dialectical structure with the publication of *The Point of View* in 1848? This would certainly change things, and I suspect that Kierkegaard realized the problem very keenly. *The Point of View* could not be published, because it would present an authoritative interpretation that would destroy the dialectical structure of the authorship.

Kierkegaard seems to be struggling with this problem in the text, particularly in his explanation of the ambiguity "that the author is and was a religious author." Again, readers find the sharp dialectical tension referred to above in the notion that Kierkegaard would have us understand that this text is conceived by Kierkegaard *qua* human being (*Menneske*) and not Kierkegaard *qua* author.[13] But if we assume that Kierkegaard did write his name on the title page, then was this done qua human being or *qua* author? *Qua* readers we have no way of knowing, no way of deciding.

Kierkegaard presents the following difficulty:

> But is there not a contradiction here? It was established in the foregoing section that the ambiguity is present up to the last, and in so far as this was successfully done, it becomes impossible to establish [*godtgjøre*: literally "make good"] what the explanation is [PV 16; SV XIII 559].

Following this penetrating argument, to present an explanation—which is what Kierkegaard is doing in this section entitled "The Explanation" (*Forklaringen*, more literally rendered "a making clear")—would prove contradictory. In the same breath, then, Kierkegaard says that "a declaration (*Erklæring*), an assurance (*Forsikkring*[14]) here seems to be the only means of canceling (*at hæve*) the dialectical tension and knot."

Kierkegaard has already affirmed his dislike and lack of faith in "assurances with regard to literary productions," and makes it clear that he shall be proceeding "in the character of a third person, as reader, in order to establish (*godtgjøre*) from the writings that what (he) says is so" (PV 15; SV XIII 559). In Kierkegaard's view, then, the argument that section B, "The Explanation," contradicts section A, "The Ambiguity," "looks very acute, but is actually only quibbling" (PV 16; SV XIII 560). For Kierkegaard, it would be a comical lack of seriousness to construct a duplicity so elaborate that one gets caught up in it and can offer no explanatory purpose. Certainly we would not expect this from someone as sharp-witted as Kierkegaard. Nevertheless, to conceive a dialectical reduplication that maintains the ambiguity as compatible with a "true explanation" is problematic. In a deep sense, the "explanation" cannot be established or proven objectively "by a third party." This means that the quibbler is right in saying that it can only be declared or assured, which fits better with the characterization of a testimony (*Vitterlighed*) given in the Introduction.

A look at "the highest example" may help to make the point clearer.

> The whole life of Christ on earth would have been mere play if he had been incognito to such a degree that he went through life totally unnoticed—and yet he was in truth incognito [PV 16; SV XIII 560].

Christ's "explanation" can hardly be proven. Nor does it require a defense (cf. the epigraph to Part Three of *Christian Discourses*).

Analogously, Kierkegaard's "explanation" is no defense, no argument. And, try as he might, Kierkegaard cannot establish or prove his explanation. Does this mean that Kierkegaard is not a religious author? No, not necessarily. Based on a comprehensive reading of the Kierkegaardian corpus, which is to say nothing with respect to the man, "Kierkegaard" the author is both religious and aesthetic. Neither solely one nor solely the other, he is one in the other. Only from this point of view can the dialectical duplicity and ambiguity be maintained. Kierkegaard's original "either/or" must give way to an ultimate "both/and," as indicated above.

It should be well noted that the only possible judgment I can form from the point of view of the reader concerns Kierkegaard qua author. Concerning Kierkegaard qua human being I can have no knowledge, make no judgment. I can understand the assurance he endeavors to make regarding his own person. I can deem him justified in making such an assurance, but I cannot justify it. Based on a metonymical reading of the texts, Kierkegaard (i.e., the body of literature that serves as the human being's incognito) is a both/and. Quite significantly, then, only this reading can maintain Kierkegaard the reader's either/or, for it is ultimately a matter of faith whether or not one accepts Kierkegaard's own explanation. This is equally true for Kierkegaard the person, for whom it is a matter of the deepest inward concern. And the same is true for any reader of any text. Thus, the positing of a both/and is a judgment on the texts alone. There is no judgment on anything, or anyone, outside the texts.

I shall now consider this holistic interpretation from a slightly different angle.

The "Higher" Dialectical Structure of Kierkegaard's Writings

A comprehensive reading of Kierkegaard's writings reveals that, once reconstructed, there is a dialectical structure "higher" than the one discussed by Kierkegaard, one that incorporates both *The Point of View* and *The Concept of Irony*. These works have traditionally been considered as lying outside the "authorship proper," and it is interesting and significant that one finds them collected in the same volume in the first and second editions of Kierkegaard's *Samlede Værker* (Collected works). How curious!

One is used to reading translators and commentators who say about any given work under consideration that it is the best introduction to Kierkegaard, the single work that should be read first. To this I would reply, Why not begin with volume 13 of Kierkegaard's collected works? It contains both his earliest writings and the later ones on the purpose of the authorship. In short, this single tome signifies the higher dialectical structure of Kierkegaard's writings.

In its simplest form, the higher dialectical[15] structure of Kierkegaard's writings looks like this.

The Concept of Irony

AESTHETIC religious

?

aesthetic **RELIGIOUS**

The Point of View

After reading Kierkegaard's supposedly "direct" claims in *The Point of View,* are we to forget all that has previously appeared concerning irony? Certainly something has been changed with the direct report to history, but does this mean that the "truth of irony" is now revoked or withdrawn? Is Kierkegaard now to be systematically characterized as purely or solely religious? The ironic "introduction" to his writings disallows such an easy, unambiguous classification. The higher dialectical structure of his writings formed by the opposing dialectical poles—*The Concept of Irony* and *The Point of View*—makes it impossible to determine if Kierkegaard was solely religious or aesthetic, for he can and should be read as both.

The intrinsically contradictory concept of irony itself expresses the ambiguity, since Kierkegaard speaks equivocally of irony. Sometimes it is solely aesthetic, sometimes it assumes a "religious" qualification. Analogously, *The Point of View* is equally ambiguous, as Kierkegaard intertwines ironic and indirect communication with straightforward or direct communication. The most conspicuous example is found in the conclusion of the piece, where Kierkegaard's "poet" speaks concerning the martyrdom of our author, which is as much an example of irony and deceit as the ones previously mentioned by Kierkegaard (e.g., that he turned up at crowded theaters to appear an idler).

Unlike other readings, to read Kierkegaard in the way that I am suggesting maintains the reader's own either/or. For it is wrongheaded to wish to stress at all costs that Kierkegaard was a Christian and can be understood only within the context of Christianity,[16] while it is by the same token misguided to argue that Kierkegaard's writings all fall together under the rubric of an implicit aesthetics. The higher dialectical structure of Kierkegaard's writings embraces the dialectical structure of the authorship and preserves the ambiguity, undecidability, and irreducibility between the methods of irony and edification. Any reader is always free to choose, or not to choose, how to read a given work. For example, one may read *Works of Love* ironically or *Stages on Life's Way* with edification, yet not have any ultimate justification for privileging one strategy over the other. This dialectical criss-cross of strategies (symbolically represented in the "X" of the author) is revealed through Kierkegaardian irony, Kierkegaardian edification,[17] which is as much a response to a very particular literary problem concerning the situation of language/reflection and the problems of reading and writing as it is a search for true, authentic human existence.

It follows from this point of view that Kierkegaard's writings are ultimately undecidable, and rightly so, for this preserves the freedom of the reader, something near and dear to Kierkegaard's heart. The insight that Kierkegaard's writings are ultimately undecidable and perhaps intentionally so (who knows?) expresses an even greater affinity between Kierkegaard and postmodernism[18] than has hitherto been acknowledged. Nevertheless, strictly speaking, Kierkegaard does not need to be deconstructed in order to be read as undecidable, although it is true that a certain false reading must be deconstructed. This different strategy of reading Kierkegaard—as a writer aware of the ultimately undecidable nature of his writings—avoids the problem of simplicity involved in the clearest attempted deconstruction of Kierkegaard's works.

Christopher Norris presents a deconstruction of Kierkegaard in a chapter entitled "Fictions of Authority: Narrative and Viewpoint in Kierkegaard's Writing,"[19] which nevertheless admits that Kierkegaard's writings "pre-empt the work of deconstruction, exhaustively rehearsing its tactics in advance."[20] Such ambivalence presents a problem for the careful reader, who cannot be sure whether Kierkegaard should be viewed seriously as anticipating postmodernism or rather as one who easily succumbs to the deconstructive project. Postmodern writings have repeatedly faced the difficulty of wanting simultaneously to hail Kierkegaard and to deconstruct him. One cannot help but wonder, then, if the supposed deconstruction is rigged from the start.[21]

Nonetheless, I can, for the most part, agree with the general gist of Norris's conclusions, while regarding his formulation of the problem as doubtful and misleading—in effect he deconstructs a bad, "mythical" view of Kierkegaard. Thus, in a sense, narrow-minded defenders of Kierkegaard's religious position are canceled out by Norris's attack. This is all right as far as it goes, but the deeper problem remains: How shall one read Kierkegaard's writings from irony to edification?

Should one look more closely at Norris's deconstructive view of Kierkegaard, one would find it recapitulated in his article, "De Man Unfair to Kierkegaard? An Allegory of (Non-) Reading." Norris writes that:

> one could treat *all* of Kierkegaard's texts (including the ethical, religious or 'edifying' discourses) as belonging to the order of aesthetic production, as written—and who is to prove otherwise?—from some pseudonymous, ironic, and noncommittal standpoint, and therefore as open to a postmodern reading indifferent to questions of ultimate truth. . . . In fact Kierkegaard himself baits the trap by organizing his entire life's work around a series of supposedly stable and controlled oppositions . . . which are only held in place by his (and the reader's) willingness to take them on faith. The deconstructionist will have no trouble in showing that these binaries are finally 'undecidable', that they rest on nothing more than the arbitrary privilege accorded to one term in each pair, and that therefore the whole project of Kierkegaard's writing—its attempt to lead the reader through and beyond the seductions of irony or aesthetic understanding—comes up against the obstacle of our simply not knowing how to take this or that particular pronouncement in context. Kierkegaard will then be seen to pro-

> vide all the materials, inducements, and rhetorical strategies for a deconstructive reading of his own texts. And this would apply not only to those works that belong to his so-called 'aesthetic' production, and which more or less explicitly ask to be read as ironic, pseudonymous, or expressing a viewpoint at several removes from Kierkegaard's own. For in the end there is no telling—so the argument would run—just where to draw the line between these strategies of aesthetic indirection and that other, authentic or 'edifying' portion of Kierkegaard's discourse which supposedly renounces such literary tricks and brings us face to face with ultimate issues of ethical and religious truth.[22]

This rich passage comes close to my own position that postmodern readers lie caught between the tension of irony and edification, and ultimately choose for themselves where to lay the privilege. Such a conclusion seems to be in keeping with many a diverse Kierkegaardian text. Norris, then, is right in stating that Kierkegaard's "writings pre-empt the very work of deconstruction, exhaustively rehearsing its tactics in advance."

He goes wrong, however, in stressing that they "lay claim to an ultimate justifying faith."[23] Here Norris simply ignores Kierkegaard's perhaps most widely known notion of a "leap of faith" (and all that lies behind it), which is so dubbed because there is no possible justification or legitimation available to be championed in the name of faith. It is particularly here, if anywhere, that Kierkegaard presents a clear anticipation of postmodernism by showing that all claims to absolute knowledge or truth are without, and will always remain without, any ultimate legitimation or justification. As is well known, Kierkegaard equates the highest truth available for an existing individual with faith, which is defined most fully by Johannes Climacus as "the objective uncertainty due to the repulsion of the absurd held fast by the passion of inwardness, which in this instance is intensified to the utmost degree" (CUP 540). For Kierkegaard, faith cannot justify itself, and persons of faith should not attempt to justify themselves, for this is a trivialization of a personal relation maintained in inwardness.

After reading Norris, one is left with the impression that there is not much that can be done to salvage any understanding out of Kierkegaard's texts. The reader is left at a loss, not knowing what to make of Kierkegaard's literature. In contrast to this view, however, my reading suggests that it is only through reconstructing the Kierkegaardian canon that the undecidable, indissoluble dialectical knot is constituted. But the impression that this reconstruction gives is that this undecidability is as it should be, it is not an aberration. To make the reader aware of his or her responsibility—of responding—has been clearly written in the subtext all along. The problem, then, is rightly left in the lap of the reader. How shall I choose to read Kierkegaard's writings? From irony to edification? From edification to irony? Or both, beginning from either end?

Nowhere is the criss-cross of irony and edification more present than in Kierkegaard's conclusive appraisal of Socrates, which is metaphorically expressed in his judgment that Socrates has become a Christian. From the beginning I have maintained that Kierkegaard's conception of Socrates gives readers the best insight into his life-view. Therefore, I shall conclude by discussing this "highest" evaluation.

How Did Socrates Become a Christian?[24]

There is much in Kierkegaard's writings that is witty and wise, much that is edifying and profound. Then there is this:

> I for my part tranquilly adhere to Socrates. It is true, he was not a Christian; that I know, and yet I am thoroughly convinced that he has become one [PV 41; SV (3rd ed.) XVIII 105].

This is an intriguing and puzzling quote. It is uncouth and problematic, to say the least, and I have yet to come across a commentator who ponders the significance of this passage. To pure common sense, the thought that Socrates has become a Christian is a hankering joke, amusing nonsense, and perhaps a justification for avoiding the knotty task of reading Kierkegaard. To reasoned opinion, it is simply bad theology or an even greater abuse of the philosophy of history. For Kierkegaardologists it might be avoided, perhaps in favor of the amusing, eschatological wish of Kierkegaard that

> Socrates, who, according to his own statement wanted to ask the wise in the underworld whether they knew something or not, may get hold of Hegel in order to question him about the absolute method. Perhaps it would become evident that Hegel, who became

> so extra-ordinarily absolute in this earthly life, which ordinarily is the life of relativity, would become rather relative in the absoluteness of eternal life [JP II 1606].

To the mind cultured by postmodernism, this passage might be read differently. But how?

Certainly, there are countless ways to approach Kierkegaard's writings, but, as we have seen, one of the clearest is to begin with the conception of Socrates and Socratic irony that resounds throughout Kierkegaard's writings, from the prerequisite starting point *On the Concept of Irony with Constant Reference to Socrates* (1841) to the posthumously published "conclusion" of Kierkegaard's works, *The Point of View for My Work as an Author* (1859), in which Kierkegaard reaffirms his loyalty to Socrates and puts the crowning touch on this conception by conceiving Socrates as a Christian. As I have argued from the beginning, a focus on Socrates provides a palpable philosophical clearing for approaching Kierkegaard's texts, and avoids the melancholy problems involved in matching Kierkegaard's personal life to his literature—problems that arise especially with regard to Kierkegaard's broken engagement to Regine and the religious conception Kierkegaard supposedly appropriated solely in inheritance from his stern father.

We have also seen how the conception of irony holds a deep relationship to Christianity, and now it is clear that Kierkegaard regards the introducer of the ironic method, his only true teacher, as a Christian. Hence, one need not search for Freudian clues to interpret Kierkegaard's Christianity through his relationship with his father. Instead, one can approach Kierkegaard's Christianity entirely textually through his appreciation of Socrates, that father of philosophy who has (supposedly somehow) become a Christian. Nor need one read the whole output of Kierkegaard through the lens of the silence he maintains concerning his mother, a silence that has recently gained notoriety in postmodernist literature on Kierkegaard.[25]

Moreover, one can look plainly to Kierkegaard's conception of Socrates for a moment of insight into the relationship between Kierkegaard and postmodernism and for the possibility that something salutary might yet be found among the ruins of nihilism's de(con)struction, through the juxtaposition of irony and edification. This new view could be called an "edifying ironism," which would then have something vital to do with Christianity. Something hidden, no doubt.

Socrates's existence is considered as presenting an analogy to faith, and, for Kierkegaard, both the ironist and the Christian always travel incognito. The following imaginary dialogue in the underworld makes the point.

HEGEL: How goes it?
SOCRATES: Very well, thank you. I do so enjoy traveling around incognito.
HEGEL: Incognito? But where is your disguise?
SOCRATES: I'm disguised as myself.
HEGEL: Don't be absurd. That's no disguise. It is what you are.
SOCRATES: Quite the contrary, it must be a very good disguise, for I see that it has fooled you completely.[26]

Conscious that one is always striving—in the process of becoming, which corresponds to the infinite in existence—the outward form is negative while the inward, in contradiction with the outward, maintains a deeper positivity. The inward (i.e., the formless), however, can never be brought out in finitude, can never be communicated directly, because of the absolute distance between both language and reality and the world and one's subjectivity. Kierkegaard, as is well known, distinguishes subjectivity from objectivity using an analogy of the "what" and the "how." Both ironist and Christian are solely concerned with the "how."

What is characterized here, again, in the case of both Socrates and Kierkegaard is that a negative (ironic) dialectic produces nothing whatsoever. Such is also the fate of the "higher dialectic" of this holistic interpretation. Whence the laughter, for the "result" is in truth a "non-result," and the simulacra of the standpoints of Socrates and Kierkegaard must be viewed as nothingness. They stand isolated and impotent, which leads us (back? forward?) to Christ and the ironically religious practice of self-denial and impotence before all earthly forms of power. Kierkegaard writes:

> Christ has no scepter in his hand, only a reed, the symbol of impotence—and yet at that very moment he is the greatest power.

> As far as power is concerned, to rule the whole world with a scepter is nothing compared to ruling it with a reed—that is, by impotence—that is, divinely . . . in the divine order, the greatest impotence is the greatest power [JP 4:184–85].

Moreover, if Christ writes to erase (cf. KW V 67), then this is the highest example. Kierkegaard, on the other hand, erases to write. His self-denial is felt in his writing, for the point of view is strained through irony, making the texts themselves impotent when it comes to expressing their deepest point of view. Spiritually understood, however, this is their power, which is communicated to those readers who choose. Rightly or not? That is not even the question.

Notes

1. In this chapter the original text references to *The Point of View* and *On My Activity as a Writer* are to the second edition of Kierkegaard's collected works, that is, SV XIII.

2. Amnesty International Lectures on Freedom and Interpretation, Oxford, London, 1992.

3. Christopher Norris, "De Man Unfair to Kierkegaard?" p. 89.

4. In his *Points of View* Louis Mackey closes by relating a dream had by Karl Barth, in which the esteemed author of *Church Dogmatics* is laughed at by "the numberless multitude of the heavenly host." Mackey concludes: "Brother Thomas and Professor Barth had attained, perhaps, the only possible point of view for their work as authors. The case of Magister Kierkegaard is not so clear" (p. 192).

Obviously, although laughter, jest, and irony remain with Kierkegaard throughout his productivity, whether or not he had the laugh on his side cannot be known with certainty. He did, however, make the following note to the "Two Notes Concerning My Work as an Author," entitled "The Individual" (*Den Enkelte*), which was published in 1859 along with *The Point of View*: "And there is—rightly understood—between laughter and me a secret, happy understanding. I am—rightly understood—a friend and lover of laughter" (PV 123; SV XIII 643).

Thus, it is a debatable point that the case is less clear with respect to Kierkegaard than with others. But even if this is this case, could it not then conceal a much heartier laughing?

5. During this year Denmark was at war with Germany and lost the area of Schleswig-Holstein. Also, there was a bloodless political revolu-

tion in Denmark that led to reforming the world's oldest monarchy from an absolute monarchy to a constitutional one.

6. Quoted by Mackey in *Points of View*, p. 160.

7. "Eyes of Argus," 37.

8. Thus, it is not the case that the Climacian account concurs with the one given in *On My Activity as an Author*, as suggested by Joakim Garff in "Eyes of Argus," 32.

9. Perhaps because a publishing writer's views are made public, whereas a reader can maintain a private inwardness.

10. The young student Johannes Climacus would certainly agree!

11. As Mackey points out, "this text is not averse to contradicting itself" (*Points of View*, p. 164).

12. Kierkegaard notes the specific works he includes in "the whole authorship," but his note contains some holes, making it necessary to distinguish between the authorship as Kierkegaard represented it and the broader category of his works and writings: "In order to have it at hand, here are the titles of the books. *First Class* (the aesthetic productivity): Either/Or; Fear and Trembling; Repetition; The Concept of Angst; Prefaces; Philosophical Crumbs; Stages on Life's Way—and 18 edifying discourses, which came successively. *Second Class*: Concluding Unscientific Postscript. *Third Class* (merely religious productivity): Edifying Discourses in Diverse Spirits; Works of Love; Christian Discourses—and a little aesthetic article: The Crisis and a Crisis in an Actress's Life" (PV 10; SV XIII 555).

This classification omits several important works crucial for forming a full, deep understanding of Kierkegaard's entire production. Most significantly, *The Concept of Irony* and *The Point of View* itself are not recognized as playing a role in the "dialectical structure of the authorship."

13. Kierkegaard never explicitly explains what it means to work qua author. In a later section he writes: "Only an author will really be able to understand what a task it is to work qua author, that is, with the spirit [*Aanden*] and the pen, and still to be at the service of everybody" (PV 47; SV XIII 583).

14. Lowrie's translation is "protestation," which does not strike me as appropriate. *Forsikkring* literally means "a making certain," and is most often used to mean "assurance" or "insurance." The word "certification" also comes to mind, because it contains the same root word "certain," and it could be maintained that the "point" of this writing for Kierkegaard, the human being, is to become subjectively certain of his personal religious faith.

15. Here, as is appropriate, we have a third perspective. The Kierkegaard of *The Concept of Irony* and *The Point of View* appears different

from the Kierkegaard behind the pseudonyms and the veronymous works within the authorship. This "existentially ironic Kierkegaard" appears simultaneously as both aesthetic and religious—like Socrates, a practitioner of both irony and religion.

Furthermore, this figure is modeled after the diagram Kierkegaard gives to elucidate the statement "consciousness presupposes reflection" (P IV B 10:12; KW VII 257).

16. To say "S.K. was a religious writer" or "S.K. was a Christian" implies a result that Kierkegaard could never in good faith claim to have attained. (Does this not in part explain why Kierkegaard himself chose not to publish *The Point of View*?) Kierkegaard could not accept any result reached in finitude. In his journal he writes: "Finitely understood, of course, the continued and the perpetually continued striving toward a goal without attaining it means rejection, but, infinitely understood, striving is life itself and is essentially the life of that which is composed of the infinite and the finite" (JP V 5796; P VI B 35:24).

The nature of existence, as Kierkegaard understands it, would not permit him to say "I am a Christian," since such a statement would abrogate the striving implied in one's desire to become a Christian. In all likelihood Kierkegaard would have appreciated Nietzsche's remark that "there was only one Christian, and He died on the cross."

17. Sylviane Agacinski is also well aware of the indistinguishability between irony and edification: "the ironic point of view resembles the religious point of view" (*Aparté*, p. 78).

18. Although the subject of "Kierkegaard and Postmodernism" has been receiving increased attention throughout the last few years, it still appears to be shrouded in confusion. To some extent this is not surprising given the confusing nature of Kierkegaard's writings and the existential proximity of the postmodern condition. Be this as it may, I think that much of the confusion can be averted by (1) establishing a comprehensive interpretive framework for the Kierkegaardian corpus, (2) setting up the problem in a satisfactory manner, and (3) specifying the conception of postmodernism under discussion. Achieving these goals may yield a critical understanding of the relation between Kierkegaard's writings and postmodernism. This study has focused on achieving goal (1) while sketching how goal (2) might be accomplished. Goal (3) requires more space than is left to the present work, and therefore remains a problem for future study.

One further comment: in general, one can avert many problems by asking the right kind questions, for the wrong questions may surely lead one astray. Was Kierkegaard a postmodernist (or pre-postmodernist, if you prefer)? Would Kierkegaard feel at home within postmodernism? Would he regret the marriage? These questions have the misfortune of conjuring up the idea of Kierkegaard, the person, in an attempt to detect what he really believed. This biographical/ psychological enterprise is doomed to failure.

19. This is the chapter 4 of *The Deconstructive Turn*.

20. Norris, *The Deconstructive Turn*, p. 4.

21. Further confusion is involved in that Norris claims to be writing for Anglo-American philosophers—the mainstream as he calls it—and focuses his attention on the philosophers Wittgenstein, Austin, Ryle, and Kripke, so that the transition to Kierkegaard is very rough indeed. The implicit supposition that Kierkegaard is within the "mainstream" philosophical tradition is mistaken. Analytic philosophers often denigrate Kierkegaard's writing and would hardly admit that he presents a link in their tradition, to say nothing of a worthy opponent. For these philosophers who do not or cannot read Kierkegaard, he is a thinker one cannot "sharpen one's wits about."

22. Pp. 90–91.

23. *Deconstructive Turn*, p. 4.

24. Part of the following section, as well as a few passages scattered throughout this text, first appeared in my article "How Did Socrates Become a Christian?"

Obviously, to say that Socrates has become a Christian is not to say that he has become Christ. So, to this extent there still remains an extreme opposition between the two. I hope to have shown, however, that throughout Kierkegaard's developing view of Socrates he moves much closer to the "father of philosophy" and appears quite content to grant him the privileged status of "the way." Needless to say, only Christ could call himself "the truth."

25. The most persuasive account is given by Sylviane Agacinski in *Aparté*. Toward the culmination of her argument Agacinski writes: "It would not be impossible to find the traces of such a strategy in Kierkegaard—should we only be willing to push an entirely conjectural interpretation even further. If the secret scene of the father had to be 'encrypted' by the son, then the simultaneous burial of the mother would be equally necessary (pp. 252–53).

Kierkegaard's writing strategy, his economy, following Agacinski's interpretation, was to inter the scene of the rape of his mother, Anne Sørensdatter Lund (Agacinski mistakenly writes Maria instead of Anne), a virgin maid-servant, by his father, Michael Pederson Kierkegaard. The churchyard (*kirkegaard*) of Søren Kierkegaard's writings now testifies to the deaths of mother and father—but of course Regine too! He buries himself a(long)side his loved ones. In writing he loses himself, when all along we had thought that his self was just what was being gained. That solitary individual was never one with himself; he was haunted by too many phantoms.

Truly an original reading, but is such a rhetorical reading—a reading of what is not written—the secret of a secret—traces of an unconscious repression—edifying? Is this what we want to call deep reading? Is it reading at all?

Such an interpretation is as convincing as it is doubtful, as pleasurable as it is disagreeable; but, then, it was never meant to be anything more than an *aparté* (aside) from beginning to end.

26. This dialogue is adapted from an epigraph to *Whole Child/Whole Parent* by Polly B. Berends (New York: HarperCollins, 1987).

Bibliography

Agacinski, Sylviane. *Aparté: Conceptions and Deaths of Søren Kierkegaard*. Trans. Kevin Newmark. Kierkegaard and Postmodernism Series. Tallahassee: The Florida State University Press, 1988.

Andersen, Hans Christian. *Kun en Spillemand* (Only a Fiddler). Borgen: Sprog- og Litteraturselskab, 1988.

———. *Mit Livs Eventyr* (My Life's Adventure). Copenhagen: C. A. Reitzel, 1855.

Aspelin, Gunnar. *Tankens Vägar* (The Ways of Thought). Stockholm: Almqvist & Wiksell, 1958.

Axelsen, Jens. *Dansk-engelsk Ordbog* (Danish-English Dictionary). Copenhagen: Gyldendal, 1984.

Bejerholm, Lars. *Meddelsens Dialektik: Studier i Sören Kierkegaards teorier om språk, kommunikation och pseudonymitet* (The Dialectic of Communication: Studies in Søren Kierkegaard's Theories on Language, Communication, and Pseudonymity). Copenhagen: Munksgaard, 1962.

Berends, Polly B. *Whole Child/Whole Parent*. New York: HarperCollins, 1987.

Bertung, Birgit, ed. *Kierkegaard: Poet of Existence*. Kierkegaard Conferences 1. Copenhagen: C. A. Reitzel, 1989.

Bigelow, Pat. *The Conning/The Cunning of Being: Being a Demonstration of the Postmodern Implosion of Metaphysical Sense in Aristotle and Early Heidegger*. Tallahassee: Florida State University Press, 1991.

———. *Kierkegaard and the Problem of Writing*. Kierkegaard and Postmodernism Series. Tallahassee: Florida State University Press, 1987.

Brandes, Georg. *Søren Kierkegaard: En kritisk Fremstilling i Grundrids* (Søren Kierkegaard: A Critical Presentation in Outline). Copenhagen: Glydendal, 1877.

Brandt, Frithiof, and Else Rammel. *Søren Kierkegaard og Pengene* (Søren Kierkekegaard and Money). Copenhagen: Levin & Munksgaard, 1935.

Brøndsted, Mogens, and Sven Møller Kristensen. *Danmarks Litteratur fra Oldtiden til 1870* (Denmark's Literature from Antiquity to 1870). Copenhagen: Gyldendal, 1963.

Caputo, John D. *Radical Hermeneutics: Repetition, Deconstruction, and the Hermeneutic Project*. Bloomington: Indiana University Press, 1987.

Cavell, Stanley. "Existentialism and Analytical Philosophy." *Daedalus*, 93 (1964), 946–74.

Climacus, John. *The Ladder of Divine Ascent*. Trans. Colm Luibheid and Norman Russell. New York: Paulist Press, 1982.

Crites, Stephen. *In the Twilight of Christendom: Hegel* vs. *Kierkegaard on Faith and Philosophy*. Chambersburg, Penn.: American Academy of Religion, 1971.

Derrida, Jacques. *Acts of Literature*. Ed. Derek Attridge. New York: Routledge, 1992.

———. *Glas*. Trans. J. P. Leavey and R. A. Rand. Lincoln: University of Nebraska Press, 1986.

———. *Of Grammatology*. Trans. Gayatri Chakravorty Spivak. Baltimore: The Johns Hopkins University Press, 1976.

Dostoevsky, Fyodor. *The Idiot*. Trans. Constance Garnett. New York: Bantam Books, 1981.

Emanuel, Steven M. Review of *Works of Love? Reflections on 'Works of Love'*, by Gene Fendt. *International Journal for Philosophy and Religion*, 33 (1993), 125–27.

Evans, C. Stephen. *Kierkegaard's "Fragments" and "Postscript": The Religious Philosophy of Johannes Climacus*. Atlantic Highlands, N.J.: Humanities Press, 1983.

———. "Kierkegaard's View of Humor: Must Christians Always Be Solemn?" *Faith and Philosophy*, 4 (1987), 176–86.

———. *Passionate Reason: Making Sense of Kierkegaard's "Philosophical Fragments*." Bloomington: Indiana University Press, 1992.

Fendt, Gene. *Works of Love? Reflections on 'Works of Love*.' Potomac, Md.: Scripta Humanistica, 1990.

Fenger, Henning. *Kierkegaard-Myter og Kierkegaard-Kilder* (Kierkegaard Myths and Kierkegaard Sources). Odense: Universitetsforlag, 1976.

———. *Kierkegaard: The Myths and Their Origins*. Trans. George C. Schoolfield. New Haven, Conn.: Yale University Press, 1980.

Garelick, Herbert M. *The Anti-Christianity of Kierkegaard*. The Hague: Martinus Nijhoff, 1965.

Garff, Joakim. "Det aesthetiske hos Kierkegaard: dets flertydighed og dets rolle i hans teologiske tænkning" (The Aesthetic in Kierkegaard: Its Ambiguity and Its Role in His Theological Thinking). *Dansk Teologisk Tidskrift*, 55 (1992), 36–55.

———. "The Eyes of Argus: The Point of View and Points of View With Respect to Kierkegaard's 'Activity as an Author.' " Trans. Bruce H. Kirmmse. *Kierkegaardiana*, 15 (1991), 29–54.

Goethe, Johann Wolfgang von. *Faust*. Bilingual edition. Trans. Walter Kaufmann. New York: Doubleday,, 1961.

Grunnet, Sanne Elisa. *Ironi og Subjektivitet: En studie over S. Kierkegaards disputats "Om Begrebet Ironi"* (Irony and Subjectivity: A Study of S. Kierkegaard's Dissertation "On the Concept of Irony"). Copenhagen: C. A. Reitzel, 1987.

Hansen, Heidi, and Leif Bork Hansen. "Maskineriets intrigante hemmelighed" (The Machinery's Scheming Secrecy). *Kritik*, 83 (1988), 118–28.

Hansen, Søren Gorm. *H. C. Andersen og Søren Kierkegaard i dannelseskulturen* (H. C. Andersen and Søren Kierkegaard in the Culture of "Refinement"). Copenhagen: Medusa, 1976.

Hartshorne, M. Holmes. *Kierkegaard, Godly Deceiver: The Nature and Meaning of the Pseudonymous Writings*. New York: Columbia University Press, 1990.

Heidegger, Martin. *Being and Time*. Trans. John Macquarrie and Edward Robinson. New York: Harper & Row, 1962.

Hegel, George Wilhelm Friedrich. *Lectures on the Philosophy of Religion*. Trans. E. B. Speirs and J. B. Sanderson. 3 vols. New York: Humanities Press, 1968.

———. *The Phenomenology of Mind*. Trans. J. B. Baillie. London: George Allen & Unwin Ltd, 1910.

———. *Science of Logic*. Trans. A. V. Miller. New York: Humanities Press, 1969.

Helweg, Hans Friedrich. "Hegelianismen i Danmark." *Teologisk Tidskrift*, 2 (December 16, 1855).

Henriksen, Aage. *Methods and Results of Kierkegaard Studies in Scandinavia: A Historical and a Critical Study*. Copenhagen: Munksgaard, 1951.

Himmelstrup, Jens. *Søren Kierkegaards Opfattelse af Sokrates* (Søren Kierkegaard's Conception of Socrates). Copenhagen: Arnold Busch, 1924.

Holm, Søren. *Filosofien i Norden før 1900* (Philosophy in the Nordic Countries Before 1900). Copenhagen: Munksgaard, 1967.

Høffding, Harald. *Søren Kierkegaard som filosof* (Søren Kierkegaard as a Philosopher). Copenhagen: Gyldendal, 1892.

Jeffner, Anders. "Vår Natur är oss en väldig borg" (Our Nature Is for Us a Mighty Stronghold). *Forskning och Framsteg* (Research and Progress) (March–April 1991).

Kaufmann, Walter. *Existentialism from Dostoevsky to Sartre*. New York: New American Library, 1975.

———. *Nietzsche: Philosopher, Psychologist, Antichrist*. Princeton, N.J.: Princeton University Press, 1974.

Kingo, Anders. *Den opbyggelige tale* (The Edifying Discourse). Copenhagen: Gad, 1987.

———. "Den opbyggelige tale: Om Søren Kierkegaards *Atten opbyggelige Taler* og deras status i forfatterskabet" (The Edifying Discourse:

On Søren Kierkegaard's *Eighteen Edifying Discourses* and Their Status in the Authorship). *Dansk Teologisk Tidskrift*, 45 (1985), 133–38.

Kirmmse, Bruce. *Kierkegaard in Golden Age Denmark*. Bloomington: Indiana University Press, 1990.

Kolb, David. *Postmodern Sophistications: Philosophy, Architecture, and Tradition*. Chicago: The University of Chicago Press, 1990.

Lang, Berel. *The Anatomy of Philosophical Style*. Oxford: Basil Blackwell, 1990.

Lapointe, François H. *Søren Kierkegaard and His Critics: An International Bibliography of Criticism*. Westport, Conn.: Greenwood, 1980.

Lübcke, Poul. Review of *Faith, Reason, and History*, by Robert C. Roberts. *Kierkegaardiana*, 15 (1992), 167–70.

———, ed. *Filosofilexiconet* (Dictionary of Philosophy). Trans. Jan Hartmann. Stockholm: Bokförlaget Forum, 1988.

Lyotard, Jean-François. *The Postmodern Condition*. Trans. Geoff Bennington and Brian Massumi. Minneapolis: University of Minnesota Press, 1984.

Mackey, Louis. *Kierkegaard: A Kind of Poet*. Philadelphia: The University of Pennsylvania Press, 1971.

———. *Points of View: Readings in Kierkegaard*. Kierkegaard and Postmodernism Series. Tallahassee: *The* Florida State University Press, 1986.

Malantschuk, Gregor. *Kierkegaard's Way to the Truth*. Trans. Mary Michelsen. Montreal: Inter Editions, 1987.

Marino, Gordon D. "S. Kierkegaard: The Objective Thinker Is a Suicide." *Philosophy Today* (Fall 1985), 203–12.

Merleau-Ponty, Maurice. "Philosophy and Non-Philosophy Since Hegel." *Telos*, 29 (1976).

Mullen, John Douglas. *Kierkegaard's Philosophy*. New York: New American Library, 1981.

Nielsen, H. A. *Where the Passion Is*. Tallahassee: Florida State University Press, 1983.

Nietzsche, Friedrich. *Beyond Good and Evil*. Trans. Walter Kaufmann. New York: Vintage Books, 1966.

———. *The Gay Science*. Trans. Walter Kaufmann. New York: Random House, 1974.

Norris, Christopher. *The Deconstructive Turn: Essays in the Rhetoric of Philosophy*. London: Methuen, 1983.

———. "De Man Unfair to Kierkegaard? An Allegory of (Non)-Reading." *Kierkegaard: Poet of Existence*. Ed. Birgit Bertung. Copenhagen: C. A. Rietzel, 1989.

O'Flaherty, James C. *Hamann's "Socratic Memorabilia."* Baltimore: The Johns Hopkins Press, 1967.

Pattison, George. *Kierkegaard: The Aesthetic and the Religious: From the Magic Theatre to the Crucifixion of the Image*. London: Macmillan, 1992.

———. " 'Who' Is the Discourse? A Study in Kierkegaard's Religious Literature." *Kierkegaardiana*, 16 (1993), 20–45.

Plato. *Dialogues of Plato*. 4 vols. Trans. B. Jowett. New York: Scribner's, 1871.

Rée, Jonathan. "The Philosopher in His Library." *Times Literary Supplement*, October 4, 1991.

Roberts, Robert C. *Faith, Reason, and History: Rethinking Kierkegaard's "Philosophical Fragments."* Macon, Ga.: Mercer University Press, 1986.

Rorty, Richard. *Contingency, Solidarity, and Irony*. Cambridge: Cambridge University Press, 1989.

———. *Philosophy and the Mirror of Nature*. Princeton, N.J.: Princeton University Press, 1979.

Roos, Carl. *Kierkegaard og Goethe*. Copenhagen: Gad, 1955.

Rubow, Paul V. *Kierkegaard og hans Samtidige* (*Kierkegaard and His Contemporaries*). Copenhagen: Glydendal, 1950.

Sartre, Jean-Paul. *Being and Nothingness*. Trans. Hazel E. Barnes. New York: Washington Square, 1956.

———. "Kierkegaard: The Singular Universal." *Between Existentialism and Marxism*. Trans. John Mathews. New York: Pantheon, 1974.

Shmuëli, Adi. *Kierkegaard and Consciousness*. Trans. Naomi Handelman. Princeton, N.J.: Princeton University Press, 1971.

Sjöstedt, Nils Åke. *Sören Kierkegaard och svensk litteratur* (*Søren Kierkegaard and Swedish Literature*). Göteborg: Elander, 1950.

Smythe, John Vignaux. *A Question of Eros: Irony in Sterne, Kierkegaard, and Barthes*. Kierkegaard and Postmodernism Series. Tallahassee: Florida State University Press, 1986.

Strawser, Michael. "How Did Socrates Become a Christian? Irony and a Postmodern Christian (Non)-Ethic." *Philosophy Today*, 36 (Fall 1992), 256–65.

———. "The Indirectness of Kierkegaard's Signed Writings." *International Journal of Philosophical Studies*, 3 (March 1995), 73–90.

———. "Kierkegaardian Meditations on First Philosophy: A Reading of Johannes Climacus." *Journal of the History of Philosophy*, 32 (October 1994), 623–43.

———. Review of *Kierkegaard, Godly Deceiver: The Nature and Meaning of the Pseudonymous Writings*, by M. Holmes Hartshorne. *Søren Kierkegaard Newsletter*, 26 (1992), 10–14.

———. "Välkomna till Djungeln: Språkets Problem hos Kierkegaard och Wittgenstein [see next entry]. *Philosophia*, 21 (1992), 167–76.

———. "Welcome to the Jungle: The Problem of Language in Kierkegaard and Wittgenstein." *Topicos*, 2 (1992), 97–110.

Sussman, Henry. *The Hegelian Aftermath*. Baltimore: The John Hopkins University Press, 1982.

Taylor, Mark C. *Altarity*. Chicago: The University of Chicago Press, 1987.

———. *Journeys to Selfhood: Hegel and Kierkegaard*. Berkeley: The University of California Press, 1980.

———. *Kierkegaard's Pseudonymous Authorship: A Study of Time and the Self*. Princeton, N.J.: Princeton University Press, 1975.

Thompson, Josiah. *Kierkegaard*. New York: Knopf, 1973.

Thulstrup, Niels. *Commentary on Kierkegaard's "Concluding Unscientific Postscript."* Trans. Robert J. Widenman. Princeton, N.J.: Princeton University Press, 1984.

———. *Kierkegaards Forhold til Hegel og den Speculative Idealisme indtil 1846* (Kierkegaard's Relation to Hegel and Speculative Idealism up to 1846). Copenhagen: Glydendal, 1967.

———. *Kierkegaard's Relation to Hegel*. Trans. George L. Stengren. Princeton, N.J.: Princeton University Press, 1980.

Troelsen, Bjarne. *Søren Kierkegaard-Ideens Politispion* (Søren Kierkegaard: The Idea's Political Spy). Herning: Systime, 1984.

Vlastos, Gregory. "Socrates' Disavowal of Knowledge." *The Philosophical Quarterly*, 35 (1985), 1–31.

Walsh, Sylvia. "Kierkegaard and Postmodernism." *International Journal for Philosophy of Religion*, 29 (1991), 113–22.

Warnock, Mary. Review of *Kierkegaard*, by Alastair Hannay. *Times Literary Supplement* (December 24, 1982).

Webb, Eugene. *Philosophers of Consciousness*. Seattle: University of Washington Press, 1988.

Westphal, Merold. *Kierkegaard's Critique of Reason and Society*. Macon, Ga.: Mercer University Press, 1987.

Index